THE ECONOMICS
OF SECESSION

THE ECONOMICS
OF SECESSION

Milica Zarkovic Bookman

St. Martin's Press
New York

© Milica Zarkovic Bookman 1992

All rights reserved. For information, write:
Scholarly and Reference Division,
St. Martin's Press, Inc., 175 Fifth Avenue,
New York, N.Y. 10010

First published in the United States of America 1993

Printed in the United States of America

ISBN 0-312-08443-9

Library of Congress Cataloging-in-Publication Data

Bookman, Milica Zarkovic.
The economics of secession / Milica Zarkovic Bookman.
          p. cm.
     Includes bibliographical references and index.
     ISBN 0-312-08443-9
     1. Europe, Eastern—Economic policy—1989- 2. Europe, Eastern-
     -Politics and government—1989- I. Title.

HC244.B695 1993
338.947—dc20
                                                                        92-24999
                                                                        CIP

To Richard

CONTENTS

List of Tables viii

Acknowledgments ix

1. Introductory Concepts and Problems 1

2. Economic Variables and Phases of the Secessionist Process . . . 35

3. The Economics of Secession: Empirical Evidence (Part I) 51

4. The Economics of Secession: Empirical Evidence (Part II) . . . 65

5. The Economic Basis of Secessionist Aspirations 93

6. The Resolution of Economic Issues
   During the Period of Redefinition 117

7. Post-Secession Economic Viability 145

8. Secession and Self-determination in the Late 20th Century . . . 161

Notes 179

References 249

Index 257

LIST OF TABLES

Table 1.1: Characteristics of Secessionist Regions 26

Table 1.2: Characteristics of Secessionist Regions, Part II 31

Table 2.1: Effect of Economic Variables
in the Phases of Secession 42

Table 3.1: Indicators of Economic Development 52

Table 4.1: Indicators of Trade Dependency
and Interregional Flows 66

ACKNOWLEDGMENTS

I would like to thank various members of St. Joseph's University for supporting the research and the writing of this manuscript. Vincent McCarthy and George Prendergast enabled my leave of absence during 1991-92 and helped secure two St. Joseph's University Summer Research Grants for study in Moscow (1991) and in Rome (1990). I would also like to thank Henri Barkey for many hours of discussion on the topic of secession. In addition, Tom Marzik, Fred Pryor, and Zora Pryor read and provided comments on earlier drafts of some chapters. I would like to extend special thanks to Irina Kutina, who was tireless as my Moscow interpreter, escort, and ultimately my friend. Finally, I would like to thank Richard for helping clarify ideas, for editing the manuscript, and most importantly, for providing consistent and invaluable support during the difficult periods of 1991.

1

Introductory Concepts and Problems

"Proposal That Quebec Secede From Canada"

"A proposal that the province of Quebec secede from the Confederation of Canadian Provinces was expressed in a motion introduced into the Provincial Legislative Assembly today."

"Ukraine in Alliance With the Cossacks"

"The Terek and Kuban Cossacks are reported to be experiencing trouble in their own territories, the hill tribes of the Northern Caucuses having risen."

"Slav Deputy Details Austrian Atrocities"

"Compelled to dig their own graves, drowned, burned alive, hanged or shot down with machine guns, the Serbians of Hercegovina, Bosnia, Istria and Dalmatia were victims of Austro-Hungarian atrocities surpassing the human imagination."

—*The New York Times*, December 22, 1917, p. 3.

The above statements are the first sentences of articles on a single page of the *New York Times* in 1917. They show a stunning resemblance to events in 1992. Despite the passing of decades, despite political and economic modernization, and despite a changing international environment, interethnic and interregional disputes persist in an almost unchanged form. In the period since World War I, there has been a relative lull in demands by ethnic and regional groups to alter borders, although some long-term efforts persisted both in Western Europe and some in the Third World countries. Some, especially in Africa and Asia, gained momentum in the aftermath of World War II. Then, as though these interethnic and interregional conflicts follow some kind of cyclical pattern, the last few years have witnessed a resurgence in secessionist movements.[1] No longer restrained by a cold war polarization and encouraged by the winds of rapid change, subnational groups are seeking to free themselves from central authorities. Unlike any other period in recent history, this unfolding decade may result in some of the most dramatic attempts at redrawing national boundaries as secessionist fever spreads. While in the past successful secessionist efforts were few (notably Norway, Ireland, and more recently, Bangladesh), today's success of Lithuania, Slovenia, and Eritrea fuels the fires in numerous regions that struggle with their unions. Indeed, the sheer number of successful secessionist movements in the past year puts this historical period in bold contrast to any other in modern history.

Eastern Europe and the Soviet Union come quickly to mind as examples of regions experiencing secessionist drives.[2] A facile explanation for these developments might be the loosening of central control associated with the collapse of Soviet-style communism. Yet, Eastern Europe and the Soviet Union are not alone in experiencing numerous drives for regional autonomy. The early manifestations of the unraveling of national unions can be encountered at various levels of development and under diverse economic and political systems: India, Papua New Guinea, Canada, and the Sudan, among others, are also contending with significant secessionist drives. Secessionist movements among ethnic minorities within secessionist regions are common, such as those of Serbs in Croatia and Bosnia, Tatars in Russia, Russians within Moldova. In this general atmosphere of boundary anarchy and regional self-assertion, territorial and independence issues have emerged: even in Taiwan, where calls for independence were punishable with a prison sentence, the parliament is currently debating whether to declare independence from China; Germany is demanding that Russia give republic status to ethnic Germans; Romanians have claimed land from an independent Ukraine;[3] and San Marino demands U.N. membership.

The objective of this study is to identify the *economic* forces associated with secessionist movements. Although the majority of these movements are largely influenced and fueled by ethnic and religious issues, these rarely exist to the exclusion of economic factors. The scholarly literature on secession, as well as the popular press, has largely overlooked the economic concomitants of nationalism, despite clear cases of its importance in determining the nature of regional demands (such as those in Lombardy, Punjab, the Russian Republic) and the use of economic policy as a tool for the appeasement of subnational regions with active nationalistic movements (Bougainville, Slovakia, and Quebec). Economic issues are relevant in the study of secession in explaining events in various phases of the secession movements. First, before secession: how do economic issues contribute to the desire to secede? What economic concessions might be made by the union in order to prevent secession or accommodate to the reality of secession? What is the nature of the cost/benefit analysis of secession both for the seceding region as well as the center? Second, once secession is in process: How do the new economic entities disentangle their economic ties? How does the new region go about setting up an independent economy, including the establishment of new currency, a new banking system, international monetary relations, and the adjustment to the loss of old markets? Third, after secession: What economic factors contribute to the success of a region's efforts to secede? Which of these also contribute to the economic viability of the region as an independent entity? The answers to these questions range from explanatory to practical and should be a crucial element in the secessionist movements presently engaging the attention of almost one-third of the world's states. To my knowledge, they have not been previously addressed, and this study attempts to fill this gap in the literature. Although secession has been studied by various disciplines such as political science and philosophy, economists have only recently begun to address themselves to the issue, and mostly in the practical sphere as consultants to the newly emerging economic entities of the former Soviet bloc.

THE CONCEPT OF SECESSION

According to a dictionary definition, secession is "the act of withdrawing formally from membership in an organization, association, or alliance."[4] In its application to international events, the term has come to be associated with the breaking of ties (political, economic, etc.) by one group of people and their territory from the larger political unit of which it was a part.[5]

The distinction between separatist, irredentist, ethnoterritorial, and secessionist movements is often blurred, both in fact and in the usage of the terms. Indeed, the popular press in the 1990s has clearly confused the distinctions, especially that between irredentist and secessionist efforts. Horowitz distinguishes between secession and irredentism in the following fashion: "Secession is an attempt by an ethnic group claiming a homeland to withdraw with its territory from the authority of a larger state of which it is a part. Irredentism is a movement by members of an ethnic group in one state to retrieve ethnically kindred people and their territory across borders. . . . Irredentism involves subtracting from one state and adding to another, new or already existing; secession involves subtracting alone."[6] Irredentism is a term originating with Italian liberation movements and thus was more popular in the description of events in Mittel Europa of the past century. Nevertheless, it is useful today to distinguish between it and secession insofar as it clearly distinguishes today's "nationalist movements" according to their aims: The desire to create a Kurdistan inhabited by Kurds residing in Iraq, Turkey, and Iran is irredentist in nature, as is the desire of Hungarians residing in Romania to unite their land with Hungary. The demand for independence by Corsicans from France is simply secessionist, as no further link is sought with another state. Sometimes the two types of movements are extremely close and the distinction between them becomes blurred, as in the case of the Tamils in Sri Lanka, whose initial desires were irredentist and then became secessionist. Similarly, the Ibo and Hausa of Nigeria, as well as inhabitants of Southern Sudan, over time became secessionists. Because of the ease with which these movements sometimes float across the borders of academic definitions, all these examples exhibit a characteristic that Horowitz describes as "convertibility of claims."[7] Other times, what begins as one type of movement among an ethnic group gives rise to another type of movement among another group that perceives a threat associated with the emergence of the former movement. Examples of this abound in the early 1990s: the secessionist movement of Croatia gave birth to the irredentist movement of Krajina where the Serbian population demands unification with Serbia; the secessionist movements of Moldova and Georgia from the Soviet Union resulted in the awakening of the Russians and the South Ossetians, who wanted unification with Russia and North Ossetian Autonomous Region, respectively. For the purposes of this study, this distinction between secessionist and irredentist movements is useful because of the implications for the "during and after" phase of successful secession. In other words, the viability of a region is clearly enhanced if that region is enveloped by a preexisting economic entity than if survival is limited to its own resources and devices.

Ethnoterritorial movements differ from secessionist movements insofar as the former is broader, and encompass both secession and irredentism. According to Thompson and Rudolph, "The term ethnoterritorial is used . . . as an overarching concept for various political movements and conflicts that are derived from a group of people, *ethnos* in the Greek sense, having some identifiable geographic base within the boundaries of an existing political system."[8] A separatist movement differs from a secessionist movement insofar as the demands of the former consist of increased autonomy in one or many areas, whereas in the latter, full independence is part of the definition of success. It is useful to distinguish between various political movements on the basis of goals. Indeed, Buchanan contrasted secession with other forms of challenge to the political authority of the center, such as revolution and civil disobedience.[9] The former entails a desire to overthrow the government, clearly not a desire of secessionists that merely want a restriction of its jurisdiction over a certain territory and population. (This distinction is clear in the two secessionist movements in Southern Sudan and neighboring Ethiopia. In the former, a change in the central government is clearly sought, while in the latter, the Eritrean secessionist movement is not concerned with the nature of the rule in Addis Ababa as long as its ties to it are cut). Civil disobedience differs from secession insofar as it is a means to achieving some change, but that change again involves the nature of the government.

There are several aspects of secession that warrant elaboration. Namely, how is the secessionist unit defined, is secession necessarily associated with territory, does it necessarily involve ethnicity, what is the difference between secession and the unraveling of states, how do we identify the popular basis of secessionist movements, and finally, what difference does voluntary or involuntary union make when regions demand secession?

(i) The Secessionist Unit

Most cases of secession involve relatively large and clearly defined political and administrative units, such as republics (Lithuania) or states (Punjab). This does not exclude the possibility of secession of smaller but still clearly defined political units. Examples of this, although rare, are encountered: Some counties of Tennessee were formed by secession from others. In Switzerland, the Jura canton split from the Berne canton during the 1970s, and recently, the Berne canton is debating a split as the French-speaking population is demanding secession.[10] Within the former Soviet Union, regions at administrative levels below the republic are proclaiming independence, including the Chechen-Ingush and the Tatar Autonomous Republics.[11] Secession attempts have occurred in cities also: Staten Island has debated seceding from New York City, Coconut Grove from Miami, and even Odessa once proposed to leave the Soviet Union. More recently, the city council of Lujansk in Ukraine voted to secede from Ukraine if Ukraine secedes from the Soviet Union.[12] In the present environment, there has been an increase in secession attempts among regions whose political definition within a state has been undefined as a single administrative unit. One attempted secession of this kind is presently proceeding in California: in January 1992, the 27 northern counties of California have introduced into the State Legislature a plan to secede from California to form the 51st state of the United States.[13] What distinguished this case from the more prominent attempts at secession of 1991 is the fact that the 27 counties form no single administrative, cultural, or any kind of unit. Another example of this is underway in the territory of post–World War II Croatia. Regions such as Krajina and Slavonia did not even have the status of autonomous regions within the republic of Croatia prior to the civil war of 1991. Indeed, they were merely a collection of counties, with common ethnicity and history providing the uniting thread. In their efforts to secede from Croatia, on December 19, 1991 they proclaimed themselves a republic: the Republic of Serbian Krajina.

(ii) Secession and Territory

Secession is associated with territory.[14] A population makes a claim on some land, its homeland, on the basis of religious, historical, or economic reasons. It is the strength of these ties to that land that give secessionists the drive that they often have. It is this same bond to land that prevents the peaceful resolution of territorial disputes by what outsiders may rationally and cold-bloodedly suggest, namely planned population movements. The partition of Punjab by India and Pakistan and the consequent population movement that ensued caused tremendous human suffering. More recently, at the suggestion that the Yugoslav crisis be resolved by the movement of Serbs out of Croatia and the relocation of Croats out of Serbia, the response of the Serbs was that it was not an option, partially because their territory, their homeland, is where they have resided for centuries and where their ancestors are buried. The same arguments lie at the roots of demographic solutions to the Palestinians and Israelis territorial debate, as well as the one between Serbs and Albanians in Kosovo. It is because secession involves territorial claims that efforts to decrease the authority of a government on a population cannot be satisfied by emigration of that group.

Since secession involves the leaving of a nation by a group of people *and the taking of some land with them,* those populations demanding secession that do not inhabit continuous territory or are widely dispersed within a state, are clearly disadvantaged. Usually, the seceding region is at the outskirts of the union. In other words, it has one international border. This does not have to be the case, as Buchanan points out by invoking the "hole in the donut secession," when the seceding region is completely surrounded by the remainder state.[15] This is the case of Tatarstan, whose secession from Russia would raise difficulties if nothing else because of its geography and its repercussions on its economic survival.

The geographical location of the seceding territory clearly plays an important role in secession: If Quebec secedes from Canada, the Maritime provinces will not be contiguous with Ontario and the rest of Canada, leading to the fear of a situation such as East and West Pakistan, divided by India. Some might argue that it would indeed be natural for the Maritimes to become independent themselves or join the United States. Another pressing example of the geographical influence of secession is the present conflict of the Serbs within Croatia. The territory inhabited mostly by Serbs, Krajina, is not continuous with Serbia, but instead is divided by Bosnia and Hercegovina. Other examples are Cabinda, the secessionist oil-rich territory of Angola that is divided by Zaire; Armenia and Azerbaijan both divided by each other; and Kaliningrad (Konigsberg), which since the independence of Lithuania, has been separated from Russia by a sovereign state. The issue of territorial continuity is so compelling and so clearly threatens the linkage between regions that the Israeli government is willing to discuss the creation of partial autonomy for Palestinian lands on the West Bank provided they are not continuous and therefore would not one day pose a secession threat.

Territory is closely related to the question of boundaries. Clearly, if secession involves the rupturing of territorial integrity of a state, the next question to be answered is how to draw the new state boundaries. Legal experts are finding the present time especially wanting in theoretical and practical answers to this question. At present, in addition to the secessionist activity, a study by Kratochwil, Rorlich, and Mahajan indicates that not more than 25 of the member U.N. states are free of boundary disputes.[16]

It is for reasons of territory that we rarely find ethnically based secessionist movements in the "New World," including the United States and Australia. Canada is a rare exception, and mention should be made of the efforts by Western Australia to secede from the federation in 1933.[17] These states are composed of immigrants that have left their historical soil, and in that process have given up the passions and rights that are associated with secessionist territorial demands. In the words of Gardels, "Perhaps when immigrants forsake their soil, they leave behind the passionate edge of their *Volksgeist* as well."[18] At the same time, the indigenous inhabitants of the New World have been so decimated and demoralized by the colonizers that they have not succeeded in making strong claims on territory: indeed, the Eskimos and Cree Indians of northern Quebec and their newly established rights to territory are an exception rather than the rule in the Americas.[19]

(iii) Secession and Ethnicity

Must secessionist activity by definition involve an ethnic group (defined loosely as a group of people having a distinct culture and kinship within a larger society)? Most examples in history and in the present time would indicate that, indeed, an identification of an ethnic group is a precondition. However, the involvement of ethnic groups gives rise to two different types of sentiments that have been described in the literature. According to Connor and later Shiels, ethnic separatism grows out of ethnonationalism, and the two are defined as follows: *ethnonationalism* is "the sentiment of an ethnic minority in a state or living across state boundaries that propels the group to unify and identify itself as having the capacity for self-government" while *ethnic separatism* is the "movement by members of an ethnic group to gain autonomy over their own destiny, with the formation of a separate state as the major option."[20] Most of the cases of secessionist activity that characterize the world in the 1990s are cases in which ethnonationalism has taken on elements of ethnic separatism.

In the absence of an ethnic group, the secessionist movement may take on several forms. It may be a simple border dispute, of which examples in South America abound, or it may be the result of problems of federalism, such as the southern confederacy that led to the U.S. Civil War. Other historical examples of nonethnic secession include Venezuela's exit from Gran Colombia in 1830, Panama's departure from Colombia in 1903, and Syria's exit from the United Arab Republic in 1961. In the 1990s, the proposed secession of northern Californian counties, as well as Staten Island from New York City, does not involve ethnicity. Lombardy represents the most glaring example of nonethnic attempts at separatism; the population of northern Italy supports a divorce from central and southern Italy, from whose population it does not differ ethnically. In all of these cases, strong economic motivations, rather than ethnicity, became a leading component of secessionist activity.

(iv) Secession vs. State Unraveling

A distinction must be made between states in which a single or several secessionist movements exist and those in which the entire political fabric is unraveling. It is becoming clear that some regions that started off the 1990s as secessionist regions (such as Lithuania) can no longer be simply termed as such, since they are part of a group of regions that are all seceding due to the total unraveling of the state. Whether the secessionist movement in one region actually causes the unraveling of the entire state is debatable and must be examined on a case-by-case basis. Indeed, there are numerous cases of ongoing secessionist attempts that have not shaken the political union at the center (such as in Indonesia), leading to the conclusion that secessions are neither a sufficient nor necessary condition for state unraveling. The distinction is clear if we compare the case of Punjab in India to Estonia in the former Soviet Union: the possible secession of Punjab (even Punjab and Kashmir) would leave the union intact, while in the case of Estonia, there is no longer a union to be preserved. Indeed, the former Soviet Union represents the clearest example of this unraveling. The Soviet Union ceased to exist as such in August 1991, therefore the regions that we termed secessionist when their parliaments voted for independence are no longer such, but rather gained their independence when the entire union disintegrated. Some of these regions then agreed to form the Commonwealth of Independent States. This unraveling has given rise to new acronyms, such as the UFFR: the Union of Fewer and Fewer Republics.[21] The situation in Yugoslavia, although similar, is not as simple. Although there are numerous regions vying for independence, so many that Andrejevich called 1991 the year of the acronyms[22], there is no consensus as to whether Yugoslavia has ceased to exist. Indeed, although the formal death sentence was pronounced in the international arena on January 15, 1992, with the recognition of Slovenian and Croatian sovereignty by Germany, it is unclear that all regions of former Yugoslavia have accepted this. One question that arises from the Yugoslav example is whether we can speak of secession if there is no union from which to secede. This question of semantics is important in the sphere of international law regarding Yugoslavia. Serbia claims that the Slovenes and Croats have threatened the integrity of Yugoslavia by their secession, while they respond that they have not seceded because Yugoslavia ceased to exist prior to their declaration of independence on June 25, 1991.

In a broader context, the unraveling of present Yugoslavia and the Soviet Union prompts comparisons with historical occurrences of multinational conglomerates of peoples in a single political system. The most frequent comparisons are with the Austro-Hungarian and the Tsarist Russian empires.[23] In all of these, numerous ethnic groups strived for power with the center, while the center strived to create a supernational identity to provide a common link among the disparate peoples. The goals pertaining to multinational cohesion, and the methods used to achieve these goals, have often differed in unraveling states and those with single secessionist efforts.

(v) The Popular Basis of Secession

How can the extent of popular support for secession be measured? Indeed, is it at all clear that the Punjabi population is in favor of an independent Khalistan, and does the Western Saharan population in fact support the Polisario? When a small group of leaders demands the severance of ties to the center, how do politicians, social scientists, and the international community that is expected to give its stamp of approval, know the degree to which their sentiments are shared by the population they profess to represent?[24] Methods of expression of popular desire vary across regions, ranging from limited due to repressive tendencies of the government (such as in the case of support for the Karen in Myanmar) to the party politics in which voting and polls judge popular sentiment at frequent intervals (such as in Catalonia and Lombardy). In the western democratic political tradition, referenda have emerged as the most democratic way of settling an issue, since they entail a direct vote on an issue. Even Lenin supported the idea of a referendum as the most democratic method of self-determination, indicating that questions of secession should be settled "only on the basis of a universal, direct, and equal vote of the population of the given territory by secret ballot".[25] The international community has also chosen referenda as the measure of legitimacy, as evidenced by the recent EEC demand for one as a precondition for recognition of the former Yugoslav republics. It is problematic to assume popularity of secessionist movements without some formal measure among the population.

Despite the legitimacy that both policy makers and academics perceive is conveyed by a referendum, this democratic act by no means provides a positive determination of popular support for secession. Indeed, numerous questions arise related to referenda that may alter its outcome. For example, the breadth of voters to be included in the referendum vote often determines the outcome, and thus reflects a bias. A referendum in a region wishing to secede may be open to the population of the region or to the entire state. In most cases, this decision has a large impact on the outcome. The numerous referenda held in Yugoslavia over 1990-1991 are a case in point: the populations of Slovenia and Croatia voted overwhelmingly to secede from Yugoslavia, but had that vote been open to the entire Yugoslav population, the outcome would have certainly been different. The population of Krajina is hoping for a referendum to be organized during the U.N. peacekeeping forces' involvement in the region to determine whether they want to be part of Serbia or Croatia. Who will be allowed to vote in that referendum? The outcome will clearly depend on whether only residents of Krajina are included or all of Croatia is included. A difficult decision lies ahead for the United Nations, similar to the one it faces in Western Sahara, where the decision to allow voting by tens of thousands of Moroccan citizens whose fathers were born in Western Sahara is perceived by the Polisario as biased in favor of annexation of the region by Morocco.[26] In the case of Ethiopia, the people of Eritrea have been promised a referendum on their future status within two years. However, it has also been proposed that the entire population should vote on whether the Eritreans should secede. In Czechoslovakia, former President Havel wanted to put Slovak secession on a national referendum. Slovaks feared they would lose because voting was to take place at the level of Czechoslovakia.[27] This raises important questions surrounding the issue of self-determination and who the self is, as well as what are the obligations and responsibilities of the remaining population. It should be noted that in France, one of the more democratic countries in the world, the referendum on self-determination and independence of New Caledonia was conducted in 1988 among the entire French population, not only the New Caledonians.

(vi) Secession vs. Independence

Increasingly, regions are questioning the historical roots of their political associations that resulted in their present unions. In some cases, this exploration into history sheds light on what is perceived as unjust assimilation and border-drawing with no concern for the local sentiment. Although such practices were the norm in past centuries, western civilizations now seem to be concerned with the morality of such deeds and are imposing this morality (albeit sometimes selectively) on those outside the confines of their culture. Thus, although the western imperialist powers were largely responsible for the boundaries that today lie at the root of secessionist movements in Sudan, Ethiopia, and Angola, they at the same time profess that secession of the Baltic states from the Soviet Union is justified on the grounds that they were never voluntarily a part of the union.

At issue is the question of whether a region can secede from a state when the legitimacy of its belonging to that state is under dispute. Indeed, is the fight for secession of East Timor from Indonesia genuine secession, since the region was invaded by Indonesia immediately following the withdrawal of the Portuguese? If the principle used rests on the voluntary status of the union, then we will find that the majority of present borders in existence across the globe would justify new "prenuptial agreements." Furthermore, there are cases of secession from regions to which one never belonged. This is exemplified by the case of the three provinces of Southern Sudan, which was entirely eliminated from the negotiations leading up to its independence and definition in today's borders: "The Southerners reject charges of secessionism on the grounds that, since they were not party to the Cairo Agreement involving Britain, Egypt, and the Arab political parties of the Sudan, and providing for the country's joint independence, they are simply not bound by it."[28] Thus, they are not seceding from that to which they never belonged.

NONECONOMIC CONSIDERATIONS IN THE STUDY OF SECESSION

This study does not negate the importance of noneconomic factors in forging both the demands for secession and determining the success of secessionist movements. In fact, issues of ethnicity, nationalism, religion, and language are often so interconnected that they blend with each other to create an atmosphere in which it is impossible to quantify, in a scientific manner, how much each of these factors has contributed to a secessionist cause.

Religion is the focus of numerous secessionist movements. Its importance is elevated when two or more religions coexist and injustice, whatever its root, is perceived as aimed at people on the basis of their religion. Religion tends to be a focal point in secession especially when religious intolerance is policy at the governmental level, and efforts aimed at religious purity are undertaken. Among the secessionist movements active at present, some are clearly religious in orientation. Indeed, the fact that the southern Sudanese rebel groups are Christian in a state populated by a Moslem majority cannot be discounted, nor can the fact that the Karen are Christians while Myanmar's official religion is Buddhism. The role of religion is even more poignant in the cases of the Catholics and Protestants of Northern Ireland and the Catholics and Eastern Orthodox in the Yugoslav civil war of 1991.[29]

Other secessionist movements are focusing on language in an effort to protect and preserve a language and script in the face of pressure from a linguistically dominant majority. Indeed, increased autonomy or independence is demanded as a result of perceived demise of minority culture as exemplified by language. Quebec comes to mind as a region in which extreme effort has been put in reviving French as the regional language, to perhaps the detriment of non-French-speaking inhabitants of the region. Catalonia is also revising regional laws to grant precedence to its language in the face of increasing popularity of Spanish. In both of these cases, language preservation, together with the culture that is embodied in it, is cited as a major reason for the desire for secession.

Closely related to the question of culture and cultural uniqueness is ethnicity. Numerous ethnic groups have demanded autonomy as a result of injustices associated with government policy or popular intolerance based on their minority status within a state. Indeed, the Ibos, Tibetans, Punjabis, Kashmiris, Kosovars, et cetera, all claim mistreatment on the basis of ethnicity. The issue of minority status on ethnic grounds raises numerous questions and triggers numerous responses among policymakers and populations. For example, how are ethnic demands to be accommodated within a multiethnic state and what are the advantages of policies of integration? One important question whose answer has wide repercussions is who is, in fact, the minority ethnic group? Depending on one's point of reference, the distinction between a minority and majority becomes blurred. For example, Tamils of Sri Lanka are attempting to defend their culture and ethnicity against the more dominant Sinhalese. However, to the Sinhalese, the oppression of the Hindus from India who speak Dravidian languages is perceived as a major threat. Indeed, according to a Sinhalese politician, "In this country, the problem of the Tamils is not a minority problem. The Sinhalese are the minority in Dravidistan. We are carrying on a struggle for our national existence against the Dravidian majority"[30] This perception is similar to that of the Serbs in Croatia, who feel their ethnic status is reduced to secondary within Croatia, while the Croats perceive they are a minority within Yugoslavia. Additional examples, such as the Russians in Latvia and Moldova, abound, and point to the numerous problems arising when secessionist aspirations are based on ethnicity.

Culture, ethnicity, language are all embodied in the notion of nationalism, defined as "the devotion to one's nation; patriotism or chauvinism."[31] The role of nationalism in the creation and destruction of states has been addressed extensively in the literature, and its role in the Austrian, Hungarian, Ottoman, and Russian empires has been established. Moreover, its role in the two world wars, as well as Third World independence movements, is indisputable. The policy towards it in communism has also been avidly debated. Nationalism has been viewed both as a progressive force, as by Rosa Luxemburg, and a regressive force, suppressing the individual rights and initiative, as by Talmon.[32] In socialist societies of the Soviet bloc, it was assumed that nationalism would be eradicated by "the socialist man" and the short-run measure to achieve this result was federation.[33] Despite Lenin's predictions, history has shown that in federations such as the Soviet Union, Yugoslavia, and Czechoslovakia, time has produced greater, not lesser regional manifestations of nationalism. Indeed, the debate on nationalism is again resurfacing, relating nationalism to other factors, including communism, democracy, and economics. The obvious question arises: Is it that the communist system did not give legitimate expression to the manifestations of nationalism of its minorities, giving rise to the present obsessive nationalistic passions, or was there too much liberty to express nationalistic tendencies, as in Yugoslavia, preventing the creation of a sympathetic sentiment towards the center?[34] Many claim that with the demise of communism, nationalist sentiment became free to be vented. Isaiah Berlin claims that "in our modern age, nationalism is not resurgent: it never died. [It and racism] are the most powerful movements in the world today, cutting across many social systems"[35] O'Brien claims that democracy and nationalism are incompatible, calling nationalism a "conglomerate of emotions" and claiming that "the early stirrings of nationalism appeared to be democratic, but later manifestations were more disquieting."[36] And Eric Hobsbawm identifies a proliferation of petty nationalisms as societies look for means to define themselves in new economic terms. In the world of interregional economic interdependence, states are no longer aiming to economic self-sufficiency and rely on international markets for the satisfaction of their needs. Therefore, the idea of a state existing along the lines of its economic interests is not relevant anymore, leading to other parameters in the definition of states.[37]

The role of nationalism is neither negated, nor explored, in this study. It is relevant for our purposes insofar as it is interconnected to economic factors. The relationship between nationalism and economics is strong in some cases, and it is with extreme difficulty that the two can be separated. Indeed, how can we distinguish between the desire for national control of resources among the Azerbaijanis and the pride in their culture and the desire to see their people in power? Which force is dominant?

WHY SO MUCH SECESSION?

A mere glance at a major newspaper in the early 1990s supports the contention that there is not only an increase in the number of secessionist movements across the globe but also in the number of successful attempts. Until 1991, when the independence of the former Baltic Soviet republics was recognized, there were very few cases of peaceful secessionist movements. Indeed, Belgium's secession from the Netherlands in 1830 and Norway's secession from Sweden in 1905 are extremely rare in their success and lack of violence. A few more cases of successful secessionist movements exist, although they were accompanied by violence and damage: Ireland in 1919, Algeria in 1956, and Bangladesh in 1971. Although more than one-half of the states presently in existence are less than 40 years old,[38] their creation did not occur by secession.

Horowitz asked, "If nearly every secession is doomed to failure, why do secessionist movements continue to arise?"[39] There is no single answer to this question, and numerous theories are bound to arise in the near future. Some of these will undoubtedly focus on the following two issues: the lack of a coincidence between ethnic and state boundaries, and the end of the cold war. These are discussed below, although neither of them provide a satisfactory or sufficient basis for explaining present secessionist activity.

(i) Ethnic and State Boundaries

In most countries, ethnic and state boundaries do not coincide, providing an excuse for ethnically based secessionist and irredentist activity.[40] A few definitions are in order: A state is a legal-territorial concept, referring to that set of structures and institutions that seek to maintain control over a population within a specific geographical area. A nation refers to a group of people who share culture, history, and usually language in a specific territory, and who give political expression to this common identity. A nation-state is a state in which national and political borders coincide. In most cases, they do not. Indeed, according to Conner,[41] of a total of 132 contemporary states, only 12 are ethnically homogeneous. In 25 states, one ethnic group accounts for more than 90 percent of the population, while in an additional 25 states it accounts for between 75 and 90 percent. In 31 states, the dominant ethnic group represents 50 to 75 percent of the population, and in 39 states, it represents less than half. It is also noted that in 53 states, the population is divided into more than five significant groups.

In many of these cases, the multiethnic states have worked out an elaborate system of mutual tolerance and a *modus vivendi* has emerged among ethnic groups sharing a common political space. This explains the numerous regions in the world in which the political and ethnic boundaries do not coincide, and yet there is no turmoil at present, such as Alsace and large parts of Africa. Switzerland is often cited as unique insofar as it is ethnically heterogeneous and has not experienced secessionist activity at the state level, nor have irredentist movements attempted to unite territory with France or Italy. The countries in Asia and Africa tend to be ethnically heterogeneous, often with compact minorities residing in compact territories. Many of those are divided by international boundaries drawn arbitrarily with little regard to ethnic composition. In Africa alone, the number of ethnic groups divided by international boundaries abound: the Yoruba in Nigeria and Benin, the Hausa in Nigeria, Niger, and Ghana, the Berbers in Algeria, Tunisia, and Libya, the Bakongo in Angola and Zaire, et cetera.[42] In the former Soviet Union, of the 23 interrepublican borders, only three are not contested.[43] In South America, although there are numerous Indian groups whose rights have unequivocally been curtailed with the advent of white man, there are no significant secessionist movements. It is likely that this absence may be explained by the fact that these groups of indigenous populations have little power and little leverage in the political arena. Others are not tied to any particular land.[44]

The lack of coincidence between national and state borders alone fails to explain the present agitation, since borders have not coincided for the entire past century, nor do they coincide in numerous regions of the world where such conflicts do not exist (as, for example, in Switzerland). The issue of ethnicity and borders therefore succeeds only in providing a historical context to the present conflicts.

(ii) The End of the Cold War

The increase in secessionist activity in the 1990s might be attributed to the end of the cold war, which enabled the release of nationalist sentiments in an era of crumbling central control. In the former Soviet bloc, it allowed the unleashing of pent-up emotions, while in other regions, it provided the backdrop of the formation of a new world order that created the right international environment for change. Indeed, Berlin claims that in the former Soviet Union, secessionist activity spurred by nationalism is a reaction, after years of oppression, that manifests itself in an outburst of national pride and aggressive self-assertion. O'Brien says that communism "was effective in sedating nationalism. As communism wore off, nationalism woke up again, and disintegration of the multinational polities set in"[45] According to Chazan, irredentist and secessionist manifestations tend to be "associated with periods of major political reordering, boundary readjustment or restructuring of the international system."[46] He adds that these movements are tied to periods of war and conflict, as well as the breakdown of empires. In the late 20th century, although there is no major war, there is a major international restructuring. The cold war's passing has brought an end to the bipolar division of the world into the communist/capitalist economic systems or the dictatorship/democracy political systems.

While the cold war may provide the causal link in demands for autonomy in Eastern Europe and the Soviet Union, it fails to explain other movements that are completely outside the sphere of bipolar politics. Indeed, the most that these secessionist movements have done for the global secessionist movements is to create a domino effect by providing an impetus to passive and dormant demands. Moreover, the state of anarchy that is developing in the world where the vacuum of the bipolar division has not yet been replaced by another structure provides an appropriate environment for testing the limits of numerous political establishments. These indirect effects of the cold war may only hope to explain some of the secessionist efforts, since many were well entrenched before the unraveling of the Soviet Union.

Instead of asking why there are so many secessionist movements in the 1990s, it may be more appropriate to ask why are there so few. The conditions for secession are certainly present in numerous parts of the world. There is a changing world order and there is some measure of anarchy as international relationships are in the process of redefinition. Furthermore, ethnic boundaries are under dispute, and ethnic groups are increasingly intolerant and self-assertive. So there must be some other considerations in the drive for greater political subdivisions, and one of these, the economic, is the subject of this book.

CLASSIFICATIONS OF CASES

The theoretical framework proposed for the study of the economics of secession is illustrated by the examples of secession attempts both past and present. Although the emphasis will be on those regions in which the author has had most direct experience, such as the Soviet Union, Yugoslavia, Italy, and India, a total of thirty seven secessionist movements is studied. Empirical evidence from these is used to identify the economic components of secession, and to offer hypotheses pertaining to economic viability of independent entities. These secessionist regions are enumerated in Table 1.1. The choice of these, and the exclusion of others, was made on the basis of the following considerations: An attempt was made to cover a broad range of geographical zones, historical conditions, political systems, and levels of development. Small and large regions were included, as were ethnically homogeneous and heterogeneous populations, and both violent and peaceful conflicts. Although the number of secessionist attempts in the former Soviet Union is presently high, only five regions were specifically studied, covering the four geographical zones of republics and different administrative levels. The self-proclaimed Autonomous Tatar Region and the Republic of Serbian Krajina,[47] both lacking international recognition, were nevertheless included in the study given the importance of these regions in current events.[48] A last consideration, but by no means unimportant, is the availability of data and information on the secessionist movements. Some secessionist activity has received more attention in the popular press and academic journals, enabling a more informed judgement on the economic components of the secessionist struggle. Furthermore, some governments have been more reluctant to collect and publish regional statistics, thus limiting some aspects of this study.

As a result of all these considerations, secessionist movements presently active in parts of France and Belgium, regions of Italy such as Trentino Alto Adige, parts of Eastern Europe,[49] as well as movements associated with the Sorbs (not Serbs) in Germany, and the Muslims in Arakan (Myanmar), although mentioned sporadically, have not been subject to detailed analysis.

There are a few anomalies that must be explained about the choice of some of these cases. First, Lombardy and Southern Sudan were included despite the fact that they are not actively demanding secession at this time, but rather vying for increased autonomy from their respective centers. Second, Puerto Rico was included although it is not attempting secession from the United States, since it was never a part of it. However, the region is exploring the possibilities for alternative relations with Washington, and the debate is largely based on economic issues. As such, the questions raised by a new arrangement are similar to those that must be answered by secessionist regions everywhere. Third, Singapore was included even though its experience with respect to "breaking up" is different from all the others: it is the only region that was formally expelled from the Malaysian Federation before it seceded. It was nevertheless included because of the economic nature of the grievances that its government had with the Malaysian Federation and because of the economic success that it achieved despite the odds against its viability.

The 37 regions in which secessionist movements are active (or have been active) are by no means similar. They differ with respect to their backgrounds, their positions within their respective unions, and the nature of their secessionist efforts. The differences are discussed below, and are captured in Table 1.1. Given the wide variations in the nature, goals and success potential of seceding regions, what is the justification for comparing their experiences? It is based on the fact that we are essentially observing their economic conditions and relations, and thereby making a cross-sectional study of one variable across different conditions. Moreover, the cases have been grouped according to some characteristic in an effort to enable comparison. In methodological terms, this follows the suggestion by Przeworski and Teune called "the most similar systems design."[50] The most important of these variables is the level of income of the seceding region, both in absolute terms as well as relative to the union. Various other economic variables are observed and an effort is made to identify patterns within these subgroups.

An explanation of the statistical basis of this study is in order. Numerous secessionist movements exist within states with highly developed statistical systems, thus providing ample evidence of economic links between regions. Moreover, freedom of study of delicate political subjects such as secession results in the publication of research that may be used as secondary evidence. However, in most countries, neither of these sources of information is available. Indeed, even countries that have sophisticated statistical collection techniques and high standards, such as India and Yugoslavia, do not have, for example, official interregional trade data. Regions such as East Timor, Iraqi Kurdistan, and the Karen region of Myanmar were included despite the lack of statistics pertaining to their economies. In these cases, government statistical breakdowns, to the extent that they exist, do not coincide with the borders of the secessionist regions. Whenever possible, estimates were made of regional economic characteristics. However, since that was not always possible, the book tends to overemphasize those regions for which there was sufficient information.

BACKGROUND CONDITIONS AND CHARACTERISTICS OF SECESSION MOVEMENTS

1. The *historical* experiences of secessionist regions differ significantly. Some were an integral part of empires that unravelled at the end of World War I, such as the Austro-Hungarian and the Ottoman Empires, which covered areas that today house numerous secessionist movements, including those by Slovaks, Slovenians, Macedonians, Kurds, et cetera. Other regions where secessionist activity thrives were colonies of the 19th-century European powers and only gained their independence after World War II. In this category are those movements such as in the Sudan, Western Sahara, Iraq, India, et cetera. Some territories were tossed around among rulers within a short period of time, so that the indigenous population never associated with any one particular culture, the way that Algerians did with France, or the Indians with England. An example of this is the island of Bougainville, whose history includes rule by the Dutch, the Australians, the British, and the Germans. Different historical experiences manifest themselves in different views pertaining to individual and group rights, constitutions, ethnic tolerance, and political culture.

2. Current secessionist movements exist under widely different *political* structures, ranging from loose federations to centralized, unitary systems.[51] The constitutions in these political systems will vary, and consequently the rights and obligations associated with each segment of the territory will also vary. Clearly, Quebec has a different political relationship with Ottawa than Transylvania with Bucharest or Eritrea with Addis Ababa. Differences in political rights and obligations of regions have an effect on the demands of their secessionist movements.

3. Secessionist regions vary with respect to the *economic* system of which they are a part. It has long been clear to economists that a classification into the traditional categories of capitalist and socialist is meaningless in light of the numerous variations within those categories. For decades, the capitalist economies have been taking on properties associated with socialism, while the socialist economies have been adopting characteristics of capitalism. Therefore, an effort to divide the secessionist movements into those that are part of a socialist system would separate the former Soviet bloc, Tibet, and Eritrea from the remaining secessionist regions. A more relevant separation of regions might take into account the various stages of the "transition to capitalism" in which some of these regions find themselves. Indeed, it is these variations in the speed and intensity of reforms that can cause friction in interregional or center-state relations, leading to an acceleration of the secessionist drive. This happened in Slovenia: during 1988-90 the reforms aimed at marketization were more radical than what was acceptable to other parts of Yugoslavia, making the speed of reforms one of the principal justifications of secession. In 1992, disagreement over economic reforms is exacerbating differences between Ukraine and Russia.

Another aspect of the regional economy that varies considerably among the regions is the degree of decentralization of economic power at the regional level. Regions such as the Yugoslav republics enjoyed great decentralization, culminating in the existence of republic central banks, while others, such as East Timor or Transylvania, have virtually no local economic powers. The disagreement over the distribution of power between the center and the regions has been one of the crucial elements underlying the failure of the Soviet Union to remain unified.

4. Seceding regions vary with respect to the *ethnic composition* of their residents. The study by Conner mentioned above shows that very few states in existence in the late 20th century are ethnically homogeneous. If these heterogeneous states have regional subdivisions that coincide with ethnic borders (such as Bougainville and Slovenia), then secession of one of those will create fewer disturbances than when ethnic groups are mixed (such as

in Moldova or Georgia) or if the populations reside in a mosaic pattern, (such as in Bosnia-Hercegovina). Out of the 37 regions studied here, fewer than 15 are ethnically homogeneous.

5. Seceding regions vary with respect to their *inherent wealth.* Some seceding regions contain lucrative raw materials (such as Katanga, Bougainville, etc.), are located in strategically important places (Biafra, Punjab, the Karen region, etc.) or have a historical tradition of high productivity and a well-established industrial base (such as Lombardy and Catalonia). Others share none of these advantages, such as Kosovo or Turkmenia.

6. Secessionists vary according to their intentions pertaining to *associations* with other countries. Independence offers novel possibilities for political alliances and economic links. Some secessionists begin their independence efforts with some form of association already in mind, based upon ethnicity (in the case of irredentist movements) or economic interests or geopolitical logic. Indeed, on the basis of geography, Bougainville is exploring links with the Solomon Islands, and on the basis of economic interests, Slovenia and Croatia have explored links with Germany and Austria in advance of their declarations of independence.

7. Secessionist movements differ according to their relative *uniqueness* within a state. The existence of secessionist agitation may be limited to one area of the country, such as northern Sri Lanka, Southern Sudan, Slovakia, and Cabinda, or it may manifest itself in a multitude of regions, such as in the former Soviet Union, Spain, Myanmar, and Yugoslavia. Although it is presently more common to witness a single region attempting to secede, when there are numerous attempts within a state, the possibility of success is higher because the center is dispersing its energies on several fronts. Indeed, this multitude of pressures may result in the unraveling of the entire state, as occurred in the Soviet Union and Yugoslavia, and as is feared by India and Britain.

8. Secessionist movements vary according to the *duration* of the secessionist effort or conflict. As evident from Table 1.1, some secessionist regions are engaged in open conflict that has persisted for decades, such as Northern Ireland and Eritrea. Other regions, such as northern Sri Lanka and Punjab, are entering their tenth year of conflict. Other conflicts are significantly more recent, such as that in Bougainville. Indeed, what that region has achieved with respect to independence in a remarkably short time is envied by the Tamils and Irish. The greater the duration of a conflict, especially if violent, the greater the economic damage with respect to loss of labor, productivity and material resources, and consequently, the greater the recovery time in the aftermath of secession.

9. Secessionist movements vary according to the nature of the conflict, namely the degree of *violence* that is involved in the expression of demands and in the achievement of goals. In some cases, localized guerrilla warfare is conducted, such as among the Karen, the Corsicans, or the Quebecois during the 1970s. The Irish struggle for secession from Britain has been significantly more violent. In some cases, civil war occurred over the secession issue, such as in the United States, Croatia, Biafra, and Katanga. Indeed, the conflict in the Congo pertaining to Katanga almost produced World War III, as international economic and geopolitical interests became threatened.

10. Secessionists vary according to the *moral basis* of their claims and demands. Some regions might be trying to redress old grievances of invasion (such as the Baltic republics of the USSR) or irrationally drawn borders (such as Western Sahara). Others are simply revolting economically against what they perceive to be exploitation (such as Lombardy and Slovenia). In some of these cases it is easier to bring about a moral judgement than in others. However, in all of these, one important consideration is the nature of the first union between region and center: was the union voluntary (such as Croatia, which later simply changed its mind) or involuntary (such as Lithuania, which was invaded)? Unlike the republics of the USSR, the regions of present Yugoslavia and Czechoslovakia were united voluntarily at the end of World War I. Bohemia, Moravia, Slovakia, Slovenia, and Croatia were minority regions within the Austro-Hungarian Empire. Serbia was independent since its liberation from the Ottoman Empire, and was instrumental in creating the Kingdom of Serbs, Croats and Slovenes after World War I. Therefore, the present regional agitation in Czechoslovakia and Yugoslavia is not rooted in the involuntary assimilation of one region by another. This is different from the experience of regions such as Southern Sudan and Punjab. The regions of Southern Sudan were never even consulted when the Arab North, in conjunction with Egypt and the British, forged the terms of the Sudan's independence. In Punjab, the concept of a sovereign Sikh state is not new to modern history. Indeed, the Akali Dal Party agitated for autonomy as early as 1944 when its goal was to "evolve a scheme for the establishment of an independent Sikh state in case India was to be divided".[52] However, the demand for an independent Khalistan differed from that of Pakistan insofar as the Sikhs were not a majority in any one region. The legality of their incorporation into the Indian union has been greatly debated at the present time and lends secessionist movements in these states a measure of historical "right" not shared by all secessionist movements across the world.

11. Secessionist movements vary with respect to the *popular support* that they receive. It is easiest to gauge popular support in multiparty systems

where the electorate expresses support for a secessionist platform through the voting procedure. However, the mere existence of a party does not lend legitimacy in representing the regional population and reflecting the regional sentiment. Some of the regions that do have parties supporting secession vacillate between legality and illegality, so it is often hard to judge what the support of a party is. In 1988, secessionist parties were in existence among the Welsh, the Scots, the Basques, the Corsicans, and the Ambonese in Indonesia. There has been a significant rise in the number of regional parties that have recently been put to test with respect to the secession issue, including the former republics of the Soviet Union and Yugoslavia.

12. Secessionist movements vary in their *demands*. Some have persistently sought full independence and have been unwilling to compromise. In this category are the Baltic republics of the USSR. Others have agitated for increased autonomy within the existing union, such as Yakutia's demand for republic status within Russia. Alternatively, a region may simply be vying for increased attention from the center, which may amount to a more favorable redistribution of benefits. Both Lombardy in the 1990s and Western Australia in the 1930s are examples of this. In other cases, the demands of a region may undergo transformation, alternating between demands for secession and increased regional powers. This occurred in Southern Sudan: During the first civil war in the aftermath of independence (1964-69), the demands of the Southerners were outright secession. However, in the present conflict, that demand has receded to the background, and is supplanted by the demand for an entirely different basis of government, with greater participation and rights ("we want in" rather than "we want out"[53]).

13. Regions aspiring to secession vary with respect to the *constitutional rights* that their administrative unit is granted by the state constitution. For example, the constitution of Yugoslavia, like that of the Soviet Union but unlike that of Czechoslovakia, grants its regions the *right* to secede. Whether this has any measure of usefulness in regional attempts to secede is unclear, but it does give Yugoslav regions a legal right to do so that Slovakia, for example, does not share. Other constitutions do not give regions the right to secede, but rather give the center the right to expel them, such as that of the Malaysian Federation, according to which a region may be "dissociated" by a mere act of Parliament.[54] The Spanish constitution even prohibits a referendum on secession.

Secessionist regions must also contend with the legal aspects of border changes, given the numerous international conventions pertaining to this. International law recognizes several ways in which a state could acquire a legal title to a territory, and some secessionist states do not qualify for international recognition.[55] Moreover, regions also vary with respect to the binds that they are legally in. For example, some countries, including the United States, Canada, and 30 European countries, signed the Helsinki Final Act of 1975, which confirmed the inviolability of the post-World War II borders. This was aimed, at the time, at securing a country's borders against invasion. Since it did not address itself to the securing of borders against internal pressures, such as that of regional self-determination of any peoples, the law's interpretation is now open to discussion by the secessionist region and the center.

14. Secessionist movements differ with respect to the degree and nature of *international intervention* that is drawn to their crisis. In most cases, secessionist problems are considered a "family matter" and outsiders are unlikely to become involved. When involvement does take place, it can be bilateral or multilateral, in the latter case often involving the United Nations (as in the failed secession attempt of Katanga and currently in Yugoslavia) or more recently the EEC (in Yugoslavia). This international involvement may be motivated by irredentism (such as Pakistani efforts in Kashmir, or the threatened Turkish efforts in Azerbaijan), or it may be based on political interests (such as Iranian support of Iraqi Kurds), or economic interests (such as German efforts on behalf of Croatia). International intervention may be limited to sending of food and nonmilitary supplies (such as to the Sudan) or military supplies (such as the Indian intervention on behalf of Bangladeshi secession from Pakistan). Intervention sometimes is limited to passive lack of support of secessionists, (such as the policy of the United States during the Biafra attempted secession, when it supported the slogan "To keep Nigeria one is a job that must be done"[56]) or the withholding of international recognition (such as the refusal of the EEC to recognize Macedonia). International intervention is sometimes symmetrical, such as when two adjoining states support each other's secessionist movements. The most glaring example of such a pattern is that of Sudan and Ethiopia: the Khartoum government supported the rebels of Eritrea and Tigre by allowing them freedom of operation on their territory, while, Ethiopia provided training and supplies to the Sudanese People's Liberation Army. This situation reflected a virtual indirect war, or war by proxy, between the two states.[57]

OUTLINE OF THE BOOK

In the Hindu religious text, the *Bhagavad Gita,* God is described first by what he is not. Without intending to give this study inappropriate stature by using this analogy, I too will first describe the book by what it is not. This study of secession does not question whether a seceding region has the right to secede, nor whether the union has the right to prevent it. It does not study the moral basis of secession. It does not prescribe how the international audience should react, nor does it delve into the various political forms that allow secession and the constitutional questions to be asked in secession.

Instead, this book is an attempt to study secession from an economic point of view while fully realizing that economics cannot by itself explain this phenomenon, nor alone present conditions for its success. Just as secession is multifaceted, so it warrants a multidisciplinary approach. The goal is to induce economists to study a heretofore ignored subject and to introduce an economic perspective in a topic dominated by political scientists, sociologists and ethnologists.

The theoretical framework for the economic study of secession is presented in chapter 2 while the empirical evidence pertaining to secessionist movements is presented in chapters 3 and 4. The topics of chapters 5, 6, and 7 evolve from the theory of chapter 2: they cover the various phases of the secessionist process in which economic issues are of relevance, namely the economic *basis* of secession, the *resolution* of economic issues, and the *viability* of regions. These three chapters draw on the empirical evidence presented in chapters 3 and 4 to illustrate the three phases. The topics covered reflect the dilemma faced by seceding regions, to the extent that they can view the subject in a rational, nonemotional manner. That, of course, remains a highly unrealistic assumption in most environments, but one that politicians and people alike need to aspire to. Finally, chapter 8 offers some concluding thoughts into secessionist activity in the 1990s.

Table 1.1: Characteristics of Secessionist Regions

The entries in Tables 1.1 and 1.2 correspond to the 14 characteristics described in chapter 1. However, item number five, pertaining to the inherent wealth of the region, is not described here, but rather in Table 3.1.

Explanation of Terms:

(1) historical=the recent past of the secessionist region.

(2), (3) system poli/econ=the political and economic system (fed.=federal, unit.=unitary, ss.=special status within the union, peas.=peasant agriculture).

(4) ethnic= the principal ethnic group in the seceding region; %=the percent of the population in the seceding region that is of that ethnic group (if ethnicity is not relevant, then the religious differences are stated here), homog.=homogeneous, hetero.=heterogeneous.

(6) irredentist/association=Is the movement irredentist in nature, and is there an association with another country that is being formulated for the future?

(7) single=Is the movement the only one in the state?

(8) onset=the year the conflict or secessionist aspirations began. (If there are two years listed, this indicates there was a respite in the conflict. Moreover, in the case of secessionist aspirations that have persisted for centuries, such as in Scotland, only the most recent episode is listed).

REGION	(1) HISTORICAL	(2), (3) SYSTEM POLI/ECON	(4) ETHNIC (%)	(6) IRREDEN-TIST/ASSO-CIATION	(7) SINGLE?	(8) ONSET
ASIA						
Bougain-ville [58] (PNG)	Australian colony	unit. (ss)/ peasant; capitalist [59]	homog. [60]	no	yes	1968/1988
Tibet [61] (China)	Chinese invasion	unit. (ss)/ socialist [62]	75 Tibetan [63]	no	no	1950/1987
N & E Provinces (Sri Lanka)	British colony	unit. (ss)/ peasant; capitalist [64]	50-95 Tamil [65]	no	yes	mid-1970s
East Timor (Indonesia)	Portuguese colony	unit. (ss)/ peasant; capitalist [66]	80 Timorese [67]	no	no	1975

REGION	(1) HISTORICAL	(2), (3) SYSTEM POLI/ECON	(4) ETHNIC (%)	(6) IRREDEN- TIST/ASSO- CIATION	(7) SINGLE?	(8) ONSET
Punjab (India)	British colony	fed. (ss)/ capitalist[68]	60 Sikhs[69]	no	no	1960[70]
Assam (India)	British colony	fed. (ss)/ peasant; capitalist[71]	50 Assamese[72]	no	no	mid-1970s
Kashmir (India)[73]	British colony	fed. (ss)/ peasant; capitalist[74]	95 Muslims	maybe[75]	no	1947/1987
Karen region (Myanmar)	British colony	unitary/ peasant; capitalist	Karen[76]	no	no	1948
AFRICA Southern Sudan[77]	British colony	unitary (fed. 1991)/ peasant; capitalist[78]	Dinka[79]	no	yes	1964-69/ 1983
Western Sahara	Spanish colony	unitary/ peasant; capitalist	Sahrawi	no	yes	1973
Eritrea (Ethiopia)	Italian colony	fed. (ss) +unitary/ peasant; socialist[80]	hetero.[81]	no	no	1962
Cabinda (Angola)	Portuguese colony	unitary/ peasant; capitalist[82]	Bakongo[83]	no	yes	1966/1991
Casamance (Senegal)	Portuguese colony[84]	unitary/ peasant; capitalist	Diola[85]	no	yes	1990
MIDDLE EAST Kurdistan (Iraq)[86]		unitary/ peasant[87]	Turkik[88]	yes	yes	1921

REGION	(1) HISTORICAL	(2), (3) SYSTEM POLI/ECON	(4) ETHNIC (%)	(6) IRREDEN- TIST/ASSO- CIATION	(7) SINGLE?	(8) ONSET
NORTH AMERICA						
Quebec (Canada)	French influence[89]	fed./ capitalist	83 French[90]	no	yes	1960s
Puerto Rico (U.S.)	Spanish colony/U.S. common- wealth[91]	fed. (ss)/ capitalist[92]	Hispanic	no	yes	1952
FORMER SOVIET BLOC						
Latvia (USSR)	Soviet invasion	federation/ socialist	53.7 Latvian[93]	no	no	1944/1988
Tadzhikistan (USSR)	Soviet empire	federation/ socialist	58.5 Tadzhiks[94]	no	no	1988
Georgia (USSR)	Russian empire	federation/ socialist	68.8 Georgians	no	no	1920/1988
Ukraine (USSR)	Russian empire	federation/ socialist	73.6 Ukrainian	no	no	1930s/ late 1980s
Tatarstan (USSR)	Russian dominance	federation/ socialist[95]	48 Tatar[96]	no	no	1990
Slovenia (Yugoslavia)	Austro- Hungarian Empire	federation/ socialist	89 Slovene	no	no	late 1980s
Croatia (Yugoslavia)	Austro- Hungarian Empire	federation/ socialist	77 Croat (12 Serb)	no	no	WWII, late 1980s[97]
Krajina[98] (Croatia)	Austro- Hungarian Empire/ Croatia	federation/ socialist[99]	62 Serb[100]	yes	no	1989[101]
Kosovo / (Serbia/ Yugoslavia)[102]	Ottoman Empire	federation/ socialist[103]	77 Kosovar (13 Serb)[104]	yes	no	1968/1981

REGION	(1) HISTORICAL	(2), (3) SYSTEM POLI/ECON	(4) ETHNIC (%)	(6) IRREDEN-TIST/ASSO-CIATION	(7) SINGLE?	(8) ONSET
Slovakia (Czecho-slovakia)[105]	Austro-Hungarian Empire	federation/ socialist[106]	85 Slovak[107]	no	yes	1939/1989
Tran-sylvania (Romania)[108]	Hungarian Empire	unitary (ss)/ socialist[109]	40 Hungarian[110]	yes	yes	1950s/1989

WESTERN EUROPE

REGION	(1) HISTORICAL	(2), (3) SYSTEM POLI/ECON	(4) ETHNIC (%)	(6) IRREDEN-TIST/ASSO-CIATION	(7) SINGLE?	(8) ONSET
Northern Ireland (U.K.)	Partition/ U.K.[111]	fed.-unit.[112] direct rule[113]/ capitalist	homog.[114] (1m Prot.; .5m Catholic)	yes	no	1921
Scotland (U.K.)	Crown of England	fed.-unit. (ss)/ capitalist[115]	homog. (Scots)	no	no	1914/1979
Corsica (France)	influence Genoa & France[116]	unitary (ss)/ capitalist[117]	homog. (Corsicans)	no	yes	mid-1970s
Basque provinces (Spain)[118]	Castillian crown	regional autonomy/ capitalist[119]	60 Basque[120]	no	no	1939/1968
Catalonia (Spain)[121]	Castillian crown	regional autonomy/ capitalist[122]	homog. (Catalans)[123]	no	no	1939/ mid-1970s
Lombardy (Italy)	Napoleonic Lombard Republic	unitary/ capitalist	homog.	no	no	1989

HISTORICAL CASES

REGION	(1) HISTORICAL	(2), (3) SYSTEM POLI/ECON	(4) ETHNIC (%)	(6) IRREDEN-TIST/ASSO-CIATION	(7) SINGLE?	(8) ONSET
Biafra (Nigeria)	British colony	federation/ peasant; capitalist[124]	hetero. (mostly Ibo)	no	yes	1962 to 1970
Katanga (Belgian Congo)	Belgian colony	unitary/ peasant; capitalist[125]	hetero.[126]	no	yes	1958 to 1963

REGION	(1) HISTORICAL	(2), (3) SYSTEM POLI/ECON	(4) ETHNIC (%)	(6) IRREDEN- TIST/ASSO- CIATION	(7) SINGLE?	(8) ONSET
Bangladesh (Pakistan)	British colony	federation/ peasant; capitalist	85 Bengali[127]	no	yes	1966 to 1971
Singapore (Malaysian Fed.)	British colony	federation (ss)/ capitalist[128]	76 Chinese[129]	no	no	1963 to 1965

Table 1.2: Characteristics of Secessionist Regions, Part II

Explanation of Terms

(9) violence/peace=Is the movement violent or peaceful in nature (P=peaceful, V=violent), as measured by high, low, or medium (med.) (C=violence from the center, I=violence internal to the region or movement)?

(10) moral basis (nature of union)=Is there a moral basis to secessionist aspirations as indicated by the voluntary (vol.) or involuntary (invol.) nature of the union?

(11) support and legitimacy=What is the basis of legitimacy of secessionist demands (liberation movt.=liberation movement; ref.=referendum)?

(12) demands=Is the region demanding secession, autonomy, independence, or control over its resources?

(13) constitutional rights=Does the constitution of the state grant the secessionist region the right to secede?

(14) international intervention=Has there been international intervention in support or against the seceding region?

REGION	(9) VIOLENCE/ PEACE	(10) MORAL BASIS	(11) SUPPORT & LEGITI- MACY	(12) DEMANDS	(13) CONSTI- TUTIONAL	(14) INTER- NATIONAL INTER- VENTION
ASIA						
Bougain- ville (PNG)	V (C) med.	invol.[130]	liberation movt.[131]	secession; then autonomy	no	no
Tibet (China)	P[132]	invol.	liberation movt.	indepen- dence	no	no
N & E Provinces (Sri Lanka)	V (C) high	vol.	party[133]	secession	no	yes (India)
East Timor (Indonesia)	V (C) med.	invol.[134]	liberation movt.[135]	indepen- dence	no	no
Punjab (India)	V (I/C) med.	unclear[136]	party[137]	secession; then autonomy	no	no

REGION	(9) VIOLENCE/ PEACE	(10) MORAL BASIS	(11) SUPPORT & LEGITI- MACY	(12) DEMANDS	(13) CONSTI- TUTIONAL	(14) INTER- NATIONAL INTER- VENTION
Assam (India)	V (I/C) med.	vol.	party[138]	secession; then autonomy	no	no
Kashmir (India)	V (I/C) med.	invol.[139]	party	indepen- dence	no	maybe (Pakistan)
Karen region (Myanmar)	V (C) high[140]	invol.[141]	liberation movt.	secession; then autonomy	no	yes (Thailand)
AFRICA						
Southern Sudan	V (I/C) high[142]	invol.[143]	party/ guerrilla[144]	secession; then federation	no[145]	yes (Ethiopia, China, Iran)[146]
Western Sahara	V (C) high[147]	invol.[148]	lib. movt.[149]	indepen- dence	no	yes (Mauri- tania)
Eritrea (Ethiopia)	V (C) high	invol.[150]	liberation movt.[151]	secession	no	yes (Sudan)
Cabinda (Angola)	V (I/C) med.[152]	invol.[153]	liberation movt.[154]	secession	no[155]	yes (Zaire)
Casamance (Senegal)	V (I/C) low	invol.	liberation movt.[156]	autonomy	no	no
MIDDLE EAST						
Kurdistan (Iraq)	V (C) high	invol.	party[157]	secession; then autonomy	no	yes
NORTH AMERICA						
Quebec (Canada)	P	invol.	party/ referendum[158]	secession	no	no

REGION	(9) VIOLENCE/ PEACE	(10) MORAL BASIS	(11) SUPPORT & LEGITI- MACY	(12) DEMANDS	(13) CONSTI- TUTIONAL	(14) INTER- NATIONAL INTER- VENTION
Puerto Rico (U.S.)	P	invol.	party/ referendum[159]	independ.; state; status quo	not appli- cable	no
FORMER SOVIET BLOC						
Latvia (USSR)	P	invol.[160]	party/ referendum	secession	yes[161]	western support
Tadzhiki- stan (USSR)	V (I)	invol.	party/ referendum	secession	yes	no
Georgia (USSR)	V (I/C) low[162]	invol[163]	party/ referendum	secession	yes	no
Ukraine (USSR)	P	invol.	party/ referendum	secession	yes	no
Tatarstan (USSR)	P	invol.[164]	party/ referendum[165]	autonomy	no[166]	no
Slovenia (Yugoslavia)	P[167]	vol.	party/ referendum[168]	secession	yes[169]	western support
Croatia (Yugoslavia)	V (I/C) high	vol.[170]	party/ referendum[171]	secession	yes	western support
Krajina (Croatia)	V (I/C) high[172]	vol.	party/ referendum[173]	secession	no[174]	yes (Serbia)
Kosovo (Serbia/ Yugoslavia)	V (I/C) med.	vol.	party/ referendum[175]	secession	no[176]	no[177]
Slovakia (Czeckoslo- vakia)	P	vol.	party[178]	secession	no[179]	no
Transylvania (Romania)	P[180]	invol.[181]	party	autonomy	no	no

REGION	(9) VIOLENCE/ PEACE	(10) MORAL BASIS	(11) SUPPORT & LEGITI- MACY	(12) DEMANDS	(13) CONSTI- TUTIONAL	(14) INTER- NATIONAL INTER- VENTION
WESTERN EUROPE						
Northern Ireland (U.K.)	V (I/C) high[182]	vol.[183]	party[184]	independence	not applicable[185]	yes (Ireland)
Scotland (U.K.)	P	vol.[186]	party/ referendum[187]	greater autonomy	no	no
Corsica (France)	V (I) low	invol.[188]	party[189]	greater autonomy[190]	no	no
Basque provinces (Spain)	V (I) low	invol.[191]	party[192]	greater autonomy	no[193]	no
Catalonia (Spain)	P	invol.[194]	party[195]	greater autonomy	no	no
Lombardy (Italy)	P	vol	party	greater autonomy	no	no
HISTORICAL CASES						
Biafra (Nigeria)	V (C) high	vol.	party[196]	secession	no	yes
Katanga (Belgian Congo)	V (C) high	invol.[197]	party	secession	no	yes (Belgium, U.N.)
Bangladesh (Pakistan)	V (C) high[198]	vol.[199]	party[200]	secession	no	yes (India)
Singapore (Malaysian Fed.)	V (I) low[201]	vol.	party[202]	economic concessions[203]	expulsion[204]	no

2

Economic Variables and Phases of the Secessionist Process

> Turning and turning in the widening gyre
> The falcon cannot hear the falconer;
> Things fall apart; the center cannot hold;
> Mere anarchy is loosed upon the world
>
> —W. B. Yeats

SECESSION IN ACADEMIC LITERATURE

Secession is a topic traditionally addressed by political scientists and historians, not economists. The former have addressed it in their attempts to understand the process of nation building, the definition of state versus nation, the integration of populations, and the political development accompanying modernization.[1] Some have specialized in the international aspects of separatism by studying the cause and effect of secession on various aspects of international relations,[2] while others have studied the role of nationalism in secession.[3] Psychological studies have emerged studying groups and their behavior in secessionist activity.[4] Historians have studied secessionist movements during and after colonial times, such as those that thrived within the Ottoman, Russian and Austro-Hungarian Empires.[5] Anthropological studies have observed secession from the viewpoint of ethnic groups and their functioning under various forms of national integration.[6] Philosophers have addressed secession from the point of view of the moral right to secede and the moral imperative to accept secession and recognize the seceding region.[7] Legal experts have even extended the concept of secession to include employment-related issues.[8] Finally, geographers have contributed to the debate by affirming the importance of territory and social space.[9]

Although these disciplines have considered the economic issues associated with secession, these were relegated to a secondary position. Indeed, some scholars stated that any emphasis on economics in the study of secession was wrong insofar as it detracted from other issues of greater importance.[10] In this vein, others claimed that interest in economic issues on the part of the secessionists implied a lack of genuine separatism, implying that an economic orientation was inferior to an ethnic one, despite the fact that it too is a challenge to center-state relations and interregional distribution of power: "Also falling short of genuine ethnic separatism and autonomy-seeking are struggles between ethnic groups after power, resources, or resource-protection."[11] The sparse and incomplete reference to the role of economics in secession can be divided into two categories: economic preconditions and the economic aftermath.

The role of economics in fueling the secessionist drive (the preconditions) has been treated on two levels, namely that of the state and that of the region. With respect to the economic development of the state, it was accepted among scholars and policymakers that economic development, as exemplified by capitalist industrialization, would have the effect of reducing group identities, and therefore would dissipate separatist tendencies.[12] However, this view was shown lacking by the proliferation of ethnic self-assertion activity of the mid-1960s in Western European industrialized countries such as France, Britain, and Belgium. There emerged another group of theories that claimed that industrial capitalism in fact was conducive to ethnic protest, and that the political arena that accompanies modernization provides a vehicle for nationalist self-expression.[13] Other scholars treated the relationship between secessionist aspirations and economic development at the level of the region. The most common description of the relationship between secessionist activity and development is an inverse one: namely, the greater the underdevelopment, deterioration, and stagnation of a regional economy, the greater the secessionist drive (Hroch found this in 19th-century Europe, Michneck in contemporary USSR, Birch in Bangladesh, etc.[14]). Indeed, Drake claims that economic inequality "was a major underlying cause of the civil war in Sudan, and it had a definite role in the breakup of Pakistan into Pakistan and Bangladesh. Within Indonesia, too, several of the regional rebellions experienced since independence have had economic grievances at their root."[15] Hobsbawm, also focusing on less developed regions, hints that underdevelopment does *not* stimulate secessionist aspirations since it behooves regions to remain unified with more advanced regions.[16] The direct relationship between economic development and secession has rarely been drawn: Wallerstein is rare among scholars to argue that the wealthy regions, as a result of their wealth, are more likely to attempt secession.[17] This relationship has also been identified and elaborated upon by the author with a comparative study of several secessionist movements.[18]

With respect to economic factors in the aftermath of secession, until recently the literature has focused on economic reconstruction in the aftermath of secessionist efforts, be they successful (as in Bangladesh) or unsuccessful (as in Katanga and Biafra). The conditions of state creation are treated as irrelevant and only the economic problems of new states are studied. However, one study by Buchanon and Faith does attempt to delineate the relationship between secession, taxation, and government transfers.[19]

It was only in 1990, with increased secessionist activity across the globe, that economists awoke to the need to identify economic aspects of secession. This took several directions: First, under the guise of aiding the governments of aspiring new states created from the crumbling Soviet bloc, consultant economists formulated steps to be taken in the process of disassociating from the state. Second, business economists speculated on the damaging effects of investment and trade with dissolving countries by studying the economic potential of individual regions, and paying close attention to individual rules pertaining to tax, profit repatriation, and so on. Third, analogies were made between struggles for power over resources in the present and the past. The realization is reached that just as economic factors often play a crucial role in expansions of states (witness Russia's occupation of Moldova for the economic benefit of the Danube, France's absorption of Alsace for access to the Rhine, Austrian movement into the Dalmatian regions for access to Mediterranean ports, British economic interests in South Asia, etc.), so too they might be relevant in the dissolution of states.

PHASES OF THE SECESSIONIST PROCESS

What is lacking at this time is a thorough and broad understanding of economic issues in all phases of the secessionist process. This is not to negate the literature on secession that has focused on the stages of secession. Indeed, this literature will be briefly described before suggesting phases useful for this study. Research by John Wood has identified five phases in secession: in the first, the preconditions of secession are created or recognized; in the second, a secessionist movements arises; in the third, the central government responds; in the fourth, events occur to directly precipitate secession; and in the fifth, the secession is resolved by armed conflict.[20] Research by Anthony Smith has differentiated secessionist movements according to their maturity, so that at first, a movement is organized and institutionalized, then it acquires mobilization capability, followed by a set of communal values that diffuse among the population and lastly, the movement takes on the properties of an ideology.[21]

This study differs from the above in the following ways: First, the studies by Wood and Smith have tended to be interdisciplinary in nature and have largely overlooked economic issues, while this study focuses on the economic, while considering other issues. Second, both studies tend to assume that the secessionist movement will not succeed, and thus they fail to carry through their analysis into the period after. In this study, the focus is on the period of actual secession and its aftermath, largely warranted by the increase in successful secessions in the period 1990-92. Third, unlike the study by Wood, here it is assumed that armed conflict is only one of the possible responses of the center to secession. Again, the possibility of a peaceful divorce, such as that of the Baltic republics from the Soviet Union, is increased in the present international atmosphere than it was one decade ago, when Wood published his work.

For the purposes of this study, it was possible to condense the evolution into only three phases through which secessionist movements evolve, unless aborted: reevaluation, redefinition and reequilibration, corresponding to the before, during, and after of secession. The following questions are relevant in these phases: What is the nature of the reevaluation of state-region relations, how do regions dissociate themselves from their centers, and how do they then survive independently? Thus, the reevaluation phase includes the first four phases described by Wood, while the redefinition phase may include Wood's last phase.

(i) Reevaluation

This phase refers to the period of time during which the seeds of secession are planted and anticenter sentiment percolates. This phase may last a few months or a few centuries. At some point in this phase, demands are formulated by a segment of the population. These greatly vary in scope and tenacity. Indeed, they may simply be demands for increased favoritism by the center toward a region or a targeted segment of the population, or they may be demands for a dramatic change in the participation of a region in the central and state affairs, or the demands may be such that nothing short of severance of preexisting economic and political ties with the center is acceptable. The latter demand, which is actually the only secessionist demand, is referred to by Leslie as the "we want out" demand,[22] while Bremmer modified Hirshman's concept and calls it the "exit option."[23]

What are those economic factors that lead a region to reappraise the costs and benefits of membership in the union? The critical consideration is the perception of economic injustice. This includes both objective macro conditions, such as poverty, as well as policy aimed at rectifying those conditions, resulting in the following: above-average contribution to the national budget, insufficient benefit from the national budget, unfavorable terms of trade resulting from price manipulation, unfavorable regulation pertaining to investment and foreign inflows of resources, et cetera. It is clear that perceptions of economic exploitation may be experienced by regions that are more *or* less developed relative to the nation, as is evident in Italy (Lombardy as well as the Mezzogiorno), India (Punjab as well as Kashmir), Yugoslavia (Slovenia as well as Macedonia), and in the former USSR (Lithuania as well as Turkmenia). The high-income, subnational regions enumerated above are presently experiencing a tax revolt, reflecting a saturation with what they perceive to be unfair drainage of their resources, while the less developed regions are lobbying for increased spread effects of national development, as well as a change in the redistributive policy. Perceptions of economic injustice influence the reevaluation of the relative costs and benefits of belonging to a national union, and when costs outweigh benefits, economic factors are then mingled with ethnic, religious, or cultural factors, to form a set of demands that sometimes take the form of "we want out."

A study of the economic origins of secessionist movements has been largely overlooked by economists. Yet, an understanding of this "before" process has enormous value for policymakers in states that may yet have time to use policy to accommodate regional demands and thereby retain existing state borders. Thus, an understanding of the "before" of secession has the greatest long-term benefits. However, one must keep in mind that there are numerous problems inherent in a study of secessionist aspirations that have not been resolved and that force scholars to be hesitant. For example, how is the link between economic conditions and aspirations to be made? Even when secession-promoting economic conditions are present, it is unclear that they get translated into perceptions, and then to aspirations. Another example pertains to the assumption of rationality in the secessionist effort. To assume rationality would be to assume perfect information pertaining to issues related to justice in economic relations, such as interregional flows of resources and trade dependency. This information is rarely available, and when it is, it is unclear that it is correct. Indeed, there are numerous cases of efforts to secede that seem clearly doomed to failure, cases in which a weak and poor region is pitted against a stronger, larger, and richer state.

(ii) Redefinition

The period of redefinition is the period during which a region is in the process of breaking its existing ties with the center and is formulating new ties to both its former union as well as to the international economy. These include, a settlement pertaining to the division of the national and international debts, the division of federal or central budget, foreign currency holdings, and other financial holdings and property. The obligations of each side must be calculated with respect to social security, armed forces, et cetera. While these ties are being severed, the new economy must introduce a new currency, a new monetary policy, a new tax system, a new army, and new border crossings and regulations. In the international sphere, trade agreements, joint ventures, and investments must be renegotiated.

The nature of the negotiations, as well as its outcome, will depend largely upon agreement, in principle, between the region and the center, pertaining to the breakup. If the idea that the region should secede is generally accepted, then negotiations about the division of assets, although turbulent and controversial, can proceed in an atmosphere of peace. So far, this is the experience of the former Soviet Union. There are clearly areas within the negotiations that are potentially explosive, such as the questions of the Black Sea fleet and the future of Crimea, but there is no question about the desirability of Ukraine's secession. If war precedes the distribution of assets, as in Bangladesh and presently in Yugoslavia, then negotiations are more difficult to conduct since there is basic disagreement on the issue of secession.

(iii) Reequilibration

A study of the "aftermath" of successful secession must address itself to the economic life of the region as an independent economic entity. The nature of the arrangements made in the "during" period, as well as other economic factors inherent in the particular situation that characterizes the region, are relevant in determining the economic future of the region, in other words, its viability. Economic viability, not unlike secessionist aspirations, is a concept fraught with imprecision. Hobsbawm recently discussed economic viability despite a disclaimer that it is not clear exactly what the term means.[24] A recent study by the Deutsche Bank calculated the viability of Soviet republics (the "Independence Potential") by identifying various economic criteria for success, and then testing for them.[25] Ding conducted a similar study of the Yugoslav republics.[26] Indeed, all attempts at defining viability must keep in mind the examples of Hong Kong and Singapore, which according to many criteria seemed inviable yet continue to experience economic progress. Indeed, just three years before its independence from the Malaysian Federation, the government of Singapore said "Singapore . . . is dependent on the Federation of Malaysia for its water supply, its trade, and its survival. It is not viable by itself."[27] For the purposes of this study, the economic viability of a region is defined as its ability to sustain economic growth at or above the preindependence levels, in the short-run aftermath of secession.[28]

Various economic factors determine the viability of regions. These include the region's level of development, the region's trade dependency *on the state,* the net flows across regional boundaries (of capital or resources), and the degree of decentralization of economic decision-making (all discussed below in detail). In addition to these, other economic factors are relevant. First, the method by which secession was achieved has an effect on the economy. If independence is achieved through peaceful means, then the new region is not encumbered with reconstruction costs, as it might be when the economy is devastated by outbursts of violence in response to secessionist demands. Indeed, the civil war that ensued from the declarations of independence in both Biafra and Katanga so devastated their regional economies that they ceased to be viable. Second, homogeneity of the population is important for the economy in the aftermath of secession insofar as it may minimize disruption within the labor force. Minorities in the seceding region might be threatened by secession, as their rights are usually reevaluated. This process of ethnic rivalries may translate into significant disruption of economic activity, as occurred when the rights of the Gagauz and the Trans-Dniesterians in Moldova were threatened by presecessionist activity, as were those of the Russians in Latvia and Estonia. Third, the degree of national price deviation from international prices is important in determining the facility with which a region can integrate itself into the global economy. Clearly, a region accustomed to subsidies will undergo a costly adjustment following independence. Indeed, it has been estimated that Lithuania will pay double for the purchase of various raw materials in the absence of central subsidies.[29]

ECONOMIC VARIABLES

In this study, the following economic variables have been chosen for analysis insofar as they contribute to the determination of secessionist aspirations, the process of disassociation, and economic viability:

1. the *relative* level of income of the region
2. the *absolute* level of development of the region[30]

3. trade dependency of the region *on the state*
4. the net flows of capital and resources across regional boundaries
5. the degree of regional decentralization of power with respect to economic issues

The hypothesized relationship between these economic variables and (i) secessionist aspirations, (ii) advantage in the process of disassociation, (iii) economic viability of the region, are shown in Table 2.1. Due to the nature of the variables, this study does not propose to test these propositions, but merely to examine them.

Table 2.1:
Effect of Economic Variables in the Phases of Secession

economic variable	stage of secession		
	reevaluation	redefinition	reequilibration
relative income of region	+/-	+	not applicable[*]
level of development	+	+	+
trade dependency	-	-	-
net outflows	+	+	+
decentralization	+/-	+	+

Note: + refers to a positive relationship and - refers to a negative relationship between the given variables—during reevaluation, between the economic variables and secessionist aspirations, during redefinition, between the economic variables and the various aspects of redefinition; during reequilibration, between the economic variables and viability.

[*] a post-secessionist region no longer has a *relative* income

Although there are numerous other variables that could have been included, these five were deemed the most important. This is in contrast with a study on economic viability of the Soviet republics, conducted by the Deutsche Bank, which includes twelve variables: the degree of industrialization, hard currency-earning capacity of industrial goods, agricultural production, hard currency-earning capacity of agricultural products, degree of self-sufficiency in terms of industrial goods, mineral resources, hard currency-earning capacity of raw materials, business mindedness, proximity to Europe, level of education, homogeneity of the population, and infrastructure.[31] Several of these are included, by definition, in one of the variables used in this study, namely the absolute level of development (degree of industrialization, hard currency-earning capacity *in general,* business-mindedness, and infrastructure). The greater these variables, the higher the level of development. Clearly, the proximity of Europe is not a universal characteristic that is applicable to the viability of, for example, Bougainville. The concept of trade dependency, as used in this study, indirectly includes the hard currency-earning capacity variables of the Deutsche Bank. As such, all their variables, with the exception of ethnic homogeneity and level of education, are accounted for with the variables studied here. Furthermore, the relative income of the region, decentralization and net outflows are included, all of which are especially relevant in the determination of secessionist aspirations. Neither this nor the Deutsche Bank study includes, for example, the relative violence associated with secession, which affects the viability of the region; it also can determine secessionist aspirations if violence is perceived against the region (for example, the Slovenian independence movement gained both support and momentum after the Yugoslav federal army interceded; the Sikh separatists gained international sympathy after the storming of the Sikh Temple in Amritsar by troops of the Indian army). However, the importance of the violence variable is not universal, and thus was omitted from this list of variables.

Moreover, in order to perform a systematic assessment of the viability of seceding region, which would have entailed an econometric model and statistical analyses, it was necessary to have sufficient and comparable data. Given the obstacles in data collection that were encountered in many of the 37 regions under study, coupled with incomparability of many of them, it seemed hopeless to attempt such a study. If the study were confined to one set of seceding regions within one country, so that the sources and units of data, as well as indicators, were the same (as was done for the Soviet Union and Yugoslavia in the studies described above), then an index of viability could have been established. Given the inability to rank seceding regions by their relative viability index, in chapter 7 the regions are divided into those with greater and lesser viability, and the reasons for that classification are discussed.

DISCUSSION OF ECONOMIC VARIABLES

(i) Relative Income

The economic status of a region *relative* to its state is determined by its wealth, including its capital, human, and natural resources. Under conditions of regional disparities in wealth, an interregional comparison may elicit feelings of injustice among regional populations.[32] Relatively low-income regions might attribute their relative economic position to unfair practices, exploitation of their resources, or inadequate assistance from neighboring regions. Relatively high-income regions may perceive themselves as the economic backbone of the state, while their neighbors drain their resources and restrain their growth. Thus, states with wide regional disparities in income constitute a ripe environment for perceptions of injustice at all levels of income. This link between the relative status of regions and either perceptions of injustice or regional movements has been identified in the literature as uneven economic development,[33] discontinuous development,[34] relative deprivation,[35] internal colonialism,[36] and differential modernization.[37]

Although injustice is perceived by both the relatively higher- and lower-income regions, a positive relationship between the relative income and secessionist aspirations is predicted because *relatively low income regions are less likely to pursue secession on economic grounds*. Given their status within the state, they are likely to be appeased by economic policy that tips the balance more in their favor. The high-income regions, because of perceptions of their economic power, are more likely to believe they can benefit from and survive secession.

Relative income does affect the secessionist period of redefinition insofar as the relatively wealthier region tends to have greater leverage in the negotiating process. However, relative income is not a meaningful concept during the reequilibration phase since the secessionist region is no longer compared to its former union.

(ii) Level of Development

The level of regional development may be measured by a variety of economic and social indicators. Since there are no absolute demarcations between levels of development across states, the conventional World Bank classification of nations is adopted here, according to which the more developed nations tend to have the following characteristics: a relatively high income per capita, derived largely from industry and services, whose population is largely literate and enjoys educational and health services that result in high life expectancy. Do high levels of development imply that a region is more or less likely to aspire to secession—in other words, what is the role of development in the reevaluation process? A large body of literature suggests that nationalism tends to decrease with modernization, and thus by implication, the secessionist drive decreases. Indeed, according to Deutsch and Huntington, with modernization, ethnic groups tend to assimilate,[38] thus decreasing the ethnic component of secession. Conner suggests instead that, with modernization and the increasing ability of a population to communicate, the tendency is to increase self-awareness and the distinction of the ethnic group is enforced.[39] Others still claim that modernization raises the educational and cultural levels of the population, thus making people think and act as members of civic societies not based on ethnic communities.[40] History illustrates that secession has been attempted and debated at all levels of development, including on one end of the spectrum, in Quebec, Lombardy, and the Baltic states of the USSR, as well as the less developed Punjab, Basque Provinces, Moldova, and Bougainville.

An interesting issue is raised by Buchanan with regard to secession by the "better off" and the "worse off" regions. He claims, correctly, that the *source* of the development of the "better off" regions must be understood as a prerequisite to the discussion of secession, since it impacts on both how the region is perceived and what its viability is. In other words, regions whose development is due to characteristics inherent to their region differ from those that have been the target of favorable policies within the economic structure of the union. An application of this distinction to the cases studied here points to the difference between Bougainville (which has such clear wealth in natural resources that are responsible for the inflow of the greatest proportion of foreign currency in Papua New Guinea) and Slovenia (which has neither abundant raw materials, ample territory, nor population, but has consistently benefited from the union). Although these two cases may differ in source of development, it is unclear whether this source is perceived, understood, and integrated into opinions by the populations that agitate for secession, and therefore whether it affects secessionist aspirations.

The level of development makes a positive contribution in all three phases of secession. During reevaluation, a higher level of development gives regional populations the confidence to forge ahead with secessionist demands because of their belief that they can survive economically. During redefinition, a developed region, with its concomitant higher standards of living and usually a more educated population,[41] is better able to maneuver its way through the renegotiation phase, or if it is in a war, is better able to withstand the impact of the war. During reequilibration, economic development increases a region's economic viability: the higher the level of development, the more likely is survival independent of the nation.[42] In all likelihood, its capital stock is high, its factor productivity is high, its infrastructure is well developed, and services such as transportation and banking are extensive. An underdeveloped subnational region is less likely to pursue secession out of economic reasons fearing the repercussions of the loss of vital inputs and infrastructure.[43]

(iii) Trade Dependency

Subnational regions are linked to each other, the center, and the international economy through a series of complex economic relationships. One of these consists of the exchange of goods, services, and factors of production across regional borders. Trade dependency of a region refers to the importance of extraregional markets for the satisfaction of its market demands or the sale of its output. For the purposes of secession, regional dependency on the state is relevant, rather than on the global economy.[44]

Trade dependency is relevant in the three phases of secession in the following ways. First, low trade dependency of the region on the state fuels secessionist aspirations because it indicates that the region does not need the state markets to sustain its economy. If this perception is in fact absorbed by the population, then trade dependency is negatively related to secessionist activity in the reevaluation phase. Second, the lower the dependency on the state, the greater the negotiating power of the region in the redefinition stage of secession. In this way, the lack of dependency has an effect on the process of breaking up that is very similar to that of economic development. Third, the lower the trade dependency, the greater the ability of the region to set up the new economic structures and relationships that secession entails. Indeed, the region least dependent upon interrepublic trade will be the one best off: according to Havrylyshyn and Williamson, "the greatest economic risk in the centrifugal process of establishing separate economic policies lies in the potential disruption of existing interrepublic trade."[45]

In the assessment of economic viability, dependency on state and international economies has different implications. A region is more likely to sustain its rates of growth in the aftermath of secession if its dependency on the state is minimal. Instead, its links with the international economy are positively related to its viability. Thus, in contrast to conventional "dependencia" theory, the prediction offered here is that the repercussions of dependency on the international economy are less threatening to the region than those associated with dependency on the state. Indeed, dependency on international markets implies an already established link with global markets and thus may be perceived as an advantage in the event of secession (provided that the international community accepts the political implications of secession).

(iv) Net Outflows

Two types of interregional flows occur in states. One of these is voluntary and private, consisting of interregional movements of resources in response to economic opportunity. Examples include the investment originating in the more developed regions and targeted for the less developed regions, or labor migrations from regions of surplus labor to those of high labor demand. The second type of flow is public, mandated by the government as an integral part of its regional development policy aimed at enhancing the economic growth of the disadvantaged region. Interregional transfers occur through the tax system, through the central budget and its various funds, through subsidies and loans, through a controlled price system (including the foreign exchange), and through manpower and investment policies. Measures include reduced import duties, selective credits by the national bank system, preferential participation in institutional borrowing abroad, tax preferences to foreign partners in joint ventures, et cetera.

Central action such as that involved in regional redistributive policies often provokes strong opposing reactions within the regions: typically, it is perceived as insufficient by the low-income regions and unnecessarily burdensome by the high-income regions. This discrepancy in the perception of central policy is due to differing interests of regions at various levels, as well as the center. The high-income regions may perceive this outflow as having a high opportunity cost, which results in the tax revolt that is presently witnessed in numerous regions. The interregional conflict that arises from this tax revolt may necessitate new central concessions, which further increase the spiraling effect of regional disparities and central intervention, as occurred in Western Australia, which in 1933 proposed to secede from the Commonwealth because its leaders believed that its economic interests were being largely ignored by the government (which was dominated by the more industrialized eastern regions), thus setting in motion a series of concessions.[46]

Given that central intervention sets the stage for the perception of economic injustices by regions, it also gives regions an economic basis for separatism. When the net flow of mandated resources has a negative value, that prompts the reevaluation of the costs and benefits of national union. This negative net balance is one of the principal economic factors cited by regional representatives in their case for secession. Thus, the greater the mandated net outflow of resources from a region, the greater the secessionist aspirations. However, when the magnitude of these flows is calculated, present or past flows may be taken into account. Often, selective memory characterizes the calculations, as secessionists focus on those flows that help solidify their case for economic exploitation.

How do interregional flows affect the ability of regions to set up an independent economy, as well as their economic viability? The severance of ties to the nation implies the curtailment of this outflow, which may translate into a larger pool of resources for regional use and thus enhance the chances of sustained economic growth after independence. Thus, the greater the mandated net outflow, the greater the bargaining power of the region during the phase of redefinition, and the greater the viability of the region during the phase of reequilibration.[47]

(v) Decentralization

States with various types of political and economic systems have grappled with the question of regional decentralization and just what is the appropriate amount of responsibility in administration and execution at various levels of administration. States such as the former Soviet Union and the United States have elaborate plans pertaining to the rules and responsibilities of governments at the federal and the state or republic levels. In numerous states, the delineation of power at various levels has been in flux and has undergone changes over time, including the ongoing debate on center-state responsibilities in India and Western Europe. Even in the less developed countries, since the 1960s, efforts at development have been rooted in the belief that decentralization is necessary for the acceleration of economic development. Indeed, numerous donor agencies have insisted on measures of decentralization as a precondition for the infusion of funds.

But as much as there has been a shift towards decentralization, there is a lack of agreement as to what that term implies. Ley and Truman claim that to the economist, decentralization can "reduce the cost (or increase the profit) of producing a given set of goods."[48] To the regional scientist, decentralization relates geography to services and events, thereby producing a working definition that is more useful for administrators. According to the United Nations, decentralization involves the transfer of authority on a geographic basis to levels of government or special statutory bodies.[49] Irrespective of whether the process of decentralization involves deconcentration or devolution,[50] it entails a shifting of power away from the center.

The actual economic role of the decentralized region is defined by the application of Pryor's study of decentralization to regional issues.[51] According to this, the more regionally decentralized a state economy is, the greater the control of regional economic assets of a region and the greater the regional experience in guiding the functioning of the economy on a regional level. The advantages, to a region, of decentralization are discussed by Havrylyshyn and Williamson, and include the following:[52] First, extreme decentralization may include separate regional currencies, enabling regions to follow monetary policies independently to guard from inflation and promote economic growth. Indeed, some regions may find it desirable to devalue, for example, while others might not. Second, if each region is responsible for its own budget deficit, then regions would become more careful in their spending and appropriation of funds. Third, regions might be faster at implementing economic reforms given their smaller scale.

Together, these features of decentralization indicate that greater decentralization encourages the self-sufficiency of regions, and thus contributes positively to both the ability of a region to set up an independent economy, and its economic viability.[53] With respect to the effect of decentralization on secessionist aspirations, two outcomes are possible. Although at first glance it may seem that the more decentralized the region, the less likely it is to pursue secession since it already has control over its local economy, an examination of cases shows that a high degree of decentralization in center-region economic relations may give rise to secessionist aspirations: regions experiencing discontent desire increased distance from the center, and those that are more decentralized will tend toward secession since they already have achieved significant autonomy with respect to control, interaction, and participation. As the recent Soviet and Yugoslav experiences of federal unraveling illustrate, republics want independence, the autonomous republics want republic status, and some minorities want the status of an autonomous region.

Several concluding points need to be made about these five economic variables that affect secession. First, no single variable constitutes a necessary and sufficient condition for the emergence of secessionist aspirations. Indeed, most of the variables are usually present in union, and well as with other noneconomic factors. Second, all five variables are independent of the economic and political system within which they exist insofar as they are present in market and nonmarket economies and in federations and unitary states. They are functions of historical development patterns, distribution of resources, and macro and micro policies. Third, clearly, not all cases of secessionist activity unquestionably fall into this category, and oftentimes it is not possible to generalize and create an explanation that will cover all cases. At times, we must simply take a case as a particular historical development that is explained in terms of local events. The following two chapters provide empirical evidence of the five economic variables in secessionist cases across the world.

3

The Economics of Secession: Empirical Evidence (Part I)

Sic Pakistan Mortuus Est!

—Craig Baxter

Chapters 3 and 4 contain empirical evidence pertaining to various indicators of the economic basis of secession in the 37 seceding regions under study. Several points warrant explanation. First, the regions are grouped geographically rather than by income to retain continuity with chapter 1 and also because income statistics are not available for all regions. Second, despite the wide gaps in the primary and secondary sources available for some regions, an effort was made to piece together the existing evidence in order to enable a comparison of regions, albeit sometimes limited. The variation in data availability and collection practices in the various countries is significant, so that not all regions are included in every analysis. Third, given the organization of the book, the two empirical chapters are self-contained and may be skipped with no loss of comprehension. Indeed, the theoretical propositions of the link between economic variables and secession during the reevaluation, redefinition, and reequilibration phases of secession are explored in chapters 5, 6, and 7.

PART ONE: RELATIVE INCOME

The evidence pertaining to relative income per capita, presented in Table 3.1, enables the classification of secessionist regions by their economic status within their unions. Three obvious categories emerge, all of which contain variations: relatively high-income, average-income, and relatively low-income. The placement of a region in one of these categories was performed, data permitting, by observing its deviation from the national average, and

Table 3.1 Indicators of Economic Development

Explanation of terms:

regional Y/P=the regional income per capita (in the case of some developing countries, this number has simply not been published).

state Y/P=the state income per capita (if available, this was given in U.S. dollars; however, in a few cases, converted data did not exist, and conversion was not attempted due to the apprehension that this would increase unreliability of the numbers).

relative Y/P=relative income per capita, and an assessment of the potential of the region is included in parentheses in the regions where relative income is low. This refers to the economic potential of the region in the aftermath of secession.

source=the principal source of the economic growth of the region.

% state Y from region=the percent of state income that is derived from the secessionist region.

% Y in II sector=the percent of income derived from the manufacturing sector.

% N in II sector=percent of the labor force employed in the manufacturing sector.

% literacy=the percent of the population that is literate. When regional data are not available, the state figure is given in parentheses, along with the regional position (described as high, low, or medium), which is derived from secondary evidence. The source of all state-level income statistics, unless otherwise noted in the note, is The World Bank, *The World Development Report 1991,* Oxford: Oxford University Press, 1991, Table 1, pp. 204-5.

na=not available (when statistics are not available for a variable, then on the basis of secondary evidence, a high, low, or average rating is inserted whenever the variable lends itself to such a description).

	regional Y/P	state Y/P	relative Y/P (potential)	source	% state Y from region	% Y in II sector	% N in II sector	% literacy
ASIA								
Bougain-ville	na	$890	high[1]	copper	17/ 45[2]	low	8.2[3]	high[4] (45)
Tibet (China)	na	$350	low[5]	wool, highland agri.	.1[6]	16.6[7]	11[8]	low[9] (69)
N & E Provinces (Sri Lanka)	na	$430	low[10] (-pot.)	agri.; commercial activ.[11]	na	na	7.6[12]	78.4[13] high

	regional Y/P	state Y/P	relative Y/P (potential)	source	% state Y from region	% Y in II sector	% N in II sector	% literacy
East Timor (Indonesia)	$130 (1979)[14]	$296 [15]	low (-pot.)	rice, coffee/ public service[16]	na	0.9 (1986)[17]	2..0 (1986)[18]	21.4[19] low
Punjab (India)	$420[20] (1988)	$233 (1988)	high	agri.	4.04[21]	14.7[22]	13.3[23]	41[24]
Assam (India)	$180 (1988)	$233 (1988)	low (+pot.)	tea/petro-leum	2.17[25]	12.7	4.1[26]	low (43)[27]
Kashmir (India)	$180 (1988)	$233 (1988)	low (-pot.)	agri./tour-ism	0.71[28]	13.9	5.9[29]	27[30]
Karen region (Myanmar)	na	na	low (avg. pot.)	smuggling, teak, timber[31]	40[32]	na	na	na
AFRICA								
Southern Sudan	Lb. Ster. 14 (1956)[33]	Lb. Ster. 29 (1956)[34]	low (avg. pot)[35]	agri.	na	na	na	low[36]
Western Sahara	$750 (1979)[37]	$880 (1989)[38]	low (-pot.)	phos-phates[39]	0.9[40]	na	na	low (66)[41]
Eritrea (Ethiopia)	na	$120 (1990)[42]	high[43]	agri./ ports[44]	na	na	na	high[45] (62)
Cabinda (Angola)	na	$610 (1989)	high[46]	oil	high[47]	low[48]	low[49]	med. (41)
Casamance (Senegal)	na	$650 (1989)	low (?+pot.)[50]	rice, cotton, corn	low[51]	low[52]	na	low[53] (28)
MIDDLE EAST								
Kurdistan (Iraq)	na	$2500 (1979)[54]	low (+pot.)	oil[55]/ agri.	na	na	na	na

	regional Y/P	state Y/P	relative Y/P (potential)	source	% state Y from region	% Y in II sector	% N in II sector	% literacy
NORTH AMERICA								
Quebec (Canada)	$21,600 (1988)[56]	$21,990 (1989)	middle	services[57]	23.6[58]	21[59]	na	med. (>95)
Puerto Rico (U.S.)	$5773 (1989)[60]	$17,596 (1989)	low (-pot.)	foreign manuf.[61]	na	38[62]	27[63]	
WESTERN EUROPE								
Northern Ireland (U.K.)	$11,390[64]	$14,610 (1989)	low/high[65] (ave. pot.)	agri./ textiles/ ship build./ services	na	40[66]	42[67]	low (95)
Scotland (U.K.)	na	$14,610 (1989)	low	oil/ whiskey[68]	na	30[69]	32.4[70]	low (95)
Corsica (France)	na	$17,820 (1989)	low (-pot.)	ports/ tourism	na	17.5[71]		low (95)
Basques Provinces (Spain)	na	$9330 (1989)	high	indust.[72]	high[73]	na	47.4[74]	med. (94)
Catalonia (Spain)	$17,250 (1991)[75]	$9330 (1989)	high[76]	indust.	18[77]	38.1[78]	46.6[79]	high (94)
Lombardy (Italy)	$16,934 (1989)[80]	$15,120 (1989)[81]	high	indust.	na	55[82]	43.4[83]	high (95)
FORMER SOVIET BLOC								
Latvia (USSR)	$6740[84]	$5000	high	indust.	1.1[85]	na	28.4[86]	high
Tadzhikistan (USSR)	$2340	$5000	low (-pot.)	grazing	0.8	na	13.8[87]	low
Georgia (USSR)	$4410	$5000	middle (avg. pot.)	agri./ minerals	1.6	na	18.0[88]	med.
Ukraine (USSR)	$4700	$5000	high (+pot.)	agri./ indust.	16.2	na	28.1[89]	high

	regional Y/P	state Y/P	relative Y/P (potential)	source	% state Y from region	% Y in II sector	% N in II sector	% literacy
Tatarstan (USSR)	na	$5000	middle	agri./ indust./ oil	na	na	na	low
Slovenia (Yugoslavia)	$5918[90]	$2920[91]	high	indust./ services	16.8[92]	47.1[93]	36.7[94]	99.2[95]
Croatia (Yugoslavia)	$3230[96]	$2920	high	indust./ tourism	25.5	38.2	26.1	95.4
Krajina (Croatia)	59,000 Din.[97]	114,000 Din.	low[98] (avg. pot.)	agri./ indust.	3.9[99]	40.7[100]	70.5[101]	med. (95.4)
Kosovo/ (Serbia/ Yugoslavia)	$662[102]	$2920	low (-pot.)	minerals/ agri.	2.2	45.2[103]	20.7	82.4
Slovakia (Czecho-slovakia)	$7140 (1989)[104]	$7880 (1989)	low (avg. pot.)	agri./ indust.	25[105]	51	na	na
Transyl-vania (Romania)	na	na	low[106] (avg. pot.)	agri./ some indust.	na	na	na	na

HISTORICAL CASES

	regional Y/P	state Y/P	relative Y/P (potential)	source	% state Y from region	% Y in II sector	% N in II sector	% literacy
Biafra (Nigeria)	21 U.K. lb.(1951-52)[107]	21 U.K. lb.(1951-52)	middle (+pot.)	port/petro-leum/manuf./ services	na	na	na	high[108] (58)
Katanga (Belgian Congo)	na	na	high	copper, cobalt, minerals	apx. 50[109]	na	36.2 (1959)[110]	high[111] (39)
Bangladesh (Pakistan)	Rs. 269 (1959-60)[112]	Rs. 355 (1959-60)[113]	low (-pot.)[114]	jute, cotton, tea	na	10[115]	10.04[116]	40 (m); 18 (f)[117]
Singapore (Malaysian Fed.)	$1500 (mid-1950s)[118]	na	high (+pot.)	finance, banking, shipping[119]	na	15.3 (1965)[120]	29.2 (1966)[121]	69.7 (77.0) (1970)[122]

subsequently creating arbitrary boundaries for each category. In the discussion below, only selected relatively high-income and relatively low-income regions are discussed in detail. The average-income regions are assumed to have no economic basis for secessionist activity on the basis of their relative status within a state. However, there are regions that have attained an average or relatively low status with respect to income per capita due to unrealized potential. This occurs when a region has an asset that it has been unable to harness and make sufficiently lucrative to tilt the balance within the nation. A compelling example is Siberia, whose economy is described by the saying "rich in oil, not oil-rich": it has the potential to exploit a lucrative resource but has failed to do so. This lack of sufficient exploitation of its resources might occur for a variety of reasons, including insufficient technological expertise, the suppression of benefits from the center, et cetera. Thus, it is necessary to distinguish between average-income regions with potential and those without, since those with potential still may have a population that perceives economic injustice in the realization of that potential, leading to secessionist aspirations.

(i) Relative High-Income Regions

According to Table 3.1, the regions that have enjoyed higher income per capita relative to their respective states are: Bougainville, Punjab, Eritrea, Lombardy, Latvia, Slovenia, Katanga, Catalonia, and Transylvania. Two points warrant explanation. First, given the lack of statistical evidence pertaining to the income of Bougainville, it was questionable whether the island in fact belongs in this category. However, the secondary evidence pointed to its above-average income, which, although it did not diffuse into economic development throughout the island, nevertheless did have spin-off effects, described in greater detail in the following two chapters. Second, Croatia was omitted from the relatively high-income category because the evidence indicates that it does not deviate substantially from the Yugoslav average.[123] In this way, it is similar to Quebec, which was also omitted from this group. The experience of some of the relatively high-income regions is discussed below.

In Bougainville, as in the rest of Papua New Guinea, the base of the economy is the agricultural sector. However, unlike the rest of the country, Bougainville has natural resources whose mining has superseded all other economic activity. Indeed, the island houses one of the world's largest copper mines, producing an average daily output of 2,000 metric tons of concentrate, as well as 600 tons of copper and 99 pounds of gold.[124] This lucrative advantage has resulted in a lopsided contribution of the island to the state income: indeed, its mining sector alone was responsible for the doubling of the national foreign earnings in 1972-73. The copper mine is responsible for 45 percent of the mainland's exports and 17 percent of the central government's revenue.[125] In addition, the economy of the island is characterized by greater productivity in a wide variety of activities: the plantation yields of both copra and cocoa are higher than elsewhere in the nation.[126] Thus, although no statistics are available pertaining to regional differences in income per capita, it can be surmised that the island, given its position in the income and foreign currency earnings of the country, is high-income.

Punjab's position within the national economy is clear (see Table 3.1): in 1988, its income per capita was $420 while that of India was $233, and its average annual rate of economic growth was 2.6 percent.[127] Punjab is, and has been for decades, the region with the highest income per capita within the Indian union. This relatively high level of income was largely due to the great strides in the agricultural sector fueled by the green revolution during the 1960s and early 1970s. This impressive agricultural performance enabled the diversification of the economy as the growth in agriculture diffused into manufacturing and services.

To characterize Eritrea as high-income seems inappropriate considering the devastation to the economy that two decades of fighting and famines have produced. However, relative to Ethiopia, Eritrea is indeed better off, both in terms of realized and unrealized potential. Secondary evidence indicates that the Eritrean economy absorbed the input provided by the Italian colonization, and during independence sustained its advantage in the following areas: education (as seen in the proliferation of schools), economic development (the proliferation of industries), political development (the establishment of political parties), and general modernization (for example, the creation of newspapers).

Lombardy enjoys a position of economic superiority relative to southern Italy (the Mezzogiorno) that it does not enjoy relative to its adjoining regions, all of which are highly industrialized and highly productive (see Table 3.1). Northern Italy, which consists of Lombardy, Valle d'Aosta, Liguria, Trentino-Aldo Adige, Friuli-Venezia Giulia, the Piedmont, and Emilia-Romagna, has attained a level of economic development comparable to that of the rest of Western Europe. The Mezzogiorno has an output per capita of 56 percent of that in the north, has an unemployment rate of 21 percent (compared to 7 percent in the north), and is significantly more agricultural than the north.[128] A comprehensive study by the Italian association SVIMEZ published in 1990 caused renewed concern because of its claim that the gap between the north and south was actually growing. It shows that the economy of Lombardy is the strongest in Italy: in 1988-89 it ranked the highest in income per capita. An average of the income in the northwest regions, which includes Lombardy, is 106.52, whereas the Mezzogiorno is 56.49 and all Italy is 84.1 (index: 100=north/center).[129]

The economic position of Latvia relative to the nation is clearly one of superiority and greater prosperity. Indeed, according to PlanEcon, output per person exceeded the overall Soviet average by one-fourth and is more than double that of many southern regions, such as Tadzhikistan.[130] Indeed, the GNP per capita in the three Baltic republics is higher than the national average and growing at an average rate of 4.9 percent yearly (1960-85) while the national average growth rate was 4.4 percent.[131] Although Latvia has an underdeveloped agricultural sector and is poor in raw materials, its industrial development made it important for the Soviet Union. Its electrical industry is the largest Soviet producer of telephone switches, electrical railway cars, buses, and motorcycles.[132] Although its territory covered only 0.3 percent of the former Soviet Union, it ranked fourth in the garment and paper industries. In addition, it has highly developed biotechnology, chemical, and light industries.

There are clear regional disparities among the republics of Yugoslavia. Slovenia is approximately three-fourths above the national average by various development indicators.[133] It is followed by Vojvodina and Croatia, both of which are above the national average by approximately one-fifth. Serbia proper is slightly below the national average, whereas Macedonia, Montenegro, Bosnia, and Hercegovina are about one-third below the national average. Kosovo, by far the least developed region by all indicators, is about 40 percent below the national average. According to Flakierski, Yugoslavia has larger discrepancies among its republics than any socialist country, including Czechoslovakia and the Soviet Union.[134]

Regional differences are clear within the former Belgian Congo, where Katanga was the high-income region. There, natural resources are concentrated in great diversity and abundance, unlike in the rest of the country. Indeed, the mineral production of Katanga represented almost one-half of the nation's earnings. According to Lemarchand, mining in Katanga represented 80 percent of Congolese mining production, and the region was the sole producer within the Congo of copper, cobalt, silver, platinum, radium, uranium, palladium, and raw zinc concentrates.[135] With a population of 1,654,000 (amounting to 12.5 percent of the Congo's total population),[136] Hernan estimated that the region was responsible for close to 50 percent of the total resources of the Congo.[137] In addition, Katanga's production of electricity exceeded local demand.

In all these relatively high-income regions, various factors have combined to create the status that they currently enjoy, including natural resources, geographical position, colonial influence, and division of labor within the state. Among these regions, Bougainville, Biafra, and Katanga have the advantage of a concentration of resources that are income-producing: copper, petroleum and copper, and cobalt and industrial diamonds, respectively.

Punjab, Eritrea, and Lombardy have the advantage of geographical position. Punjab has extremely fertile land that has enabled the green revolution in agriculture, Eritrea has ports that give it a clear advantage relative to the landlocked Ethiopia, and Lombardy has extremely fertile land due to the Po River. In addition, Lombardy is situated in the northern part of the nation, bordering on Switzerland and Austria. This location has historically enabled the region to benefit from the stimulation of technological innovation in France, Germany, and Switzerland, and its rail connection with the rest of Europe has facilitated economic integration through trade and foreign investment.

With respect to the capital infusion during the colonial period, it is clear that Punjab greatly benefited from the British investment in the form of irrigation and the canal system that still provides the backbone to the water management in the region. Eritrea also benefited from the Italian investments, especially in the building of the port of Massawa. Bougainville and Katanga were also the recipients of foreign capital aimed at developing the extraction industry. Indeed, in Bougainville, the period of Australian colonial rule marked the beginning of the development of the mining industry and the concomitant infusion of capital into the region for supporting industries. To this day, the principal mine is in the hands of the Australian subsidiary of Britain's Rio Tinto Zinc. In Katanga, the Belgian Union Minière du Haut-Katanga provided the necessary infusion for the development of the highly lucrative mining industry.

Some of these relatively high-income regions may have a cultural predisposition to their economic status. It has been claimed that the cultural characteristics of a population have an effect on their relationship to work and productivity.[138] Latvia, Slovenia, Punjab, and Lombardy may be characterized as populated by people whose culture predisposes them to valuing hard work and its rewards.

Oftentimes, a division of labor develops within a state so that different regions emerge as the principle producers of some products, usually because they have a comparative advantage in their production. Once recognized, that advantage is further reinforced by central aid and guidance. This was clearly the case in Punjab and Slovenia. In the former, the fertile land, coupled with the irrigation system, produced high yields of agricultural products. In an effort to stimulate that production and thereby satisfy the demands of the food-deficit regions of India, the central government used policy to reinforce the division of labor according to which Punjab continued to be the principal food producer. In Slovenia, where industrial production was more developed than in the rest of the country, the policies of Tito's communist government reinforced and stimulated a division of labor according to which Slovenia became the primary provider of industrial goods for domestic markets and the principal exporter and earner of foreign currency.

(ii) Relative Low-Income Regions

The regions listed in Table 3.1 that are clearly of lower income than the state average are: Kashmir, Casamance, Puerto Rico, Northern Ireland, Tadzhikistan, Kosovo, and Slovakia. Several points need to be made about these regions. First, in the case of Puerto Rico and Northern Ireland, their *relative* positions vary according to the *fixed point*. In other words, if their economies are compared to those of their union countries, namely the United States and the United Kingdom, then they are unequivocally of lower income. However, if the fixed point becomes their immediate neighboring region (or the region they strive to become a part of), such as the Caribbean nations or the Republic of Ireland, then they may be classified as higher income.[139] Second, in all the cases, the ethnic or religious majority in the secessionist regions is not the dominant one in the state, leading to the perception of a link between a religious or ethnic group and poverty (or relative deprivation): Kashmir, Kosovo, and Tadzhikistan are highly Muslim regions, Puerto Ricans are Hispanic, and the Northern Ireland secessionist efforts come from the Catholic population. Third, the relative position of these regions persists *despite* high infusions of investment and capital from the center, as is discussed in detail in chapter 4. Kashmir and Kosovo were recipients of massive per capita investment, which in the case of the latter translates into significant numbers since the population is so high relative to the state. Puerto Rico has been given the advantage of a tax-free zone, thus attracting business and benefiting from the concomitant employment and income externalities. Fourth, it is unclear where to place Quebec. According to its per capita income it is slightly below the state average, but as with the case of Croatia discussed above, it did not deviate so far from the average to warrant being included in this group.

Reasons for these regions' relative low positions within the state economies are mirror opposites of those listed above: in other words, these poorer regions often have no special advantage such as mineral deposits, tourism potential, geographical location, a highly educated and modernized labor force, and so on. When they do have some advantage, they often do not have the knowledge or infrastructure to exploit it (such as the tourism industry in Kashmir and raw materials extraction in Kosovo). Their development has furthermore often been neglected by both colonial and post-colonial governments, and their economic roles within the division of labor were established historically and little effort was expended to change them (with the exception of Slovakia[140]).

PART TWO: ABSOLUTE LEVELS OF DEVELOPMENT

(i) Classifications According to Development

The level of regional development may be measured by a variety of economic and social indicators. Since there are no absolute demarcations between levels of development across nations, the conventional World Bank classification of nations is adopted here. The World Bank identifies GNP per capita as the crucial indicator and divides the countries of the world into a simple three-tier classification of low income, middle income, and high income.[141] The low-income economies are those with a GNP per capita of $580 or less in 1989, the middle-income economies have a GNP per capita of more than $580 but less than $6000, and the high-income economies are those with a GNP per capita of $6000 or more. The middle-income category is further subdivided into lower middle income and upper middle income (divided at a GNP per capita of $2335), while the high-income category is subdivided into OECD members and Others. Although Table 3.1 includes additional economic and social data, no effort was made to classify regions according to the more complex Human Development Index that the United Nations adopted.[142] This index provides a more comprehensive picture of countries since it combines GNP data with indicators of actual standards of living, such as life expectancy and education. However, a regional breakdown of the large number of statistics required for the establishment of this index was simply not available. Although high levels of GNP per capita do not always positively correlate with some social indicators of development,[143] Kuznets's long-term modern economic growth indicates that certain changes in the economy do in fact occur with long-term sustained increases in GNP per capita.[144] These include the structural transformation of the economy, according to which the relative importance of agriculture (in terms of the sectoral distribution of both income and the industrial classification of the labor force) decreases over time, while the importance of industries and services increases. For illustration purposes, according to the World Bank classification, the sectoral distribution of GNP in high-income economies ranges from 3 to 32 percent, whereas in the middle- and low-income economies the range is from 5 to 31 percent, and 3 to 24 percent, respectively. Two comments are warranted by this data. First, the figures seem lower than what one would expect, especially in the high-income economies. This is at least in part due to the subdivision of the secondary sector data into industries and manufacturing, and the numbers above reflect only manufacturing. Second, these numbers are based on individual government statistics and are consequently somewhat unreliable because of the differences in definitions and collection and compilation methods across the countries. Therefore, regions listed in Table 3.1 that fall into the World Bank high-income category will also tend to have high proportions of income derived from industries and a high proportion of workers employed in industries. They will also tend to have a literate population. The accumulation of these characteristics in a region, in all likelihood, implies that its capital stock is high, its factor productivity is high, its infrastructure is well developed, and services such as transportation and banking are extensive.

Few of the secessionist regions listed in Table 3.1 fall into the high-income category: those that do are Quebec, Lombardy, Catalonia, Latvia, Slovenia, and Slovakia.[145] These regions have all experienced significant structural transformation of their economies, and their sectoral distribution of income from industries is relatively high. The case of Lombardy is the clearest: its economy is highly industrial; 55 percent of its state income is derived from manufacturing, 40 percent from commercial activities, and 5 percent from agriculture (which is the most productive in Italy).[146] The Spanish regions of Catalonia and part of the Basque lands contain the concentration of Spanish industry, and Quebec has undergone a significant transformation in the last two decades: manufacturing accounts for 21 percent of the gross domestic product, while agriculture accounts for 3 percent. The remainder is derived from various categories of services, including financial, legal, construction, real estate, education, and health.[147]

(ii) Unrealized Potential of Regions

The distinction between realized and unrealized potential becomes relevant in a discussion of the levels of development since it logically contributes to the viability of regions. Indeed, there are regions among those listed in Table 3.1 that, although they have low absolute levels of development, have potential that, if realized, might stimulate rates of economic growth. The most clear example of this is Biafra, whose regional income per capita in 1950 (it was then called the Eastern Region) was at the national average.[148] However, during colonial times, the entire southern region was the center of economic activity.[149] This was stimulated in part by the proximity to ports and in part by the receptiveness of the southern population to modernization. Indeed, the entire south, including the Eastern Region, became the center for manufacturing and service activities. The Eastern Region is also an important producer of rice, cassava, and yams. Commercial crops include palm oil and rubber. The area is well irrigated because of the delta of the Niger River. But it is the mining, especially of petroleum, that constitutes the principal economic asset of this region. Approximately one-half of the petroleum reserves of Nigeria are concentrated in what was the Eastern Region. Given the importance of petroleum for the Nigerian economy (in early 1970, earnings from oil were four-fifths of all export earnings),[150] the loss of these oil fields in a possible Biafran secession would certainly affect the economic life of the entire nation. Furthermore, the loss of Port Harcourt and some minor delta ports would have a significant impact on the state's ability to export oil.[151] Large quantities of natural gas have been found in the delta area, further increasing the potential for foreign exchange earnings. In addition, lead, zinc, coal, and iron are concentrated in this region.

In some cases, unrealized potential comes from mineral deposits. Indeed, the Bougainville copper mine is the largest in the world, capable of producing an average daily output of 2,000 metric tons of concentrate. However, even in times when this production is realized, the benefits of it are not so clearly visible to the island population. Similarly, Katanga is capable of producing most of the world's cobalt and industrial diamonds. This, combined with ownership of one of the world's most important copper mines, should make the region exhibit more characteristics of development than it does. In other cases, a geographical location close to ports or river transport systems creates a crucial advantage. Indeed, the Karen headquarters is at Manerplaw, a city whose strategic importance cannot be discounted. It is a river city on the way to the Andaman Sea. The blockage of that city and the port facilities would have a detrimental effect on the economy of Myanmar while providing great potential for the economy of the Karen. Similarly, Port Harcourt in the river delta in former Biafra is a main hub for imports and exports from Nigeria. The example of Eritrea and the strategic importance of the port of Massawa both with respect to economic potential and its role in the fight for independence cannot be discounted.[152] Other regions, such as Scotland, Assam, and Kurdistan, have potential as oil-producing regions. Presently, Assam is the foremost producer and supplier of petroleum to India. Kurdistan contains the oil fields on the territory around Kirkuk and constitutes a large percentage of total Iraqi production. If the full benefits of these advantages were absorbed by the regions without dissipation to a center, the chances of increasing the levels of economic development would certainly increase.

(ii) Regions with High Income, Low Levels of Development

In some regions, mixed results emerge from the study of development characteristics. According to some indicators of development, a region may seem highly developed while by others, it is clearly less developed. Two examples of this come to mind: Punjab and Katanga. In the former, the income per capita has consistently been the highest in India, which in dollars makes it comparable to middle-income nations according to the World Bank, in other words, nations such as Indonesia, Sri Lanka, and Yemen. With respect to social indicators such as literacy rates, Punjab is above the national average (41 percent, compared to the Indian 36).[153] Yet, it is a highly agricultural region whose wealth and income are largely derived from the primary sector. Indeed, only 14.7 percent of its income is derived from manufacturing.[154] Similar ambiguities are evident in Katanga, where an analysis of the industrial classification of the labor force shows that in 1959, 36.2 percent of the population of Katanga were employed as wage workers outside the "traditional milieu" (agriculture and small-scale household industries).[155] This implies some form of industrialization and leads to the expectation of concomitant indicators of development. Yet, according to information on infrastructure (such as roads and banking), education, and health care, Katanga is clearly less developed.

4

The Economics of Secession: Empirical Evidence (Part II)

It took 12 years to federate the loose American confederation when the parties were all allies against a common outside enemy; it may therefore be unreasonable to expect an analogous process to occur at the outset among a group of nations that carry a legacy of resentment against a center that is still a member of the group, as well as against each other in some cases.

—Oleh Havrylyshyn and John Williamson, in reference to the Soviet Union

The previous chapter established the secessionist region's level of development and income position relative to the state economy. This chapter contains data pertaining to trade dependency, interregional flows, and decentralization in the seceding regions. Interregional trade and financial flow data are extremely meager, even in countries with relatively sophisticated statistical systems, necessitating the extensive use of secondary evidence. The analysis of the empirical evidence presented here is conducted in chapters 5 through 7.

PART I: TRADE DEPENDENCY

Evidence of trade dependency is found in statistics pertaining to trade between the secessionist region and the domestic and international economy. Clearly, those regions that do not conduct a large portion of their trade with their state are characterized by a low level of dependency *on the state* and either a high level of self-sufficiency or a high level of dependency on the global economy. It is the dependency on the state that is relevant in a discussion of secession in both the reevaluation and redefinition stages of secession. The highest level of trade dependency is found in Lombardy,

Table 4.1:
Indicators of Trade Dependency and Interregional Flows

% X (foreign)=the proportion of output from the region that is exported to foreign markets.

% X (domestic)=the proportion of output from the region that is exported to the state markets, namely outside of the region but within the state borders.

price adjustments=is there intervention in the prices pertaining to goods traded by the secessionist region?

foreign trade barriers=are there barriers to foreign trade in the goods produced by the secessionist region?

capital/tech.=flows of capital and technology across regional boundaries, either from the center, other regions, or foreign sources.

labor=flows of labor as measured by migration, to any destination and from any source.

raw materials=flows of raw materials into and out of the region.

tax=the direction of net tax payments by the region.

	TRADE				FLOWS			
	% X (foreign)	% X (state)	price adjust-ment	foreign trade barrier	capital/ tech.	labor (migration)	raw materials	tax
ASIA								
Bougain-ville (PNG)	45 total X[1]	na	yes[2]	no[3]	(+)[4]	(+)[5]	(-)[6]	(-)[7]
Tibet (China)	low[8]	high[9]	yes[10]	na	(+)[11]	(+)[12]	na	(+)[13]
N & E Sri Lanka	low[14]	15/ 83[15]	yes[16]	yes[17]	low (+)[18]	(+)[19]	na	na
East Timor (Indonesia)	0.4[20]	3.1[21]	yes[22]	yes	(+)[23]	(+)[24]	(+)[25]	(+)[26]
Punjab (India)	low[27]	77-98[28]	yes[29]	yes[30]	low (+)[31]	low (+)[32]	local	unclear[33]
Assam (India)	high[34]	high[35]	yes	yes[36]	(+)[37]	na	(-)	unclear
Kashmir (India)	low	med	yes	yes	(+)	na	na	unclear[38]

	TRADE				FLOWS			
	% X (foreign)	% X (state)	price adjust- ment	foreign trade barrier	capital/ tech.	labor (migration)	raw materials	tax
Karen region (Myanmar)	high[39]	high[40]	na	yes[41]	na	(-)[42]	(-)[43]	44
AFRICA								
Southern Sudan	na	high[45]	na	na	low[46]	(-)[47]	(-)[48]	(+)[49]
Western Sahara	na	na	na	na	na	(-)[50]	(-)[51]	na
Eritrea (Ethiopia)	na	na	yes[52]	na	(+)[53]	(-)/(+)[54]	na	na
Cabinda (Angola)	high[55]	low[56]	na	na	(+)[57]	(+)[58]	(-)[59]	na
Casamance (Senegal)	low[60]	low[61]	yes[62]	na	(+)[63]	(-)[64]	0[65]	na
MIDDLE EAST								
Kurdistan (Iraq)	high[66]	na	na	na	(+)[67]	na	(-)[68]	na
NORTH AMERICA								
Quebec (Canada)	77[69]	low[70]	yes[71]	na	na	na	na	(+)=(-)[72]
Puerto Rico (U.S.)	high[73]	na	na	yes[74]	+$22b[75]	-2.5m[76]	(+)[77]	+$6b[78]
WESTERN EUROPE								
N. Ireland (U.K.)	high[79]	high[80]	yes[81]	no	(+)[82]	(-)[83]	(+)[84]	(+)[85]
Scotland (U.K.)	na	high[86]	na	no	(+)[87]	(-)[88]	(-)[89]	(+)[90]

	TRADE				FLOWS			
	% X (foreign)	% X (state)	price adjust-ment	foreign trade barrier	capital/ tech.	labor (migration)	raw materials	tax
Corsica (France)	low	na	na	na	na	na	na	na
Basque Provinces (Spain)	na	na	yes[91]	na	(+)/(-)[92]	na	na	(-)[93]
Catalonia (Spain)	8.2[94]	40.3[95]	na	na	(+)[96]	na	na	(-)[97]
Lombardy (Italy)	high[98]	na	na	na	(+)	(+)[99]	na	(-)[100]
FORMER SOVIET BLOC								
Latvia	5.7[101]	64.1	yes[102]	yes	(+)[103]	na	na	(+)[104]
Tadzikhistan	6.9	41.8	yes	yes	(+)[105]	na	na	(+)
Georgia	3.9	53.7	yes	yes	(+)[106]	na	na	(+)
Ukraine	6.7	39.1	yes	yes	(+)[107]	na	na	low (+)
Tartarstan	na	high[108]	yes	yes	(+)[109]	(+)[110]	(-)[111]	(+)
Slovenia	apx. 33[112]	apx. 33	yes[113]	no[114]	(+)/ local[115]	low (+)[116]	(+)/ local[117]	(+)[118]
Croatia	(7.1)[119]	(54.1)[120]	yes	no	(+)	na	na	unclear[121]
Krajina	na	na	yes[122]	no	na	(-)[123]	na	na
Kosovo	(0.9)[124]	(64)[125]	yes	no	(+)[126]	(+)/(-)[127]	(-)[128]	(+)[129]
Slovakia	na	na	na	na	(+)[130]	(-)[131]	(-)[132]	(+)[133]
Transylvania	na	na	yes[134]	na	(+)[135]	(-)[136]	na	na
HISTORICAL CASES								
Biafra	high[137]	na	na	na	local[138]	(-)[139]	(-)[140]	(-)[141]

| | TRADE | | | | FLOWS | | |
	% X (foreign)	% X (state)	price adjust-ment	foreign trade barrier	capital/ tech.	labor (migration)	raw materials	tax
Katanga	80[142]	low	na	na	(+)[143]	(+)[144]	(-)[145]	(-)[146]
Bangladesh	high[147]	low[148]	yes[149]	yes[150]	(+)[151]	(-)[152]	0[153]	(+)[154]
Singapore	na	na	yes[155]	yes[156]	(+)[157]	(+)[158]	(+)	0[159]

Slovakia, Kosovo, and Corsica, and all the former Soviet regions, among others. The economies of these regions are oriented toward domestic markets in either the sale of their output (Lombardy, Tadzhikistan) or the purchase of inputs necessary for production (Slovakia, Kosovo). Regions that seem to have the least trade dependency on the state are ones that have isolated themselves from the state economies by producing goods primarily for the external markets and are thus integrated into the global economy (Bougainville, Katanga and, to a lesser degree, Slovenia and Quebec). Others yet seem to have introverted economies and give the impression of self-sufficiency, which may mask an underdeveloped system of trade linkages and infrastructure (Tibet and East Timor). Due to space and data considerations, not all the cases will be discussed in detail. The experience of several regions warrants elaboration, such as the former Soviet Union (due to the sheer volume of its trade), Yugoslavia (due to the fragmentation of its economy), India (due to the regulation of its trade). Although the regions discussed below have been classified by the degree of trade dependency they experience (high or low), it is with great hesitancy that this classification is made since it is so difficult to make specific demarcations when dealing with social science indicators.

(i) High Trade Dependency

The Soviet Union has been classified as high in trade dependency although this does not apply to all the republics, Russia being the crucial exception. This dependency is due to several factors: development policy has dictated a geographical diversification of the economy, and economic policy has attempted to reap the benefits of specialization and economies of scale. These together have resulted in a high degree of interdependence among regions. According to Havrylyshyn and Williamson, "in the Soviet Union the planners' infatuation with scale economies and the underpricing of transport may well have nurtured an artificial volume of interrepublic trade." Regional dependency on the state is lowest in Russia, highest in Belarus, while Latvia, Tadzhikistan, Georgia, and Ukraine export to domestic markets the following percentages of their product: 64.1, 41.8, 53.7, and 39.1 respectively. This interdependency seems even more remarkable when observing particular sectors: according to the Lithuanian State Planning Commission,[160] before independence Lithuania depended on the Soviet Union for 100 percent of its automobiles, tractors, metals, and cotton; 97 percent of its energy; and 58 percent of its sugar. On the other hand, the Soviet Union depended on Lithuania for 100 percent of its household electric meters, 70 percent of some television components, 30 percent of some tractor components, and 1.5 percent of its total economic production. This indicates a high degree of concentration in the economy, a finding supported by statistics from Goskomstat, including numerous current studies.[161]

Lombardy is also highly integrated into the Italian economy. Numerous studies have been published pointing out the interdependence of the various provinces, as well as the north and the south.[162] A study by Ferrara uses input/output analysis of principal economic activities to establish a high degree of interdependence between the northern regions, including Lombardy, and the southern regions.[163] The evidence points in the direction of specialization in manufacturing industries in Lombardy, especially chemical, clothing, consumer durables, wood products, and agro-industries. The dependency on the state seems to be in the markets for the sale of Lombardy's output, rather than for markets in which to purchase inputs. The only input that has for decades sustained the regional economy is labor. Indeed, during the decades between 1950 and 1980, in-migration of labor from the surplus labor regions of the south helped satisfy demand at a relatively low cost. Unlike labor, capital has largely been generated within the region. Given the region's level of income, it was not a recipient of government-sponsored development plans, but rather the capital that did flow in was in response to economic incentives created by economies of scale and a well developed infrastructure.

Given the largely agricultural and subsistence base of the Slovak economy during the Austro-Hungarian Empire and the interwar period, the region was incapable of generating its own capital to fuel economic growth. This continued, despite the investment in industrial development that occurred in the aftermath of World War II. The principal source of capital in Slovakia was the center, which during 1949-1965 contributed on the order of 30.8 percent of its total allocations to Slovakia, exceeding the region's per capita entitlement. With the partial introduction of the market system associated with the New Economic Model (the reforms of 1967) and again in 1990, interregional competition for capital ensued and the Slovak economy was at a disadvantage in securing capital. Thus, the dependency on the center with respect to capital inflows increased over time as development demands on capital increased while private and internal sources failed to keep up.

With respect to the flow of technology, the centralized nature of the Czechoslovak economy dictated the nature of technological innovation in its regions. It has been said that Slovakia was dependent on inflows from the center and that there has been discrimination against Slovakia with respect to the technology that it received. According to Dean, a technological imbalance emerged between Slovakia and the Czech regions that manifested itself in several ways. First, production in Slovakia was largely extensive rather than intensive, implying that central investment was geared toward amplifying already existing capacity, rather than applying new innovative technology into other branches of the economy. Second, the production process further intensified the concentration of innovation in the Czech lands insofar as manufacturing tended to occur outside of Slovakia: indeed, raw materials were brought from Slovakia (and the Soviet Union over Slovakia) to the Czech lands, and then the finished products were returned to Slovakia for sale. This is clear from the PlanEcon statistics pertaining to the location and nature of output of the top 100 Czechoslovak firms.[164] The existence of this technological imbalance is evident even in the primary sector: Teichova shows that the ratio of motors applied to agricultural land in the Czech lands and Slovakia is six to one.[165] It is likely that there was not greater generation of innovation within Slovakia because of the inferior education and training of the regional population, as well as the limited regional power to change the situation. In other words, the Slovak population is less educated than its Czech counterpart,[166] thus providing less ability and adaptiveness to new techniques.

The evidence with respect to the labor markets is quite clear: Slovakia remains a net out-migrating region, as employment opportunities in the growing sectors of the Czech economy attracted manpower from the low labor demand regions of Slovakia. Steiner estimated that tens of thousands of Slovaks were forced to emigrate to the Czech lands for employment.[167] Koctuch claims that the oversupply of labor in Slovakia is on the order of 200,000 people.[168] Thus, the dependency with respect to the labor component of production is opposite from Lombardy insofar as Czech labor markets are an important source of employment for the Slovak population.

(ii) Low Trade Dependency

An example of the lack of trade dependency is Yugoslavia, which developed in an environment of fragmented markets during the years from 1974 to 1991. Despite the lack of official statistics pertaining to interregional trade, estimates were made by the author that indicated relatively low levels of interregional trade.[169] This is supported by empirical studies of the Yugoslav economy conducted by Bicanic, Ocic, and Ding.[170]

Given the importance of the industrial sector in Slovenia, the spatial destination of the region's industrial exports was assessed in order to determine whether the local economy is dependent on state markets for the marketing of its supply. It was found that the local, state and international markets are equally important for the marketing of its supply. According to official statistics, 33 percent of the value of Slovenian trade is accrued in the local markets, leaving roughly one-third for national markets, and another 30 percent is marketed internationally.[171]

Dependency on the state may also result from reliance on state markets for the purchase of productive inputs. To assess the relative importance of these markets, the spatial origin of raw materials, labor, and technology were observed (measured by quantity, population in-migration, and know-how). In the case of raw materials, it was found that Slovenia is characterized by extreme vertical integration, especially in the chemical, textile, and paper industries. Indeed, the inputs for these industries come from the local markets. The insignificance of the state markets for raw materials is shown by the fact that over the past three decades, the percent of wholesale trade in raw materials never exceeded 3 percent of total trade.[172] It is the international markets for raw materials that supplement the local markets. Indeed, 50 percent of Slovenian imports in 1984 (57 percent in 1986) were in the category of raw materials.

With respect to the spatial source of the labor input, clearly the majority is from the local population. However, Slovenia has been a net absorber of population since World War II to 1981.[173] Are these migrants satisfying the local manpower demands? The evidence in the literature is conflicting: according to Prout, migrants into Slovenia account for an insignificant portion of its labor force, mostly in the category of unskilled and semiskilled laborers.[174] However, Schrenk estimates that 20 percent of the total employment in Slovenia is performed by workers of other ethnic groups not permanently settled in the region.[175]

Regional contribution to technological advancement is measured by regional investment in science and research. According to official statistics, during the 1980s, Slovenia allocated significantly higher resources to this endeavor, amounting to 38 percent of total national investment in 1985.[176] This is true over time, indicating that Slovenia is training its population and building on its technological base to a greater degree than other regions. The international component is also very strong: Slovenia is the greatest importer of foreign technology. It imports approximately 25 percent of the nations goods in the category of "highly manufactured goods."[177] In addition, according to Lamers, Slovenia absorbed 35.3 percent of total foreign investment in Yugoslavia.[178]

The spatial destination of output is a critical aspect of dependency. Seventy-seven percent of Quebec's output is destined for markets outside of Canada, mostly in the United States.[179] Furthermore, Quebec's foreign exports are increasing more rapidly than those from any other province in the union. It is only in the recent decade that Quebec took greater control of its own resources and engaged in active long-term planning, enabling the economy to shift away from dependence on dying industries such as textiles, apparel, and sale of natural resources, and into the high-technology manufacturing sector (which has quintupled in size since 1979). The benefits of this changing economic base, coupled with the changing ethnic composition of the economic and business leaders, served as indication to the Quebec population that their economic matters are best served with greater independence from the center.

Another example of relatively low level of dependency on the state economy is that of Bougainville on Papua New Guinea. The copper mine in Bougainville is responsible for 45 percent of the mainland's exports and 17 percent of the central government's revenue.[180] Its closing due to secessionist activity is said to cost the central government $1000 a minute in foregone revenue.[181] Moreover, the copper mine is the country's largest employer, and its closing has put numerous people out of work. As a result of the hardships caused by both the cutoff of the foreign currency and increased unemployment, Papua New Guinea had to ask for help from the IMF and accept its austerity conditions. The closing of the mine had international repercussions insofar as it caused turmoil in the market for copper futures.

Thus, the economic dependency of the mainland on Bougainville is clear. Is there dependency in the opposite direction—in other words, what is the loss to Bougainville if it secedes from the mainland? There is indirect evidence that Bougainville received little from the mainland. Griffin claims that the central administration felt that "compared to other areas of Papua New Guinea, Bougainville was doing more than nicely."[182] He attributed this "tradition of neglect" of Bougainville partially to the extensive activities of the missions, which provided many services and in the process freed the administration from the responsibility of providing them. However, there are no data on which to base these allegations. One might infer that the loss to Bougainville might have repercussions in terms of the labor force, access to urban centers, services, and capital investment provided by the mainland. To counter this argument, one might argue that the labor force that was not indigenous tended to be the managerial class, which was foreign anyway. Furthermore, the urban center of Kieta/Panguna/Arawa in Bougainville is as urban as any center on the mainland. With respect to other services, these have been developed in Bougainville soon after the opening of the mine: for example, in late 1972 a trans-island road was built that provided access from all regions to the world port of Kieta, enabling transportation for international trade. In addition, it must be noted that the opening of the mine brought profound changes in the economy of the island that were not shared by the mainland. Indeed, this enables one to argue that those areas of the island that were directly affected by the mine are more developed than districts on the mainland: the multiplier effect of mining resulted in the construction of roads, hospitals, and schools; it increased urbanization, it increased cash income; it stimulated agricultural production; and it necessitated external communication. The mainland remains essentially rural, based on subsistence agricultural and some cash crops, and dependent on the income from Bougainville to pay for its development efforts. With respect to capital investments, there is evidence of capital infusions from the center in the development of the mines.[183]

Estimates of interregional trade in India point out that while most regions are highly dependent on the center and each other's markets, Punjab is different. It has proved to have a low trade dependency on India with respect to the inflow of inputs for production. This was assessed by studying the spatial origin of several inputs, including agricultural machinery, labor, and agricultural technology.[184] It was found that a large proportion of local demand of tractors was satisfied by local production, that Punjab did not depend on in-migration of labor (with the exception of peak agricultural seasons), and that it was highly independent of both national and international markets for its agricultural technology.[185]

Yet, with respect to the export of Punjab's output, there is seemingly a dependency on Indian markets. Indeed, wheat, the principal crop of Punjab, was found to be destined largely for the national markets (77 to 98 percent of the wheat trade, encompassing private trade and government procurement).[186] This leaves an insignificant residual for local marketing and international markets. However, the low proportion of international trade results from the central imposition of a ban on exports of foodgrains in order to satisfy the demand in deficit states. It is likely that, in the absence of that ban, Punjabi farmers would respond to the economic incentives that exist in the form of higher international wheat prices.[187]

India is an example of a country where interregional trade dependency is influenced by government intervention. Central regulation introduces biases in free trade, and thus determines the trade patterns and the importance of various spatial markets. These regulations are less stringent for non-foodstuffs, and hence affect the two other secessionist regions, Assam and Kashmir, differently from Punjab. In Assam, the principal industries are tea and petroleum-related products. Tea is one of India's principal exports, and Assam is responsible for the production of 60 percent of the national tea. Assam produces 50 percent of the nation's total petroleum and natural gas output.[188] The remaining agricultural production is largely used for internal consumption, since the state is classified as a deficit food producer. This is also true of Kashmir, whose agricultural production is insufficient to satisfy regional needs. There are no significant industries except for tourism, and that is mostly international in nature. All of these economic activities are encouraged, and those that bring in foreign currency are valued all the more as part of a central policy of export promotion.

PART II: INTERREGIONAL FLOWS

Ostensibly, the primary motivations that underlie the interregional shifting of resources by central governments are (i) to maximize economic growth and (ii) to alter regional disparities and rectify regional imbalances (all too often, decisions are made on the basis of politics, power groups, and competition for central resources). The central government faces a tradeoff in the choice between these two policies, since the former contains a bias in favor of the more developed regions while the latter is biased in favor of the less developed regions. Thus the response to either central policy will depend upon the relative position of the region within the country, at some point in time.[189] It follows that countries with the highest levels of regional disparities in income will be the ones in which populations perceive injustices of both government policies. Two countries that are characterized by large regional discrepancies, India and Yugoslavia, are studied with respect to the interregional flows.[190] It is very difficult to make an assessment of net interregional flows because flows from and to the center occur in so many different categories. Attempts to identify the net flows have been made in numerous studies in various settings. Even the U.S. Civil War has been studied from the point of view of the flows between the north and the southern secessionist states. In the two decades preceding secession, the north invested heavily into the southern states, yet at the time of secession, no effort was made to compensate the north for their appropriated property. Aranson claims that this was not done because, according to economic data, the federal investment in the south was exceeded by the revenue the south paid in the form of tariffs.[191]

Another example is Canada, where the Frazier Institute in British Columbia found that the outflow from Quebec to the federal government is roughly equal to what the province gets back in various social payments and government contracts.[192] Indeed, the net flow from the center has been calculated at a mere $300 per year per inhabitant, certainly not sufficient to create dependency on the center.[193] Some even argue that in the last four years (1986-90), Quebec was a donor province, giving more to the federal government than it got in return.[194] Others claim that the data are inconclusive in this respect.[195]

Studies have found that Katanga's contribution to the national income was substantial relative to the other regions of the nation. One estimate of the interregional flow indicates that while the region contributes 50 percent of the center's earnings, its share of central budgetary expenditure is some 20 percent.[196] That constitutes sufficient grounds for the perception of economic injustice and might underlie secessionist aspirations. Indeed, Katanga was perceived among some as "the cow that the other territories never tired of milking."[197]

In Nigeria, prior to 1960, revenue allocation among the states was determined on the basis of regional contribution. At this time, oil had not yet been an important element in the national economy, and the primary sources of export revenue were groundnuts and cocoa. These crops were grown in the northern and western regions, in exactly those states that supported the derivation principal of revenue allocation. Data pertaining to federal contribution by region shows that over the course of 1960-65, the Eastern Region consistently derived the smallest proportion of its revenues from the center.[198] When petroleum was discovered in the Eastern Region, then the arguments became reversed and the Eastern Region favored revenue allocation according to contribution.

(i) India

What is the evidence of interregional flows in India?[199] Numerous statistics are available on this issue. The center-state flows[200] fall into the following three categories: tax sharing, grants, and capital accounts. Under the system of tax devolution presently in effect, income tax revenue is distributed on the basis of population (90 percent) and contribution (10 percent).[201] The most industrialized states object to this and urge greater weight on the basis of contributions. This is clearly a point of dispute since four states contribute nearly three-fourths of the income tax collections.[202]

With respect to regional outflows, the evidence from India does not indicate a pattern according to income. Given that the most significant portion of tax revenue siphoned to the center comes from the income tax, it should follow that the states with the highest income pay the highest amount and thereby contribute the most revenue to the center. However, this is not confirmed by the data collected by the Reserve Bank of India. With respect to per capita tax shares, Punjab, Assam, and Kashmir are neither the highest nor the lowest contributors, but rather are close to the lowest.[203] Inflows, indicated by central budget per capita transfers, show that Punjab is neither among the highest nor among the lowest of the states. Assam is ranked the highest, and there is no data for Kashmir.[204] Thus, although the low-income states are indeed the greatest per capita recipients of central budget transfers, the high-income states are not the lowest recipients. Indeed, the percent deviation from the average indicates that Punjab was slightly higher (107.9), although other states deviated further from the average. Qualitative evidence indicates that the more developed regions of India have benefited from the union. Various studies have found that central banks tend to channel funds to states and regions where the profits are the greatest. Among these, Prasad claims that states such as Punjab received two and a half times more credit than the less developed regions from the public sector banks for development.[205] During 1973-74, 54 percent of total financial assistance from the Industrial Finance Corporation of India was allocated to the more developed states, compared to 25 percent to the less developed regions.[206] A similar pattern is identified in agricultural financing. In addition, K. K. George's study of the fiscal transfer mechanism in India claims that regional disparities in India have in fact increased because of the overwhelming transfers to the more developed regions, despite the professed national policy of redistribution and balanced development.[207]

(ii) Yugoslavia

An indicator of the outflow from the republics is the subscription to the Federal Fund for Underdeveloped Regions.[208] According to official statistics, the relative contribution of the republics to the Federal Fund shows that Serbia and Croatia paid out the greatest proportion of the funds.[209] If the payments from Serbia are added to those of its autonomous provinces, then unequivocally the proportion of the Federal Fund funded by Serbia is the highest. The outflow into the Federal Fund is the lowest from the least developed regions, such as Kosovo and Montenegro. Slovenian contributions are similar in proportion to those of Bosnia and Hercegovina, and consistently slightly higher than from Vojvodina. However, a measure of absolute flows does not account for interregional differences in population or territory. According to a per capita comparison, by far the largest contributing region is Slovenia, followed by Vojvodina. The position of Serbia is ambiguous: if Serbia proper is observed, then it ranks below Croatia. An inclusion of its autonomous republics would not be useful in improving Serbia's position, since Kosovo makes the lowest contribution, whereas Vojvodina makes among the highest. The two regions do not offset each other, since the population density of the former so greatly outweighs that of the latter.

Although the more developed regions do not qualify for inflows from the Federal Fund, they are eligible recipients of other investment funds from the federal budget, including grants and credits. According to official statistics, it seems that the more developed regions (Slovenia and Vojvodina) have a smaller proportion of their investment credited from federal sources. The percentage for Croatia is similar to the Yugoslav average, while the percentage for Macedonia, a less developed region, is lower than that of Slovenia.[210] The statistics pertaining to grants are equally perplexing, preventing the drawing of conclusions pertaining to inflows into regions. A similar absence of pattern is evident in the statistics of the regional distribution of Yugoslav investment from federal sources. Vojvodina ranks low with respect to both credits as well as grants, while Croatia and Serbia lead in the proportion of Yugoslav credits, and Slovenia leads in the proportion of Yugoslav grants. This high proportion allotted to Slovenia (38.7 percent) translates into a substantial inflow per capita, relative to other regions.

The magnitude of interregional transfers is currently under dispute, as various regions are attempting to engage in interregional accounting. Since there are no official statistics on the amount of the transfers by region in the post-World War II years, some secondary evidence is presented. Ding studied interregional transfers and found that with respect to federal revenue collected during 1988, Croatia and Serbia both contributed 25 percent, while Slovenia contributed 20 percent.[211] He furthermore appraised the fiscal burden of each republic relative to the strength of its economy, and found that by this measurement, Serbia ranked the highest, followed by the less developed Bosnia and Hercegovina. Singleton and Carter analyzed regional transfers in their study of Yugoslavia, and found that in fact, the more developed regions received a greater quantity of investment funds from the central budget: "during the period 1947 to 1963, . . . with the exception of Montenegro, the less developed republics received a lower than average per capita investment than did the more developed. Slovenia, for example, received three times more per capita than did Kosovo."[212] In other words, contrary to the stated regional policy of decreasing disparities, in effect the emphasis was on profitability (*rentabilnost*).[213] A statement to this effect, made by Boris Kidric, a Yugoslav partisan actively engaged in post-World War II economic policy, recently came to light. In discussing the allocation of federal industrial capital to regions, he claimed that until 1949, Slovenia, which contains 8.8 percent of the population, received 11.1 percent of the investment funds, whereas those numbers for the other republics were as follows: Serbia, 41.4 and 37.4, Croatia, 24 and 24, Bosnia 16 and 18, Macedonia 7.3 and 5.9.[214] Denitch also studied interregional flows, and found there to be no basis to Croatia's claim that their economy was exploited by the center by substantial outflows into the less developed regions. Indeed, he finds that, from the mid-1950s, Croatia fared very well as part of the Yugoslav union.[215]

This evidence is corroborated by research at the Economic Institute in Belgrade that attempted to trace the post-World War II policy of industrialization of Slovenia. The questions raised include: where did the funds to fuel Slovenian industrialization come from, and at which republic's expense? As a result of political consideration, Dordevic argues that during 1948-53, some Serbian industry was relocated into the western regions of the country.[216] In addition Mijatovic claims that foreign capital, which was essential for the reconstruction of industry during this decade, was allocated to regions on a biased basis, favoring the western regions.[217] These scholars are arguing that location of industry during this period was the result of political considerations rather than rational economic calculations. The economic arguments for investment by region emerge only at a later date, such as during the 1960s, when, for example, investment in the tourist industry on the Dalmatian coast (within the republic of Croatia) was viewed as lucrative for the federation, and it required funding from all republics on the basis of the potentially high rates of return.[218]

PART III: DECENTRALIZATION

A broad spectrum of political and economic systems of regional governance is covered by the countries listed in Table 1.1. Indeed, although the only political distinctions contained in the table are unitary and federal, variations within these categories are numerous. Data permitting, the regions under study have been divided into the following four categories: highly decentralized (Slovenia and Croatia before 1991, Quebec, Catalonia, and Basque Provinces), limited decentralization (Punjab, Assam, Slovakia), special status regions (Tibet, Kashmir, Bougainville, Puerto Rico, Corsica, Kosovo, Krajina, and Transylvania between 1952 and 1960), and highly centralized (East Timor, northern Sri Lanka, Kurdistan, Southern Sudan, Lombardy). The difficulty of classification of regions into these categories is exacerbated by the dynamism that characterizes center-region relations and the evolving distribution of power among administrative levels. Even interregional relations that have been static for decades have not been immune to the recent worldwide shifts in the balance of power. Although most of these changes have been in the direction of increased decentralization of regions, as in the former Soviet Union and Yugoslavia, we are also witnessing a trend toward increased centralization, such as in Tibet.

What is the difference between a decentralized and centralized state with respect to the powers at the central and regional levels? Following is a list of involvements and responsibilities that are distributed among the various levels of power. In all the states under study, the central government is responsible for foreign affairs, defense, criminal law, and state security. In addition, some centers also have the right to abolish states, to reorganize states, or to take over the administration of states, such as in India, while others have the right to expel regions, such as the Malaysian Federation. In the realm of economic responsibilities, foreign economic relations, general economic policies such as state plans, monetary policy, some fiscal policy, some price controls, exchange rates, customs duties and interregional aid all fall under the control and guidance of the center. In addition, the center is responsible for setting the regulations pertaining to the mix of private and public ownership, as well as the regulation of monopolistic activities.

In some highly decentralized regions, this list exhausts the responsibilities of the center, leaving ample power at the regional level. Regions then divide remaining powers among the regional and local levels, a distinction that is not relevant for the purposes of this study. The domain of responsibilities in the areas below are what distinguishes regions: some regions regulate regional banking systems, control prices of regulated goods and services, levy some taxes, and collect assistance for the less developed regions. Debates exist as to the level of administration that needs to be responsible for the social security system, transportation, law and order, and social issues such as the educational and health systems (indeed, presently Quebec and Belgian Flanders are attempting to wrest control of social security from the center). The preparation of regional plans, some interregional trade, and land questions are the undisputed responsibility of the region.

This division of the responsibilities at various levels has connotations pertaining to financing. High degrees of decentralization tend to imply that a greater proportion of government expenditure is controlled at the regional levels. There are great variations on this among the regions: for example, in India, one-quarter of the expenditure is controlled by Punjab, Kashmir, and Assam, while Slovenia and Croatia controlled three-quarters of the government expenditure.

(i) Regions With a High Degree of Decentralization

Spain

In Spain, the post-Franco government introduced sweeping changes with respect to power distribution between the center and regions. In contrast with the previous period of centralization, the 1978 constitution took regional demands into account by recognizing Spain's distinctive populations and their needs. In 1983 the state of autonomous communities was created, and regions assumed jurisdiction over matters like town and country planning, public works, environmental protection, culture, and education. Financial arrangements are negotiated with each autonomous community on a five-year basis, beginning in 1986. The Basque Provinces have the greatest amount of decentralization, insofar as they control their own health and educational systems, they control the police force, and they levy local taxes. That last privilege is not shared by Catalonia, for example.[219]

Further evidence of Spain's decentralization is found in the cultural autonomy that the Spanish provinces have enjoyed, as exemplified by the thriving of local languages. In the last ten years, Catalan has essentially replaced Spanish in all areas of public and private life of Catalonia. That is in stark contrast with the nearly four decades of Franco's dictatorship, as well as during the 1920 regime of Primo del Rivera, during which all regional differences were suppressed: local languages, dances, and culture were all forbidden. The language issue has gained such prominence that Catalan has become an official European Community language, the first minority tongue to have this status.

How does this system of autonomous communities differ from a federation? In the latter, powers are shared on the basis of the inherent rights of both levels of government, whereas in the former the devolution of authority and resources from the center to the regions occurs on a negotiated basis.[220] The experience of Spain in during the 1970s and 1980s is similar to that of several West European states, including Britain and Belgium, which have also attempted to resolve interethnic and linguistic disputes entirely through the use of the constitution and the devolution of powers. Indeed, in Belgium, the discrepancy between ethnic population and economic power in the state led, in the 1970s, to constitutional reform that increased the decentralization of power by setting up and redefining the power in three administrative regions: Flanders, Wallonia, and the bilingual Brussels.[221] The regions had control over public works, the environment, employment, health, and transport.[222] There are indications that the next session of Parliament will bring further reforms of the constitutional system, devolving powers to the regions including foreign trade, overseas aid, and farming. In addition, the regional and communal assemblies will be directly elected. The Flemings resent subsidizing the poorer Wallonia and are presently proposing the devolution of social security to the regions in order to redress that problem.[223]

Canada

The relationship between Quebec and the Canadian federation has undergone a transformation in the past several decades. During this transformation, the line dividing regional and central responsibilities has slowly been altered. Leslie describes the federal response to Quebec's demands for increasing regional control as consisting of a mixture of incomprehension, accommodation, and rejection. Policies of accommodation that were favorable to Quebec included the increased participation of Quebec in the state-level activities (this effort was mostly aimed at economic revival), as well as granting the region cultural rights, as embodied in language policies aimed at increasing the importance of French at the federal level. Negotiations pertaining to decentralization, entailing control over policy and fiscal resources, have produced conflict since decentralized measures were first introduced by the Pearson government, only to be rejected by Trudeau.[224] It is during this time that the tax system was changed so that revenues and expenditures involving the center and Quebec were largely equated (before 1968, Quebec received only 16 percent of federal spending, while paying 25 percent to the center).[225] The accumulated changes over the past decades have resulted in the decentralization that the Quebecois presently enjoy, consisting of the following: the regional government has exclusive responsibility over social matters, education, culture, health, housing, natural resources, training, and municipal affairs, while the regional government shares joint responsibility with the center in 11 other areas, including energy, immigration, industry, and language. Moreover, Quebec has its own legal code, based on the French civil code.

This decentralization and the political demands for its enhancement are an integral part of the negotiations that have taken place over the past two decades concerning the Canadian Constitution. Two sets of negotiations produced consensus (1965 and 1971), but were later repudiated by Quebec. One was rejected by Quebec but was imposed on the province anyway in 1982 as the Constitution Act of 1982, and one, in 1987, resulted in no agreement among the provinces.[226] This impasse led to the Meech Lake Accord of 1988. This accord was reached in negotiations between the regions and Ottawa and included the following: (i) recognition of Quebec's character as a distinct society, (ii) limitation of the federal government's spending power in areas of provincial jurisdiction, and (iii) changes in the formula for amending the Constitution of Canada, giving Quebec veto power. Ratification of the accord had been completed by January 1989; however, since two regional governments were replaced in the interim, new resolutions were required (in Manitoba and New Brunswick). The ensuing debate over the Meech Lake Accord is a debate about the role and responsibilities of the provinces, and therefore the future of federal relations in Canada. It has shaken the fabric of the nation and raised questions that were previously unnecessary. For Quebec, ratification of the accord had symbolic importance; it was viewed as the test of its acceptance by the rest of Canada. Failure to accept Quebec as such would result in the shedding of the 1982 constitution in Quebec and would imply the reevaluation of Quebec's position within the union. Outside Quebec, 66 percent of the population oppose the proposal and the granting of such special status to Quebec.[227] When Newfoundland decided not to proceed with the ratification vote, the nation was thrown into a peaceful crisis.

Yugoslavia

Yugoslavia during 1974-89 was among the most decentralized federations in existence, with extensive powers allocated to the republic and very few to the center. The first sign of a loosening of central ties came with the 1965 economic reforms and was followed by amendments to the constitution in 1967 and 1968 that increased control of republics over federal policy-making.[228] Further amendments to the constitution in 1971 included the decentralization of economic functions, including the transfer to republics of capital resources (previously controlled by the federal leadership), and the adoption of new principles of procedure for their disbursement. The 1974 constitution introduced widespread micro-level changes, such as the breakup of firms into constituent units, and gave regions priority in taxation and monetary and fiscal policy, as well as balance of payments recording. Banking also became highly decentralized, with financial concerns operating on a republic level. Some of these measures gave regions the incentive for increased regional economic self-sufficiency, whereas others gave them the capacity for it. In addition, the regional powers extended to the financial affairs of enterprises and to communes. Moreover, the regional administrations became responsible for social issues, the social security system, transportation, and law and order. Under these conditions of extensive decentralization, regions had ample flexibility in the interpretation and implementation of central policies. Regions took liberties to push federal policies to the limit, reflecting an effort to satisfy their regional demands, protect their regional needs, and pursue their regional self-interest. This interpretation of central policies to suit regional interests resulted in the fragmentation of the national economy. The most serious aspect of this trend was the fragmentation of markets, which entailed duplication of production and services as part of the general waste at each spatial level. Thus, in Yugoslavia, one ramification of regional decentralization is the ungluing of the national economy and the ascendancy of the regional economy.

Greater detail on the repercussions of decentralization on the Yugoslav economy is warranted. With respect to agriculture, Cochrane points out that the decentralization by region is responsible for setting incentives to the region to provide all economic services and engage in irrational trading practices.[229] For example, she notes that in 1982 Vojvodina exported corn while the rest of the country imported it and in 1983 the same pattern was witnessed in the case of wheat. In industry, Lydall writes, "investment projects are duplicated, enterprises in one republic or province are protected from competition from enterprises in other republics and provinces . . .

obstacles are put in the way of financial flows across republican and provincial borders."[230] The evidence underlying these findings has been the subject of discussion both in the popular press as well as among scholars.[231]

The repercussions of decentralization on industrial interregional trade are exemplified by Slovenia's experience. The evidence presented in Table 4.1 indicated that Slovenia relied on inputs, such as raw materials and technology, from local and international markets rather than the national economy. Although it might be argued that Slovenia's demand for technology cannot be satisfied by the national supply as a result of the latter's lower level of sophistication, that argument cannot be generalized for all raw materials, as some of them are indeed produced in the national markets, and for these materials the regional variation in sophistication is not as large. This pattern of trade, characterized by foreign imports of goods by one region that are produced by a neighboring region, was not limited to raw materials but has been observed so frequently that it became unclear what was the norm and what was the exception to the rule. Indeed, the pattern seems incongruous with concepts of internal trade that are inherent in economic definitions of a nation.

This centrally induced political basis to regional autarchy may explain the relatively low interaction between the Slovenian economy and the rest of Yugoslavia. Given no barriers to foreign exports of industrial goods, such as those that existed in the case of foodstuffs, Slovenia was motivated to expand its international exports not only because the potential size of its markets was greater, but also in order to accumulate foreign currency. This accumulation was facilitated by the Yugoslav policy toward distribution of foreign currency, according to which earners were required to divide earnings among suppliers of the goods at *all* production levels. Given the widespread vertical integration in Slovenian industrial production, this policy implied that foreign currency earned from exports was largely retained within the republic. It was clearly more desirable to receive payments in foreign rather than domestic currency, and in the absence of legal measures to induce domestic sales, or significant cost advantages, Slovenia had no reason to increase its domestic sales at the expense of its other two markets. A similar argument applies for the input markets. The vertical integration of industries implied a high degree of self-sufficiency, and the inflow of foreign currency allowed the purchase from abroad of inputs of higher quality than comparably priced domestic equivalents. Moreover, foreign investors were more likely to invest in Slovenia, where the risks were the lowest and the economies of scale the greatest, thus further increasing the region's capacity to accumulate foreign currency, compete on global markets, and distance itself from the national economy.

To a significantly greater degree than in any other seceding region under study, the last year has witnessed changes in Yugoslav regional constitutions that have enlarged significantly the economic powers of the region, culminating in the final declaration of independence and secession in October 1991. Prior to that date, Slovenia had amended its constitution to give its laws supremacy over those of the center. In October 1990, together with Croatia, it drafted a proposed constitution of a confederacy, according to which the central role would be purely advisory, with no authority of its own.[232] Before the civil war, there was a discussion of an "asymmetric community" that would give some republics tighter ties while giving Slovenia and Croatia a confederate status.[233] Despite this trend towards increased decentralization, until the outbreak of the civil war (June 1991), the republics had agreed to follow a common monetary policy in order to assure the success of President Markovic's economic reforms.[234]

(ii) Limited Decentralization

Czechoslovakia

Czechoslovakia became a federation in 1969, an act which implied, in principle, that regions granted to the center only those responsibilities they were willing to surrender. The outcome of federation was that the center controlled foreign policy, national defense, material resources of the federation, and protection of the federal constitution, while the economic jurisdiction in the following areas was shared by the regions and the center: planning, industry, currency, transport, and wage and social policies. The center alone was responsible for the administration of national budgets. The main function of the center was "to influence the principles which determine the division of the social product and of the national income, to develop economic relations with other countries and to safeguard the principle of equalization of both [Slovak and Czech] national economies by creating equal conditions and opportunities for them."[235] Despite this scheme for center-regional relations, there was a centralizing trend, as exemplified by the restoration of the crucial role of the center when measures were adopted, only one year after federation, to give federal organs the power to abolish policies that conflicted with the central plan.[236] The trend was further intensified with the constitutional amendment of 1971, according to which various economic powers granted to the regions during federation were returned to the center: planning, finance, labor and social welfare, and construction. Lastly, those matters that previously were of joint jurisdiction came under the power of the federal ministries. This was done with the aim of "integrating" the economy and "consolidating" the regions.[237]

This centralizing trend continued until the elections of 1990,[238] after which the parliament passed laws outlining regional power that reflects an enlargement of the regional role.[239] According to these, the center retains responsibility for national defense, foreign policy, and economic and financial strategy, despite efforts by the Slovak leaders to decrease the center's authority in these matters. In addition, the crucial question of oil has been resolved by the establishment of a corporation, controlled by the central government, to oversee the nation's pipelines from the former Soviet Union. Moreover, final decision-making power on questions of national minorities are to rest with the central government. As a concession to the Slovaks, the presidency of the national bank is to rotate between the Czechs and Slovaks every year, thus giving the regions equal say in monetary affairs. The republics are responsible for remaining matters.

India

Although India is said to have a decentralized political system characterized by grassroots popular participation, the power allotted the states lags behind other decentralized nations such as Yugoslavia and Canada. Indeed, the concept of a strong center underlies the principles of the Indian constitution, and results in the following division of power among the center, state, and local levels:[240] Economic issues, foreign economic relations, and general economic policies such as the federal-level plans, monetary policy, some price controls, exchange rates, customs duties, and interregional aid all fall under the control and guidance of the center. In addition, the center is responsible for setting the regulations pertaining to the mix of private and public ownership, as well as the regulation of monopolistic activities. The center assumes the responsibility for banking and some taxation, as well as issues pertaining to social welfare. The Indian Constitution divides responsibilities by placing them on one of three lists: the union list, the state list, and the concurrent list. The first two contain matters whose jurisdiction is clear, but the last list refers to those items that are jointly determined by the parliament as well as the state legislatures.[241] This leaves to the states and the local levels[242] essentially those issues that are of regional concern, such as land issues, some transportation, some interregional trade, et cetera. In the agricultural sector, trade and commerce, as well as production and distribution, are on the concurrent list insofar as the parliament may intervene if it deems that central intervention is in the public interest.[243] With respect to financing, less than one-quarter of expenditure is controlled by the states.[244]

Over time, while other countries experiencing regional pressure for secession have also experienced a decentralization of power at the expense of the center, the positions of Assam, Kashmir, and Punjab have been ones of centralization as federal rule has been extended to all three in the course of 1990-91. Indeed, president's rule, which entails the suspension of the elected state governments and the transfer of crucial decision-making powers to the center, has ostensibly been imposed in order to curtail the violence that the state governments seemed unable to control. Skeptics note that president's rule was imposed in all cases before election time to prevent a democratically elected anti-Union government.

Thus, although the three Indian states enjoy less regional decentralization in economic issues than many federations, they are equal in their bind to the center, during times of both state and federal rule. This is true despite the special constitutional status granted to Kashmir by Article 370 of the Constitution, which is insignificant with respect to autonomy since it only restricts the settlement and the acquisition of property in the state by non-Kashmiris.[245]

(iii) "Special Status" Decentralization

There are some regions listed in Table 4.1 in which the nature and degree of decentralization differs according to region, so that the seceding region enjoys a special status within the state. Examples include Scotland, Tibet, Kosovo, Corsica, Bougainville, Transylvania, and Krajina. In some of these, state centers introduced special autonomy measures as a policy of appeasement when popular demands caused sufficient pressure. This policy of appeasement is evident in unitary states as well as federations and cuts across levels of development and economic systems. Indeed, in a variety of political and economic systems, regional appeasement is perceived as a way to placate a demanding region without giving comparable autonomy to other regions whose conditions do not warrant it.

In Corsica, autonomy laws were enacted in 1982 and 1983 as part of the decentralization efforts of the Mitterand government. These measures gave the island powers to legislate in the areas of agriculture, coastal fishing, communications, land-use planning, transport, technological research, vocational training, education, and culture.[246] The central government retained powers of police and financing, thus not weakening the integrity of the state.

The effort of appeasing the Corsicans is similar to that exerted by London aimed at appeasing the Scots. The nationalist party in Scotland demanded increased decentralization in 1974, after the discovery of the North Sea oil. While other nationalist groups within the United Kingdom, notably the Welsh, were concerned with language and culture issues, the Scots were concerned with having to share the revenues of the oil with the center. However, a referendum to create a Scottish Assembly and to devolve numerous powers to the region showed insufficient support among the population, which decided that the benefits of union outweighed the benefits of increased decentralization.[247] The elections of 1992 did not indicate a dramatic swing in the sentiment of the population; however, the question of increased Scottish political power and representation will have to be addressed.[248]

Bougainville was also able to extract special concessions from its center. Papua New Guinea is a unitary state that exerts central control over its territories and in which regions do not have well-developed bureaucracies to address themselves to regional issues.[249] However, Bougainville differs from other regions insofar as it has proven most capable of exploiting a central concession on regional power. Indeed, in the aftermath of independence from Australia (1975),[250] under pressure from the Bougainvillians (and Papuans),[251] the central government agreed to set up a provincial government with some measure of financial and administrative autonomy, as well as a ministry of decentralization. In 1977, the Organic Law on Provincial Government was passed, which spelled out the mechanics of local governance as well as the source of local revenues.[252] However, the revenues that could be raised by this law were insufficient for the running of local government, let alone to fund activity in the regional economy.

Kosovo is one of the special status regions within Yugoslavia. It is a subrepublic region in which ethnic and religious issues dominate in the power struggle among peoples with mutually exclusive demands and conflicting claims on land and history. In 1947, Kosovo was the "Autonomous Kosovo-Metohija Region"; it became the "Autonomous Province of Kosovo and Metohija" in 1963, and then graduated to the "Socialist Autonomous Province of Kosovo" in 1969. The distinction between these titles is not purely semantic, but rather reflects differences in power within the federation. This ascendancy in the power of the region dates to 1966, when, following the ousting of Rankovic, policy toward the minorities took a turn. The Kosovars were appeased by various components of a new regional policy: First, there was an increased inflow of money in development projects, amounting to 30 percent of the Federal Development Funds and 24 percent of the World Bank development credit to Yugoslavia. In a five-year period during the 1970s, some 150 million dollars were pumped into it annually.[253] Second, the Kosovars were given cultural rights by the introduction of Albanian as the main language of education and the media. The 1974 constitution further gave the region de facto republic status, with a separate assembly. In March 1989, there was a reversal of this political decentralization, when the Serbian government made constitutional amendments and lifted the autonomous status of the region and thereby once again integrated Kosovo into Serbia in the way that it was prior to its separation by the Tito government. In October 1991, the Kosovo Republican Assembly met in secret and approved a measure to declare that "the Republic of Kosovo is a sovereign and independent state."[254] Serbs had always perceived that the carving of Serbia into three parts, Serbia proper, Vojvodina, and Kosovo was an effort to break up the power of the largest republic, rather than the formal reason given, namely that these boundaries reflect the populations of the regions. This argument did not make sense in view of the fact that the Serbs in Croatia were not given autonomous status, as neither were the Dalmations in Croatia. Therefore, the reversal of the status of Kosovo was perceived as long overdue justice in Serbia, while it was perceived by the Kosovars as unjust repression by a minority.

(iv) Secessionist Regions in Highly Centralized States

Center-region relations in some countries are characterized by highly centralized ties that grant little power and responsibility to the regional level. Although this category includes regions such as Lombardy, Tibet, East Timor, Casamance, southern Sudan, and Transylvania, only the first two cases are discussed in some detail. In some of these centralized countries, center-region relations are very dynamic as the struggles for power are ongoing, and central concessions and international intervention alternate between seeming imminent and remote. This dynamism is evident in Iraqi Kurdistan, where the Persian Gulf war of 1991 altered relations with the Kurds somewhat, raised and then deflated hopes for a regional solution to the Kurdish problem. Similarly hopes rose and fell in East Timor, where the massacre of Timorese at the hands of the Indonesian forces in November 1991 gave rise to increased public attention to an issue the Indonesian government has tried to sweep under the carpet.

The Italian Constitution adopted in 1948 provided for 15 ordinary regions and five special regions. Although the latter were set up immediately and the former were to be set up one year later, they did not get set up until 1970, and the regional statutes were only drawn up in 1972. The special regions received greater autonomy and more regional powers, but they also had greater problems: Val D'Aosta had a large French-speaking population, Trentino-Alto Adige had a German population, Friuli Venezia Gulia had a considerable Slovenian population, and Sicily and Sardenia were islands and therefore isolated naturally from the nation. Although these special regions have greater powers than the ordinary regions such as Lombardy, they are nevertheless subservient to the center. All regions are under stringent surveillance by the center, and none of them have powers comparable to those of regional units within federal systems found elsewhere in Western Europe.[255] Indeed, this centralization in Italy is so strong that, according to Palombara, the Italian region is little more than a tool for the preparation and execution of the national economic plan.[256]

China is also a highly centralized state, in which Tibet has little political and economic power.[257] The center-region relations that involve Tibet have undergone a centralizing transformation since the Chinese invasion of 1950, as the central government attempted to integrate the region ethnically, economically, and politically. China is divided into provinces, counties, and districts. When the non-Han population makes up a majority of the population, then the area becomes "autonomous." As such, a region simply enjoyed a non-Han local leadership that had to conform to the policy of the center pertaining to their minority status within the state. And this policy has undergone a transformation: The first communist constitution of 1931 claims that "the Government of China recognizes the right of self-determination of the national minorities of China, their right to complete separation from China and to the formation of an independent state for each national minority... All... Tibetans... may either join the union of Chinese Soviets or secede from it and form their own state."[258] However, after 1936, there was no more mention of possible secession, and by 1952, the minority rights had dramatically been reduced so that each national autonomous region became an integral part of the territory of the People's Republic of China, inalienable.

Furthermore, in the aftermath of the invasion, ethnic Tibet was divided into several administrative units, but the long-term goal was to integrate Tibet into China under a Tibet Autonomous Region (TAR), which would have more local autonomy than other provinces, but certainly not independence. In 1955, the Preparatory Committee for the Autonomous Region of Tibet was set up to study this path of integration. However, this did not proceed very far, since a rising sentiment of the population, as well as some external involvement by the CIA,[259] led to a revolt against the Han administrators. The response to the Tibetan revolt of 1959 was to proclaim martial law and dismiss the local Tibetan government in the form of the Dalai Lama's administration, replacing it with the preparatory committee as part of the government.[260] To further dissolve ancient feudal lines, the region was changed into new administrative units (72 counties, 7 administrative districts, and one municipality). The actual TAR was not set up until September 1965, and at this time, there was an all-out effort to integrate Tibet politically (as well as socially and economically).

Since the Tiananmen Square incident of June 1989, the trend in China seems to be one of increased centralization, as reins are tightened not only on individuals but also on regions and group demands. The lack of information emerging from China pertaining to political dissidence of regions limits us to few sources. There is no doubt that the breakup of the Soviet Union has produced uneasiness among the Chinese leadership, with the prospect of solidarity of the numerous border ethnic groups with their brethren in the Asian republics of the Soviet Union. Although there are no large-scale efforts at reformulating center-region relations, the questioning of central authority has come from the leaders of the 30 provinces. In November 1990 they met to protest the central government's plans to increase the power of the center. Specifically, they perceived that the center wanted to increase its authority by demanding the power to approve investment projects within the regions. In addition, the center wanted to adjust the taxation system so as to increase the flows to the center.[261] The questioning of these moves was followed by violence and street activity motivated by a desire for increased regional autonomy. Nationalist riots occurred in Xinjiang in 1991 and were suppressed by troops (this is the region where most of China's 14 million Muslims live).[262] By spring 1992, the central government reported a further crackdown in the region, in response to sabotage and other terrorist activities. It claimed that secessionists were colluding with outsiders in order to achieve independence.[263]

5

The Economic Basis of Secessionist Aspirations

Secession and autonomy movements are rife . . . members of international fo-
rums are collared to listen to the aspirations of serious-minded groups once
seen as colorfully costumed denizens of the peripheries, nurturing dying
tongues and worshipping strange gods or God strangely.

—Frederick Shiels

Arabs, who talk of "legitimate rights" of Palestinians, fall silent at the mention of the Kurds, who want only the autonomy that Palestinians have already
been offered.

—William Safire

In this chapter, the experience of the 37 secessionist cases is brought to bear
on the following questions: To what degree are secessionist demands economic in nature, and to what degree is there an economic basis to secessionists' demands? A discussion of the first question exemplifies clearly
the regional variation in demands that was discussed in chapter 1. In other
words, there are secessionist movements in which economic issues are of
primary importance, such as Lombardy and Slovenia, and those in which
they are secondary although nevertheless important. Even in regions such as
Catalonia, the Basque Provinces, and Quebec, which are mostly concerned
with linguistic freedom and cultural autonomy, the economic question
nevertheless arises. In an effort to assess whether there is an economic basis
to their demands, the five economic variables deemed to impact on secessionist aspirations are studied, data permitting.

ECONOMIC DEMANDS: GENERAL OVERVIEW

The importance of economic factors in secessionist aspirations varies widely among the cases. In some cases, the perception of economic injustice has been a very important, if not the single most important, issue that has given the movements substance. One must be hesitant in scaling complaints and measuring the importance of various disagreements in relations, and it must be recognized that a certain degree of subjectivity is inevitable. The study of demands during the reevaluation phase can shed some light on which issues are deemed important by secessionist leaders, and thus secessionist efforts were divided into those where the economic considerations were very important and those where they were secondary. Those efforts that were classified as being primarily, but not exclusively, motivated by economic factors included Slovenia, Slovakia, Punjab, and Singapore, among others. Within the region/center economic relations that these regions have experienced, several issues have consistently emerged as imperative. These are (i) the share of central budget and capital investment allocated to the regions, (ii) the proportion of input in the form of taxes that the region contributes to the center, (iii) the degree of autonomy in decision-making pertaining to economic issues, (iv) central bias favoring a sector that is underrepresented in the region in question, such as pricing policies biased against agriculture and in favor of industry, and (v) the share of foreign exchange and external funding.

Regional perceptions pertaining to these issues are dependent upon the region's relative economic position within the state. Indeed, the regions that have relatively lower incomes tend to believe that their region receives an insufficient share of capital investment, enjoys insufficient autonomy in the decision-making over their resources or in their representation at the center, is subject to biases in pricing policies and allocation of foreign exchange regulation, and receives a small share of foreign investment, aid, and other forms of foreign intervention. The perception by the population in the relatively high-income regions tends to be that they receive insufficient capital and budget allocations while making high contributions to the central budget. In addition, the population deems to have too small a role in decision-making relative to the region's economic importance, and too little power over their own resources. These regions also tend to demand increased shares of foreign exchange and foreign funding on the grounds that they are often most responsible for the accumulation of foreign currency and, given that their environment is conducive to growth, investment on their territory is most likely to result in growth. Numerous countries in the world contain both high- and low-income regions that have made these respective claims, for example, Yugoslavia (Slovenia and Kosovo), India (Punjab and Kashmir), the USSR (Ukraine and Tadzhikistan), and Italy (Lombardy and the Mezzogiorno[1]).

These economic concerns thrive even in cases in which other concerns, such as culture, politics, religion, and language, dominate secessionist aspirations. For example, the civil war in Northern Ireland, although predominantly religious in nature, is also based on the economic advantages that Protestants have and Catholics do not share. Linguistic issues seem to dominate the Catalan efforts at increased autonomy; however, the economic strength of the region is not forgotten or negated by the leaders of the nationalist movement.

Secessionist aspirations in some selected regions are discussed below in depth. They are divided into "Primarily Economic Demands," and "Primarily Non-Economic Demands." The first category is further subdivided into those regions that demand to leave the union (cases of "we want out") and those that demand an alteration of their relations with the center and their role in their unions (cases of "we want change"). The selection process by which movements are placed in one of these categories is almost arbitrary, since no clear lines of demarcation exist. Rather, a review of voiced demands are the basis of the classification.

PRIMARILY ECONOMIC DEMANDS

(i) Cases of "We Want Out"

Slovenia

What did the Slovenians want prior to their secession from Yugoslavia on June 25, 1991? *Culturally,* they wanted to assert their independence: although the constitution of Yugoslavia allowed them the use of their language, as a minority within the nation their language and traditions obviously did not take supremacy in the country.[2] *Economically,* the Slovenes did not want to share their wealth. They wanted to decrease their contribution to federal coffers and thus end what they perceived as their support of the less developed regions of the country. In the first place, this included their participation in the Federal Fund. In mid-1990, Slovenia withdrew its support from the Federal Fund and proclaimed that it was no longer willing to foot the bill for projects that benefited neither them nor the people they were aimed at.[3] Second, it wanted to decrease its contribution to federal expenditures such as the military, both in terms of equipment and personnel.[4] Third, it wanted to decrease its contribution to the support of the federal administration. Unrelated to federal expenditure but nevertheless a center-region economic issue is the fact that Slovenia wanted to shift to a market economy at a pace that it considered to be faster than that of the remainder of Yugoslavia, and it perceived central policies as preventing that process. *Politically,* the salient demand was the introduction of a multi-party system, direct elections, and the overthrow of communist rule, both locally and on the national level. Although other republics were also moving in this general political direction, their slowness became unacceptable to Slovenia, implying the necessity for an alteration in the federal rules pertaining to republics rights to follow independent paths at independent paces. Indeed, the political decentralization that characterized interregional relations within Yugoslavia was deemed insufficient by Slovenia. And this is despite the fact that Slovenia already had more political rights allotted it than would be its share by proportion: President Tito decentralized power, granting all six republics equal rights and right of veto, *irrespective of their size.* This political oddity is described by Kostunica: "Such equal representation of the constituent units in both chambers of a bicameral federal legislative assembly is not found in any other contemporary federation . . . the principal feature of the Yugoslav solution is that small federal units are highly overrepresented while large units are correspondingly underrepresented".[5]

Despite such obvious political advantage in central representation, the Slovenes demanded increased power. During 1990-1991, there was extensive debate on the degree of autonomy that Slovenia should strive for: Should it pursue complete secession, or some alternative form of unity that would retain some ties to the remaining republics of the state, such as a confederation? A referendum indicated clearly that the population was in favor of secession.[6] That was a change over the course of half a year, when secession had less support. Indeed, a poll conducted by *Delo* in Ljubljana in early 1990 showed that 52 percent of the population was in favor of a confederative association with Yugoslavia, 28 percent was for total secession, and 8 percent was for the continuation of the present status.[7]

The economic considerations underlying Slovenian disillusionment with the federation warrant some explanation. First, its contribution to the federal budget was claimed to be proportionally higher than its population or territory. This was because its population of approximately two million, or 8.4 percent of the total, produced 16.8 percent of the national domestic product.[8] Given the decentralized nature of the Yugoslav tax system, the issue of contribution is best exemplified by the Federal Fund, which makes available capital for the less developed regions. Slovenia has deemed its contribution too high.[9] Second, the Slovenian contribution to the federal budget, it was claimed, is largely used for projects that are of little interest to the Slovenes, such as the federal army. Third, the Slovenians had perceived that they do not receive a proportional share of capital investment, although this is not a large issue since the region is the greatest generator of internal capital. Fourth, it is claimed that various federal regulations had a negative impact on Slovenian development. An example of these is the regulation requiring the pooling of foreign currency at the federal level. Slovenia, a significant exporter, would have been entitled to more foreign currency in the absence of this regulation.[10] All these factors taken together had given the impression that the economy of Slovenia would flourish without the drain of the federal commitments. In its economic cost-benefit analysis, Slovenia had clearly determined that the ties to the center, such as the use of Yugoslav markets for inputs and outputs, were a benefit too low relative to the costs of union.

Slovakia

Slovaks and Czechs have fewer cultural, linguistic and religious differences than the peoples of Yugoslavia. Although they have different histories, they were both part of the Austro-Hungarian empire and as such developed within the same general culture. Their languages are mutually understandable, and their religious differences are ones of degree. Nevertheless, the Slovaks perceive themselves to be sufficiently different that one of their demands is for their culture, as embodied in their history, religious fervor and language, to come to the forefront. With respect to culture, they have often perceived themselves to be unjustly treated as inferior in the union with the Czechs.

In addition to cultural autonomy, the Slovaks are very aware of economic factors in their quest for secession. They perceive themselves to be less developed than the Czech lands, and for this they blame their union. Indeed, despite infusions of capital during the communist rule, Slovakia's economy has remained inferior to that of the Czech lands. Indeed, there is no doubt that with respect to a wide variety of indicators, the Slovak economy is not equal to that of the Czech lands. According to Komalek, all macroeconomic indicators studied indicate a wide regional disparity.[11] Koctuch contended that the absolute differences in macro indicators actually increased over time.[12] Pavlenda and Locke found this disparity during the postwar development, as did Teichova for the interwar period.[13] Slovakia contributed approximately 25 percent of the national income, less than proportional to its population of 31 percent.[14] With respect to income per capita, Slovakia has persistently lagged behind the Czech lands: If the Czech lands are 100 index, Slovakia was 71. According to Steiner, "In 1968 Slovakia's per capita national income had reached that of the Czech lands in 1958."[15]

The key economic issue fueling secessionist aspirations has been capital investment. Slovakia, although acknowledging the investment and inflow of funds that it enjoyed in the postwar period (as well as during the First Republic and the Austro-Hungarian Empire[16]), has the following complaints pertaining to that investment. First, investment did not contribute to long-term economic growth since it was limited to the raw material sector. Indeed, the division of labor that emerged within the state indicated a bias towards the location of final production in the Czech lands.[17] The emphasis on primary production in Slovakia resulted in the continuance of a largely agricultural labor force and rural population, while the structural transformation of the economy that characterizes economic growth took place in the Czech lands. As a result, the growing labor force could not be absorbed locally, and much out-migration into Moravia and Bohemia occurred. The second claim pertaining to the nature of the investment is that the technology adopted in Slovakia was so detrimental to the environment that its human and material costs are presently unbearable to the Slovak economy. Third, investment also supported the building of military equipment factories that are presently obsolete given the decrease in demand for this product in the new climate of peace. Fourth, some have made the argument that there was not sufficient industrialization forthcoming from Prague. Although the strength of this perception varied with changing leadership, Leff shows that since the creation of the republic in 1919, it has always been an issue.[18] Even after the implementation of the economic reform of 1991, there is a clear discrepancy between the two regions with respect to some aspects of their economies, such as joint ventures and privatization.[19] All of these, it was claimed, happen in the background of a deliberate policy of giving priority to Czech economic interests.

Baltic Republics of the Former Soviet Union

The three republics of Estonia, Latvia and Lithuania expressed demands that are in the category of "we want out." They have been relatively unified on most of their economic demands and complaints, despite the differing conditions of their economies. Latvia, followed by Estonia, had the highest income per capita in the Soviet Union while that of Lithuania was similar to that of Russia and Belarus. Moreover, all three regions have great trade dependency on the Soviet markets, as indicated by the fact that over 50 percent of their output consists of imports and exports. Their economic complaints to the center were unified and can be divided into the two categories: those perceived problems that arise from the nature of the union, and those problems that arise from the reforms associated with perestroika.

Perceptions of economic injustice and exploitation have been shared by virtually all the former Soviet republics. Decisions pertaining to production, allocation, prices, and other economic matters were made at the central level, and thus were not in the interest of any one region consistently. The complaints of the Baltic republics varied, but the following have been identified as persisting over time. According to Havrylshyn and Williamson, discriminatory credit allocation gave advantages to some regions, as they were better able to secure credit for development from the center.[20] Below world prices for exports were also deemed unfair, since trading in the world markets would have increased the inflow of foreign currency. In addition, it was perceived that foreign exchange was allocated among the regions on a discriminatory basis, without regard for the source of that exchange nor for the greatest need.

The economic complaints arising from central economic reforms have intensified along with the acceleration and momentum of the reforms, especially after 1989. There are several ramifications of reforms that are discussed here: inflation, shortages, and pace of change. First, inflation was a by-product of the freeing of regulated prices, and when the ruble began experiencing inflationary pressures, no independent policy at the regional level was capable of restraining it in the absence of central policy. One way for the Baltic republics to avoid this inflation was to introduce an independent currency. In the words of Estonian economist Otsason, new currency must be brought into circulation as soon as possible, since "with every week that we wait, our national worth declines".[21] This opinion was prevalent despite some measure of economic independence that was granted to the Baltic republics by legislation of November 1989, which, however, did not authorize the creation of separate banking systems. Second, shortages of goods occurred in the course of reforms as supplies decreased while demand increased. The perception in the Baltic republics was that such shortages were the result of the central control of trade and that regional trade policy would eliminate such discrepancies between supply and demand. This perception led Lithuania to introduce export restrictions to retain selected goods for internal consumption. Indeed, shortages led numerous republics, including Ukraine, to introduce laws prohibiting the exports of some items across borders, and even between cities. Third, the Baltic republics, like Slovenia, differed from the center with respect to the desired pace of economic reforms. Indeed, when Latvian policymakers attempted the introduction of consumer price reform not mandated by Moscow, they were countered by regulations and red tape preventing the execution of these experiments.[22] It was deemed by Moscow that these moves would imperil the stability of the entire Soviet economy, especially since all republics tended to favor market prices when selling and fixed prices when buying. As a further sign of disapproval of the pace of economic reform in Lithuania, Gosbank announced that it was taking full control of the ruble holdings deposited in Lithuanian savings banks in December 1989. In January 1990, the central foreign trading bank refused to honor the signatures of the three foreign trade bank chairmen in the three republics. This meant that as of that date, the central bank took the right to approve all Baltic commitments of foreign currency. It in effect gave Moscow veto power over their foreign ventures and joint commercial efforts. Actions such as this strengthened the resolve of the Baltic republics to determine the pace and direction of their economic reforms.

Scotland

According to Birch, the leaders of the Scottish Nationalist Party (SNP) are "modernizers rather than traditionalists, concerned with economic and social policies rather than with culture."[23] Although their platform has undergone transformations since the party's inception in 1934, they focused on economic questions even prior to the discovery of oil in 1971. They were not very interested in promoting a distinctive language or culture. Indeed, their growth in popularity in the few years after 1966 was largely due to economic policies of the central government that were unsuccessful in fostering economic growth (such as the Industrial Relations Act of 1971, the unpopular wage freeze of 1967, the abandoned national plan of 1964-66, etc.), and the Scots became aware of the slipping position of Britain within Europe and the world. Scotland had not even recovered from the decline of the 1930s of its industries such as shipbuilding and coal-mining. In addition, the economy of Scotland seemed to reflect all the economic woes of Britain, except in a magnified fashion. Indeed, the unemployment rate at this time was twice what it was in England.[24] These circumstances became a prime target for the SNP, which exploited the popular sentiment of discontent.

The discovery of the North Sea oil produced a plethora of facts and fantasies about how Scotland would fare as an independent economy. It became popular sentiment that the center was siphoning too large a portion of the revenues, and that economic growth would skyrocket if local management of revenues replaced centralized control. Birch notes that "it also became clear that under existing constitutional arrangements the British government would simply add the oil royalties and profits to general revenue, without any intention of earmarking a proportion of them for the special benefit of Scotland."[25] The North Sea oil became a great boost to the Scottish economy, in both absolute and relative terms. With respect to the latter, gross domestic product per capita, as a percentage of the British figure, jumped from 86 in 1964 to 97 in 1979.[26] Clearly, the principal question raised by the nationalists to the electorate was, Why should we share this?

Therefore, those in favor of greater decentralization or independence from Britain deem that the benefits from the oil could clearly offset the inflow of subsidies from the central government that Scotland presently gets. Scotland, as a poorer region of the union, contributes less than average to the center while, at the same time, it receives more than average. This element of regional policy has been behind the relatively low regional disparities in social services that have characterized Britain during the past three decades.

The issue of decentralization was brought to the Scottish electorate in the form of a referendum in 1979 to decide on the creation of a Scottish Assembly. A study by Keating shows that this measure failed because, although a majority of those who voted approved it, the turnout fell short of 40 percent of the registered electorate.[27] In 1992, SNP members hold only 5 of the 72 parliamentary seats in Scotland.[28] The elections of spring 1992 are presently a battleground once again for economic arguments pertaining to self-control of oil and whisky.

Punjab

In Punjab, various political groups have put forth a set of religious, economic, and political demands. The most extreme expression is in the demand for secession and the establishment of sovereign religious-based or ethnically pure homelands.[29] On what *economic* grounds does Punjab demand greater autonomy from the national union?[30] The economic considerations underlying Punjabi disillusionment with the federation are listed below. First, Punjabis are reticent to share their economic achievements: they want to ensure that the prosperity they achieved is maintained and is not dissipated among the Indian population. Second, Punjabis feel injustice in various forms, based on their economic status. Indeed, they claim "we are being penalized for producing plenty."[31] They feel they are discriminated against in the central allocation of funds: according to Hapke,[32] they perceive they receive reduced central funds for industrial and social projects since it is deemed that they can provide for themselves.[33] They see themselves as carrying a greater burden of supporting the center than other states. Their population of approximately 17 million, or 2.5 percent of the total, produces approximately 4 percent of the national domestic product.[34] They also feel that they are being discriminated against in their capacity as the principal producer of foodgrains in the nation: Punjab exports foodgrains to the deficit states at prices perceived to be unfairly low.[35] Lastly, perceptions of injustice apply also to the question of interregional sharing of river waters. Especially poignant is the flow of one of Punjab's five rivers into the irrigation system of Pakistan. The Sikhs believe that the system of canals, built by the British, was disproportionately divided at the time of Partition so as to benefit the Pakistanis, and they demand the central government support them in the effort to rectify this injustice. Since the second partition of Punjab in 1966 into the states of Punjab, Haryana, and Himachal Pradesh, further water problems arose insofar as Haryana became the recipient of a larger share of irrigation sources than was deemed fair by Punjab. According to a study by Mohan, these economic aspects are extremely important in Punjab. He states, "the conflict in the Punjab cannot be considered in the simplistic terms as an ethnic conflict."[36] He says that Sikhs want (i) Chandigarh to be the capital of Punjab, without giving up the revenue rich districts of Fazilka and Abohar to Haryana, (ii) the question of the use of rivers to be deferred to the Supreme Court of India, and (iii) increased autonomy as part of a new constitutional scheme expanding powers of all states.

Bougainville

What does the Bougainville Revolutionary Army want? According to Amarshi, Good, and Mortimer, "revenue demands certainly figured high on the programme of the secessionists."[37] Critical among these is that the revenues of the mines should be retained to benefit the island. This mining sector alone was responsible for more than doubling the state foreign earnings in 1972-73. The demand for decentralized control over the mines has remained a critical point in negotiations with the center, both in 1975 as well as today. Currently, however, new demands have been added. The present leader, Francis Ona, insists that the copper mine be filled and that the land be made fertile again. This request has been supported by environmentalists across the globe and has given Ona the reputation of a Robin Hood.[38] In addition, he demanded that the local landowners should be paid $11.5 billion in compensation for the use of their ancestral land. Lastly, Ona demanded that the island should be granted the right to secede if a referendum of the island's inhabitants should so determine. The rebels moved along their path to independence unilaterally: they declared their own independence, made Ona their president, and gave cabinet posts to members of the former local administration. There has been no response to this from the mainland, nor has any foreign government recognized this new nation. Yet the magnitude of the economic statement that the separatists have made is a clear indication of the importance of Bougainville's resources to the mainland.

The economic argument of the Bougainvillians is strengthened by the fact that they are significantly more educated than the average population, a fact attributed to the proliferation of missionary schools in the region. This contributed to the positioning of Bougainvillians in all parts of the nation as well as in the important positions in administration, army, and police.[39] Furthermore, the economy of the island reflects greater productivity in a wide variety of activities: the plantation yields of both copra and cocoa are higher than elsewhere in the nation.[40]

Singapore

Although Singapore in effect did not secede but was expelled from the Malaysian Federation, center-state relations deteriorated due to economic factors. Singapore had numerous economic grievances against the federation that would have flowered, over time, into demands for secession.[41] The delay was due more to a fear of viability than a desire to remain in the federation. Indeed, just two months prior to independence, Lee Kuan Yew, the man who forged the economic miracle of Singapore, exclaimed that "the question of secession is out!" largely because of viability considerations.[42]

What were those economic grievances? First, federation in 1963 alienated Indonesia, which responded with violent activities that disrupted trade. This represented a cost to the Singapore economy that it was unwilling to bear for the benefits to Kuala Lumpur. Second, to offset the new defense expenditures, the central government demanded extra revenue from the island. Third, island industrialists complained that they were treated unfairly by the center in the granting of export quotas, especially in the textile industry. They had assumed that federation would eliminate such regional biases. Fourth, some Singapore Malays assumed that federation would bring about more opportunity for employment in the mainland, as well as for advancement in the largely Chinese community within Singapore. However, they were disappointed to find that the island had autonomy within the federation with respect to education and labor, hence none of the benefits of the mainland would be available to them. Fifth, the center and Singapore began having disputes over the division of revenues, especially in December 1964 when the contribution from Singapore was to be raised.[43] Sixth, the benefits of a common market, which were the principal reason that Singapore joined the Malaysian Federation, did not materialize. Indeed, it was perceived that policies in Kuala Lumpur, such as tariffs on some island goods, were aimed at decreasing the economic advantage of the already wealthier Singapore.[44]

In addition to the economic factors, an ethnic issue was also present: the population of Singapore is largely composed of ethnic Chinese (approximately 75 percent) who have excelled and provoked resentment from the Malays, who, although a clear majority on the mainland, perceive injustice on the island. Race riots were common during the period of the federation, as both ethnic groups attempted to advance their lot in terms of education, employment, and subsidies.

Biafra

The demands made by the Biafran government for secession from Nigeria are rooted in perceptions of economic injustice. The economic aspect of the attempted Biafran secession is best illustrated by the location of important resources and activities. During colonial times, the entire southern region was the center of economic activity.[45] This was stimulated in part by its proximity to ports and in part by the receptiveness of the southern population to modernization. As such, the entire south, including the Eastern Region, became the center for manufacturing and service activities.[46] The Eastern Region is also an important producer of rice, cassava, and yams. Commercial crops include palm oil and rubber. The area is very rich in irrigation because of the delta of the Niger River. But it is the mining, especially of petroleum, that constitutes the principal economic asset of this region. Indeed, prior to the discovery and exploitation of petroleum in the region, the income per capita was exactly at the national average.[47] Approximately one-half of the petroleum reserves of Nigeria are concentrated in what was the Eastern Region. Given the importance of petroleum for the Nigerian economy (in early 1970, earnings from oil were four fifths of all export earnings),[48] the loss of these oil fields would certainly affect the economic life of the entire nation. Furthermore, the loss of Port Harcourt and some minor delta ports would have a significant impact on the nation's ability to export oil.[49] Large quantities of natural gas have been found in the delta area, further increasing the potential for foreign exchange earnings. In addition, lead, zinc, coal, and iron are concentrated in this region.

The specific case of oil may be used to illustrate how economic factors underlie regional disputes: revenue allocation among the states prior to 1960 was determined on the basis of regional contribution. At this time, oil had not yet been an important element in the national economy, and the primary sources of export revenue were groundnuts and cocoa. These crops were grown in the northern and western regions in exactly those states that supported the derivation principal of revenue allocation. As noted in chapter 4, over the course of 1960-65, the Eastern Region consistently derived the smallest proportion of its revenues from the center. When petroleum was discovered in the Eastern Region, then the argument became reversed and the Eastern Region favored revenue allocation according to contribution. Clearly, this region was at a disadvantage, and it hoped that secession would grant it control over its economic resources.

The attempted secession of Biafra is yet another case in which the ethnic and the economic issues are intertwined. With respect to the ethnic component, there is no doubt that it played a dominant part in the conflict at the level of the masses as well as the government. While the Ibos were envied by other ethnic groups, they perceived the dissipation of their achievements and resources. Their cultural characteristics predisposed them to higher levels of economic development, although many had to migrate to urban centers outside of their region to make use of greater opportunities.[50] The Ibos had adopted many aspects of European political systems, technology, and values. In short, they became, during the time of the empire, more modern than their counterparts in the north. They had taken advantage of educational opportunities and thus held better positions both in the government and the private sector.

The concentration of natural resources in the Eastern Region explains both why the Ibos assumed their economy was viable without ties to the center and why the central government was unwilling to give up its claim to the territory. There exist no adequate statistics on interregional trade within Nigeria prior to the civil war upon which one might base a precise assessment of interregional flows. Yet the obvious wealth of the region's economy relative to the rest of the nation lead us to infer that, in all likelihood, the contribution of the Eastern Region to the center exceeds the value of its benefits from the center. When the concentration of a potential source of long-term wealth is coupled with underrepresentation in the federal structure, perceptions of injustice are understandable, and secessionary aspirations seem justified.

Katanga

The demands of Katanga's secessionists entailed economic power over their territory. A short background will explain the importance of the economics underlying the interregional conflict in the Congo. At the time of independence, the Belgian Congo was by various estimates the most developed country in Africa. By the end of the 1950s, it was enjoying the highest wages and the highest literacy rate in tropical Africa. In the period preceding independence (1950-57), its real rate of growth averaged 6.7 percent. This was due in part to a well-developed manufacturing sector, the local production of numerous consumer and producer goods, and a relatively efficient agricultural sector.[51] The export of primary products was of great importance: the nation produced 8 percent of the world's copper and most of the world's cobalt and industrial diamonds. This economic success of the Congo is largely due to Katanga, where the natural resources are concentrated in great diversity and abundance. Indeed, the mineral production of Katanga represented almost one-half of the nation's earnings.[52] According to Lemarchand, mining in Katanga represented 80 percent of Congolese mining production, and the region was the sole producer within the Congo of copper, cobalt, silver, platinum, radium, uranium, palladium, and raw zinc concentrates.[53] With a population of 1.6 million (amounting to 12.5 percent of Congo's total population),[54] Hernan estimated that the region was responsible for close to 50 percent of the total resources of the Congo.[55] In addition, Katanga's production of electricity exceeded local demand.

(ii) Cases of "We Want Change"

Lombardy

The Lega Lombarda is the party of Lombardy that favors increased autonomy from Italy. Although their concerns and demands coincide on some issues with similar parties in the adjoining states of northern Italy, including the Piedmont and Friuli Venezia-Gulia, the Lega Lombarda has gone the furthest both in expressing its goals as well as in achieving support among the population. Indeed, in the national elections of April 1992, the Lega Lombarda captured between 8 and 10 percent of the national vote, clearly the biggest winner among the parties.[56] The following are some of the salient features of its platform:[57] First, it wants to create a federal system of states, patterned on the Swiss association, which would give Lombardy greater autonomy, especially with respect to financial matters and legislation. This desire for increased decentralization to the regional level stems in part from the belief that the central government is too big to effectively and efficiently control the economy.[58] Second, the Lega Lombarda reflects the tax revolt that many residents are experiencing insofar as they view that the north has supported the south for many decades, at no benefit to them. In the aftermath of World War II and up to the present, the central government has been engaged in development projects in the Mezzogiorno, funded by tax money from the entire country. Given its high concentration of wealth, Lombardy pays 25 percent of the national taxes, while it receives only 18 percent of that back in the form of various services.[59] Furthermore, the average worker from Lombardy consumes 15 percent more than the average Italian, but he produces 34 percent more output.[60] The Lega therefore proposes that the system of taxation should be redesigned so that the central government receives some taxes for defense and foreign policy but the rest of the taxes stay where collected. In other words, the burden of the less developed south is to be lifted from Lombardy.[61] Third, they wish to curb the inflow of population into their region. This implies the arresting of the inflow from southern Italy as well as from outside the nation. It would entail tougher immigration laws as well as controls on the inflow of unemployed workers from the south. Indeed, the leader of the Lega, Senator Bossi, plans to push for a national referendum to abolish the current immigration law and an amnesty law that, in his view, was too generous to Third World immigrants (while contributing in an unemployed underclass in the urban areas of Italy).[62] It is this demand of the Lega Lombarda that has given the party a racist reputation.[63] Fourth, the Lega wants to protect the northern workers by creating a trade union for the whole northern region. Its goal is to protect the interests of the northern workers by differentiating them and their needs from their southern compatriots, such as in the case of pay scales, which the Lega claims should be higher in the north because of the higher cost of living. If Bossi, its leader, succeeds in this effort, it would cause significant turmoil within the unions, which would be politically destabilizing since the unions have traditionally had power unmatched by unions in other western countries such as the United States.

Quebec

Quebec is the second largest of the Canadian provinces with respect to area: its territory spans from the United States to the Hudson Bay, dividing Canada. In 1989, the gross domestic product (GDP) of the province was $129 billion, amounting to 23.6 percent of the national total.[64] It is second only to

Ontario, which accounts for 41.5 percent of the total. Although Quebec ranks second with respect to total GDP, it ranks sixth with respect to per capita GDP. Presently, Quebec's economy is fairly diversified, with the following breakdown in the GDP: manufacturing accounted for 21 percent, agriculture for 3 percent, services (health, education, legal, etc.) for 20 percent.[65] In addition to regional variations in the Canadian economy, the population is not homogeneous in its ethnic and linguistic composition. One-quarter of the total population are descendants of the French colonists and speak primarily French. Although this francophone minority is present in all the provinces, 90 percent of them reside in Quebec, giving the province a francophone majority (83 percent of the population).[66] The region is also inhabited by Indians, Eskimos, and anglophones, whose insignificance with respect to numbers and role in the economic and cultural life of the province is increasing.[67]

The economic basis of the separatist aspirations in Quebec rests with the recognized fact that the francophones in Canada did not enjoy the same economic benefits and opportunities as other ethnic groups.[68] The complaints against the central government rest on the fact that the culprit in Quebec's lower standard of living than that of Ontario is the economic system of the federation. Its national policy, it is claimed, equated national development with the development of Ontario.[69] In addition, the policies of appeasement from Ottawa, including those associated with the textile and fighter airplane industries, did not represent significant improvement in the economic structure and performance of the region.[70] It is only in the last decade that Quebec took greater control of its own resources and engaged in active long-term planning, enabling the economy to shift away from dependence on dying industries such as textiles, apparel, and sale of natural resources, and into the high-technology manufacturing sector. The benefits of this changing economic base, coupled with the changing ethnic composition of the economic and business leaders, served as indication to the Quebec population that their economic matters are best served with greater independence from the center. The economic basis of Quebec's discontent with the federation has been discussed by the province's premier, Robert Bourassa. According to him, three areas of conflict exist in the economic relations between the center and the state, all having to do with the macroeconomic policies of the central government.[71] First, Quebec disagrees with the policy of high interest rates enforced in Canada, which slow down investment and production. Given that Quebec has embarked upon a "take-off" phase in its economy, it wants to expand its production and its exports, and a central policy of high interest rates slows down that effort. Furthermore, high interest rates cause an artificial rise in the Canadian dollar with respect to other currencies, further reducing Quebec's ability to compete in the global economy. Second, Quebec does not share the central governments's goal of deficit reduction by provincial austerity. The center has demanded that the provinces reduce their expenses and raise taxes, whereas Quebec wants to address deficit issues in a different manner. Third, the provincial government in Quebec claims that too many public services are duplicated at the federal and provincial levels. Given that the province wants to retain its control of these services, Bourassa claims that the center must relinquish its control to ensure efficient management and fiscal responsibility in these services.

It is unclear to what extent the Quebecois want complete independence or whether they want some kind of confederal agreement. The adherents to the views of the Parti Quebequois favor leaving the Canadian confederation while retaining a common army and use of the Canadian dollar. This does not imply that people are in favor of guarded border crossings, but rather there has been vague talk of "sovereignty-association" and "superstructure" modeled on the European Community. The exact form that the future relations will take is to be decided upon by a referendum on sovereignty set to take place no later than October 26, 1992. Reports of the mood in Quebec today indicate that people are tiring of the constitutional debate, and are becoming increasingly concerned with dollars and cents, given the general bleak economic conditions.[72]

Puerto Rico

What are the demands of the Puerto Ricans with respect to their future relations with the United States? The arguments surrounding the future status of the island—namely commonwealth, statehood, or independence—center around economics. Statehood would increase the ties to the United States, while at the same time it is estimated that the majority of the population would get $300 to $400 per month in welfare payments. On the other hand, statehood would mean the loss of the tax status of the island and consequently the probable relocation of industries and the hardship of the population, which will be forced to pay taxes. Proponents of independence argue that as an independent state, the island would continue to offer cheap labor and therefore it is not certain that the companies would vacate. If they were to do so, independent policy-making might contribute to reversing the slide into poverty: for example, the island might use tariff policy to protect its agricultural sector, or by controlling its air and sea landing rights, open itself to traffic to and from Latin America. Of the noneconomic issues that concern the *independentistas* are the right to the use of Spanish and the removal of the U.S. military installations.

PRIMARILY NON-ECONOMIC DEMANDS

Kashmir and Assam

The demands of Kashmir and Assam tend to be largely religious or ethnic in basis. Kashmir is the only state of the Indian Union whose population is over 90 percent Muslim, while in Assam, 50 percent are non-Assamese. The primary demands of the Kashmiri leaders is secession from India and the creation of an independent Muslim state which would, they hope, encompass the parts of Kashmir currently under Pakistani and Chinese rule.[73]

The economic demands of the three Indian secessionist states, Assam, Kashmir, and Punjab, differ because of their differing relative status within the union: Assam and Kashmir are less developed while Punjab is more developed. Although Assam is very rich in resources (it is India's biggest producer of tea, contributing to inflow of foreign exchange,[74] and it has India's largest onshore oilfields), it remains less developed by numerous economic and social indicators. Kashmir's principal industry is tourism, and thus it attracts both foreign and domestic currencies. Assam and Kashmir, although acknowledging the investment and inflow of funds that they enjoyed since 1946, have the following complaints pertaining to that investment. First, investment did not contribute to long-term economic growth since it was limited to the raw material sector. Indeed, the division of labor that emerged within the country indicated a bias towards the location of final production in the industrial belts of Maharashtra, Madhya Pradesh, and West Bengal. The emphasis on primary production in Assam and Kashmir resulted in the continuance of a largely agricultural labor force and rural population, while the structural transformation of the economy that characterizes economic growth took place in other regions of the country. As a result, the growing labor force could not be absorbed locally, and much out-migration occurred. The second claim is that there was not sufficient industrialization forthcoming from New Delhi. In the case of Assam, the United Liberation Front of Assam (ULFA) has protested the fact that the wealth accumulated from the tea industry has not benefited the majority of the population, but rather has been repatriated by foreign and Indian firms. Also, the Assamese have perceived economic hardship associated with the influx of foreigners that have competed for employment.[75] The Kashmiri population deems that the state did not do well economically as part of a union, so it thinks it can do better alone.[76] In addition, the population perceives as humiliating the dependence on India for the state's supply of necessities.[77]

Catalonia and Basque Provinces

The demands of the Spanish separatist parties in Catalonia and the Basque country are based on the regions' linguistic differences with Spain. The Basque movement is irredentist in nature, favoring unification with the Basque regions in the south of France, across the Pyrenees. Catalonia's geographic position speaks for its mood: it is turned toward Europe, and it wants to be a part of Europe as a linguistically separate state, while turning its back on Spain.

Many Basque separatists merely want greater autonomy, rather than full independence. They already have the right to raise their own taxes, create their own police force, speak their own language, and elect their own parliament. This is similar to the demands of Catalonia, where the president recently said, "We don't ask for independence but greater autonomy."[78] Although they may only want increased autonomy, some proponents of independence have been selling Catalan passports in the streets of Barcelona.[79] They consider themselves different from the rest of Spain, citing the source of this difference as the eighth century, when they were part of Charlemagne's empire (and consequently, Europe) while the rest of Iberia was under Arab domination. Critics claim that both Basque and Catalan separatists only want more money. Indeed, the regional president of Extremadure, a less developed region of Spain, recently claimed that extremists in the Basque Provinces and Catalonia are merely trying to obtain more money from the center by threatening to secede.[80]

Transylvania

The Hungarian population in Romania is treading slowly with respect to its demands for increased autonomy. Although the leaders of the Hungarian Democratic Union, which claims to have 650,000 members, have slogans that clearly imply irredentist goals—"A home in our homeland" and "the future lies in unity"[81]—at the present time they are primarily concerned with linguistic rights. Rulers of the party, representing Romania's ethnic Hungarians in the new Parliament, have decided to stay out of the coalition with the ruling National Salvation Front because they deem that the current government has introduced decrees that are less favorable to minorities than what existed under the former communist dictatorship ("the new law provides for no local autonomy and inadequate availability of instruction in Hungarian"[82]). These decrees pertain largely to education and language usage. Their 41 seats in parliament constitute the largest block of seats after the 354 won by the National Salvation Front. They have immediately pressed to make Hungarian the official language in the counties where Hungarians live (mostly in Transylvania). These language fights in Romania presently are reminiscent of the language rights fights of the last century in Europe, when the Hungarians pressed for language rights from Austria, while Romanians pressed for similar rights from Hungary's government.

Kurdistan

What do the Kurds want? There are some 20 factions that vary in their demands and there is much difference in the demands of Kurds in the various parts of the Middle East. While the main Kurdish group in Turkey is determined to achieve independence,[83] a survey of Kurds living in the diaspora indicated that 77 percent of Iraqi Kurds would presently be satisfied with autonomy; however, in the long run, they too were interested in independence.[84] Presently, the Kurdish groups in Iraq have scaled back their demands, acknowledging that independence is out of the question at this time. They are demanding autonomy in their internal affairs, and cultural freedom in their territory.

Contributing to the content of the present demands made by the Kurdish leadership is the success of the economic blockade imposed on the Kurds by Saddam Hussein, which has essentially closed off the southern part of the Iraqi Kurdish region. Kurdish leaders have been reluctant to proclaim an independent state for fear of antagonizing neighboring Turkey and Iran. Given the blockade by the Iraqi government, the open borders with those two countries are the only lifeline that the Kurds have. Claiming independence would alienate those countries, which have large Kurdish populations that might be tempted to make similar claims.

Another component that influences the demands of the Kurds is the lack of agreement among themselves as to what they in fact want. There are numerous groups vying for leadership of the Kurds, each with their distinct objectives and platform. At this time, some central authority is necessary to coordinate the effort of the resistance, but no such authority exists. The two major groups, the Kurdistan Democratic Party and the Patriotic Union of Kurdistan, are unable to resist competition and to cooperate. These and other Kurdish groups have held elections in May 1992 to elect one leader and a Kurdish parliament to establish order. The general feeling among the population was expressed by the following quote: "Saddam Hussein may have tried to destroy us once, but what we are doing to ourselves is ten times worse."[85]

Northern and Eastern Provinces of Sri Lanka

Although the Tamils of Sri Lanka may vary with respect to which of the Tamil parties they sympathize with and the degree of their demands, most do agree on the following set of grievances aimed against the Sinhalese government: They perceive that the government laws and regulations have consistently discriminated against the Tamil population in education, employment, and economic development. Therefore, they demand to assert their cultural rights, their political rights (such as the right to self-determination), and the territorial rights of their regions. Tamils of all persuasions remember that prior to the arrival of the British administration, the Tamil regions were an entirely separate administrative unit, called the Tamil Maritime Provinces. During the British times, this region was renamed the Northern and Eastern region, but its administrative functions were decentralized to the district level, rather than the provincial, and all the districts were in the hands of Tamil representatives. Since independence, the Tamils have perceived discrimination in education insofar as Sinhalese was made the official language of the nation (1956). The Tamils, who were largely educated in English, were at a disadvantage with respect to entrance into higher education institutions. Therefore, the Tamils demand genuine equality with respect to language. The new constitution adopted in 1978 made what appeared to be substantial concessions to Tamil complaints regarding the language question by adding a new status of "national languages." However, it was too little and too late, as the momentum of the separatist movement indicated that, in the words of Kearney, "events had outrun the language concession." [86]

With respect to discrimination in employment, Tamils were disqualified from numerous jobs that necessitated Sinhalese, such as those in the government service sector. Furthermore, the anti-Tamil sentiment that was aggravated by the violence of the civil war increased the discrimination against the Tamils in the private sector. The Tamils demand that employment, at least in the public sector, reflect the proportionality of the population.

The Tamils also perceive discrimination with respect to agricultural and industrial policies. In the case of the former, Manogaran raised the issue of the pricing policy, associated with the liberalization of international trade, when the government imported cheaper onions from India and thus depressed the price of onions, upon which the Tamils depend (43 percent of the land in Jaffna, for example, is devoted to onion cultivation).[87] Furthermore, industrial development has been stagnant, as no government has been forthcoming with sufficient capital to alter the existent situation. Indeed, it is claimed that no major industries have been established in the Jaffna district since the 1950s.[88]

With respect to territorial integrity, the Tamils dislike the forced changing demographic balance of the Northern and Eastern Provinces. The Colombo government sponsored migration of people, many of whom were Sinhalese, to the sparsely populated areas of the north and northeast. Given that these areas are the ancestral home of the Tamils and that this demographic shift would obviously entail competition for employment and services, the Tamils were dissatisfied.[89]

The Tamil separatists, known as the Tamil Tigers, vow to accept only an independent state called Tamil Eelam.[90] However, other Tamils would be satisfied with increased representation in the government structure and increased autonomy. This in fact was granted in 1987, when, with the help of Indian mediation, negotiations produced an agreement to create an autonomous Tamil homeland out of Northern and Eastern Provinces. Under this accord, Indian army troops were send to Sri Lanka to enforce a cease-fire and protect the Tamils who promised to disarm. However, they soon resisted pressures to give up arms, and the violence resumed and persisted after the withdrawal of the Indian troops in 1991. It is a clear example of too little, too late.

CONCLUSIONS

The overt focus on language in Quebec, Catalonia, the Basque Provinces, Transylvania, and among the Tamils and Kurds masks but does not negate the economic factors. Indeed, as shown in Table 3.1, the region inhabited by the Hungarians contains much of Romanian industry and fertile agricultural land. Similarly, Catalonia contributes nearly 20 percent of the state income, and the Kurdish regions in Iraq contain some of the primary oil fields. In Northern Ireland, where the conflict seems essentially religious in focus, economic factors have aggravated the conflict. There are proportionately fewer Catholics in high-income occupations (10.5 percent, compared to 17.8 percent of Protestants), their unemployment rate has been higher (14 percent, compared to 7 percent among the Protestants), the Catholic farmers have on average cultivated inferior land than the Protestants, nine-tenths of the judiciary posts were in Protestant hands, and so forth.[91]

Do the regions discussed in both categories above have an economic basis for their secessionist aspirations? Most of them seem to, at least with respect to the flows of resources and the degree of decentralization. All regions may claim that they are giving too much or that they are getting too little from the center, so that both relatively low- and relatively high-income states have a basis for complaint. And a region can always aspire to more decentralization of economic power until full sovereignty is reached. Indeed, decentralization is perceived as a panacea by most substate regions.

6

The Resolution of Economic Issues During the Period of Redefinition

No states have been born of an immaculate conception.

—Nigel Harris

Although there are numerous examples of regions attempting to secede, and scholars can theoretize about the sources of and reasons for their secessionist desires, there is very little information on the actual *process* of disassociation. Scholars and policymakers tread on thin ice because most past examples of attempted or successful secession have been shrouded in violence, obscuring the details of the process. The fact that independence was achieved so rapidly in numerous regions intensifies the problems, as with a premature birth. Indeed, an Estonian government official remarked recently: "We are not prepared for independence . . . We have to improvise all the time, to barter. We don't really know yet how rich or poor we are."[1] Moreover, when the outcome of a secessionist attempt is decided by violence and war, the issues to be negotiated are fewer since force has determined the distribution of assets. In the late 20th century, the increasing number of successful secessions, many of them in relative peacetime, has led to the need to carefully map out this process.[2]

There are several categories of issues that warrant attention in the process of disassociation of regions from an economic union. There are internal questions that need addressing, external issues that tie the regions to the international economy, and questions of future associations, including with the ex-country. This chapter addresses itself to these three categories of concerns. Since these issues are ones that arise at a stage of secession that few of the 37 regions have reached, the examples used in this and the following chapter tend to be restricted in number.

Secession is similar to divorce, and as there are variations in divorces, so there are in secessions. In traditional western settings, as in numerous non-western cultures, divorce often entails the wife's getting less than 50 percent of the family holdings, while the husband retains most assets and retains control over the negotiations and the outcome. That may be comparable to secession of one region while the remaining country remains united and strong. However, increasingly we are finding in modern western societies, especially among the educated and urban partners, that divorce entails an equal division of the spoils so that no single party is left with an advantage. This situation is comparable to secession that is part of a general unraveling of the union, such as in the case of the Soviet Union and possibly Yugoslavia.

Upon divorcing, two individuals must decide upon the division of common property and must make new arrangements pertaining to their new life. Some of the issues they need to resolve are economic, while others have to do with social and "historical" questions. Some are even symbolic. So too with secession. Seceding regions must resolve economic issues such as the division of public property, division of public debt, banking and currency issues, and issues pertaining to the labor force. They then must create a new tax system, a legal system, and institutions capable of carrying out the new demands on them. Among the noneconomic questions are issues pertaining to the establishment of embassies, an army, customs offices, stamps, media, and a new flag. Many of these are also very symbolic and play upon the secessionist sentiments of the population. Oftentimes, these symbolic steps are taken against better economic judgement. For example, the Ukrainian Parliament passed a measure to create an army without clear examination of what it would do, and who would pay for it.[3]

The analogy with divorce can be taken one step further. Since 1988, some courts in the United States have required divorcing parents to undergo training in the repercussions of divorce prior to the granting of divorce.[4] Similarly, it might be useful to have a set of guidelines for states and secessionist regions for the resolution of all aspects of a breakup that might be available before the splitting up. Something along these lines was attempted by the Law on Secession, proposed by the Soviet Parliament in 1990—namely the requirement of a five-year interval from the time of request of secession until independence, during which negotiations pertaining to territorial, financial, and other matters may take place.

INTERNAL ISSUES TO BE RESOLVED

The outcome of all internal economic disputes arising during secession is dependent upon the relative strength of the seceding region and the remaining state. This strength is measured in both its inherent wealth, its international support, the nature of its popular support, et cetera. Furthermore, the outcome is affected by the existence of a war and violence in the course of secessionist attempts.

(i) Public and Foreign Debt

Many of the countries currently experiencing secessionist drives have a national debt of significant proportions.   In Canada, it is estimated to be C$ 350 billion, in Yugoslavia, on the order of $20 billion. At the time of dissolution, this debt must somehow be apportioned among the various regions. However, the grounds on which this division should take place are not clear, since regions have differing proposals depending upon their self-interest. The seceding region tends to favor the leaving behind of the debt as part of the negative baggage that it chooses to forget, while the center tends to try to make the seceding region pay for its secession by forcing it to shoulder as large as possible a share. Within these extremes, on what principle does one base the division of the debt? It is possible to use a per capita calculation or to base responsibility on the basis of territory. However, either of these are bound to raise numerous accusations of injustice, as populations begin to demand justification for the expenses incurred by the debt. For example, did the population of Quebec really benefit sufficiently to justify accepting over approximately $90 billion of debt, which is arrived at on a per capita basis?

Alternatively, the basis for the division of the debt might be the relative benefit derived from it. In other words, a link might be made between debt and assets, so that the same percentage share in the payment of debt and in the receipt of central assets is used. This is a path that Estonia is following, saying that they will pay the same percentage that it receives from the Soviet Union in its gold and currency reserves.[5] However, the calculation of the benefit from the public debt, as well as its precise division, is a laborious task with insurmountable hurdles since it is bound to elicit facts and fiction from both sides of the negotiating table. For example, upon the first inklings that Slovenia was contemplating secession, studies were published both in Serbia and Slovenia claiming that each side had benefited unjustly from the public debt.[6] Similar attempts were made in the former Soviet Baltic republics: despite possible benefits from the allocation of funds from the central public debt, Summers claimed that the Soviet center should pay the Lithuanians for having caused a decrease in their standard of living, which before the war was comparable to that of the Finnish and now lags behind by 50 percent.[7]

Another aspect of the question of who benefited from the public debt is what the debt was used for. If the use in one region had positive or negative externalities, how should those be accounted for in the division of the share of the debt? Furthermore, if those externalities extended beyond the confines of the seceding region, how does the spillover effect enter the calculations? An example of this recently emerged in the discussion of the secession of Slovakia. The Slovaks are charging that, despite the investment from the central budget that was injected into their industry, they should carry less than per capita share of the public debt since that investment proved to be at a great expense to the environment, and the Slovaks will alone be responsible for the expenses of cleaning up.[8]

It is clear that the scope for debate and disagreement in the division of the debt is great. To enforce its decisions pertaining to the division of the debt (as well as other assets), the center has the power to freeze all assets of the seceding region that are under its jurisdiction. Meanwhile, the seceding region has the power to confiscate all federal assets on its territory. A simple solution, such as the canceling of all preexisting contracts, including the debt, and calling a moratorium on the discussion of debt division, might serve to start off new relations with a clear slate; however, it still leaves someone holding the bill, and all sides harboring resentment.

The division of the foreign debt raises similar issues as with the public debt, except that it is more complicated and more sensitive since it involves the international economy. First, it entails the use of foreign currency, which in most countries under discussion is in scarce supply. The seceding region, as well as the remaining region, needs to maximize its foreign reserves to tide it over the initial disruptive period associated with secession. Second, foreign debt includes foreign countries and institutions with whom commitments must be honored. Indeed, failure to shoulder one's responsibilities has a long-term effect on future access to funds and generally on financial ties to the global economy.

The experience of the former Soviet Union in servicing its external debt of over $89 billion and dividing the principal has received much attention recently.[9] It shows how the newly independent regions favored leaving as much debt as possible with the center, which became equated with Russia, and also shows how international pressure was put to bear to ensure a unified approach to debt repayment. At a meeting in July 1991, representatives of the former Soviet republics agreed on the use of the following indices for the division of the federal foreign debt: share of federal national income, the share of federal exports and the share of the Soviet Union's population.[10] Initially, Ukraine had promised to serve and pay off its share of the foreign debt, which it estimated to be 16 percent.[11] Prior to March 1992, it insisted first on receiving its fair share of Soviet assets of gold and hard currency income. However, after that date, it agreed to shoulder a greater share of the debt because there are clearly regions, such as Moldavia, that cannot pay their share. This change occurred as a result of pressure from the Group of Seven, which refused to grant Ukraine credits until it signed the debt repayment deal that it had worked out with the former Soviet Union in 1991.[12] Clearly, the loss, in terms of foregone credits, to Ukraine if they refused to sign this agreement was greater than the cost of signing. The division of hard currency holdings has been linked to the sharing of the foreign debt in Slovenia also. Yugoslavia's hard currency reserves are estimated to be between $4 and $7 billion, and the central bank had not relinquished any of that to Slovenia, which is claiming one-third.[13] The claim is not made on the basis of population or territory, but rather on a subjective estimation of its contribution to the economy.

(ii) Public Assets

How are state-owned companies and buildings, national airlines, museum contents, and other public assets to be divided among the seceding region and the remaining state? Two principal questions arise: what is up for negotiation, and how is its price to be determined?

One possible method of division merely entails the taking over by the seceding region of the public assets on its territory. This would be the principle of "finders keepers," according to which legal possession of an asset is determined by its physical location. Such a unilateral decision on the part of the seceding region would almost certainly provoke retaliation by the ex-center in the form of confiscation of its assets held on the remaining state territory. This in fact occurred when Biafra attempted secession from Nigeria in 1967: when the secessionist government in Biafra declared independence, it took over federal assets on its territory, provoking retaliation from Lagos. Sometimes, the value of assets within the region is roughly equal to those outside the region, making a simple exchange possible. This arrangement has the advantage of simplicity and expediency. This was, in fact, proposed by Estonia in the dispute over public assets: Estonia is willing to drop its claims on property in other regions of the former Soviet Union if it can keep Soviet property in Estonia through a simple legislative act.

Short of this simple (and perhaps not entirely fair) policy of tit for tat, under which each territory inherits assets on its territory, another path to follow is to evaluate the value of assets and then make an exchange. This clearly raises the question of how to determine prices of assets. The simple neoclassical approach of determining price by supply and demand is inappropriate under conditions in which the market has not functioned as a pricing device and public goods are involved. How does one calculate the price of a museum containing the historical and cultural heritage of a people—surely not by how much somebody is willing to pay for it, as in a simple real estate evaluation. The process of price determination is no simpler in the case of a factory. After summing the value of the real estate, the building, the infrastructure—no easy feat in states with high interest rates and without functioning markets—there are inevitably questions of justice arising from past decisions, such as the opportunity cost of placing assets on a given territory and the interest rate that was charged (indeed, after Slovenia's bid for secession, the Yugoslav central government began questioning its past industrial location policies, as well as biased monetary policy that favored credits for industrialization). In the course of 1991, the central government of the Soviet Union devised a pricing scheme according to which it set prices for its state companies at which the departing regions could buy central assets on its territories. The prices were deemed too high in most cases. Indeed, the Estonian government went so far as to refuse to pay for those companies at all, on the grounds that part of their budget was used to invest in public projects throughout the country, including government buildings in Moscow, and none of those assets could be recouped.

In some cases, future ownership may be determined by what was brought into the union. This is clearly possible only when the union is relatively young, and when there has been little economic growth and proliferation of assets during union. In the case of a recent union, the seceding economy might not have been yet fully integrated, and investments and allocations for it might still be treated separately than the rest of the state. For example, valuations of property in East Timor may be feasible, given that it has been part of Indonesia for less than two decades and has a special status in government bookkeeping. However, this type of calculation is extremely difficult in the case of, for example, Kazakhstan, which has been intricately tied to the Russian economy for centuries. The question of public assets that were brought into the union is presently discussed in the breakup of Yugoslavia: Serbia, victorious after World War I, brought into the Kingdom of Serbs, Croats, and Slovenes more physical, cultural, and territorial assets than Slovenia and Croatia. Is that to be weighed more in the present division than the fact that the benefits of economic growth since 1918 have been more concentrated in the latter two regions?

In the case of assets that are not physically located in a seceding region, money and power seem to be the basis for ownership. The region that has subsidized the assets tends to inherit the right to them in the absence of international opposition. A clear example of this is the unilateral decision taken by the Russian government with respect to Soviet assets in November 1991, which entailed the taking over of the foreign ministry and embassies abroad. Ostensibly, this was done because the central government did not have the funds to keep it going. However, international outrage was not forthcoming, and Russia was accepted as the inheritor of these assets.

The question of the distribution of assets is not limited to seceding regions but is shared by those regions that are searching for increased autonomy. This autonomy in part consists of increased power over resources on one's territory, including federal or state assets. Under those circumstances, a simple taking over of assets without compensation is not advisable because not all economic and political relations are to be severed, and there remain ample avenues for retaliation. This is clearly exemplified by the discussions presently taking place between Quebec and the central government in Ottawa. The provincial government in Quebec has recently debated which federal assets should be taken over by the Quebec government and how. The post and telegraph is a candidate for this transfer, although the determination of its price has been a stumbling block.

The recent experience of successful secessions indicates that the center takes a big risk in placing its assets on the territory of a region that has joined the union involuntarily. Buchanon aptly draws an analogy with the following: "If you force your way onto my land, take over my house, and then proceed to make improvements in it, I owe you no compensation for your investment when I finally succeed in expelling you."[14] This argument is not limited to regions that have joined involuntarily, since there are counterexamples (such as Slovenia and Croatia) of regions that have joined voluntarily and subsequently changed their minds. Indeed, the question of the location of assets is bound to become an issue as states begin to evaluate potential secessionist regions. Surely, new investments entailing central assets in, for example, Catalonia, Scotland, Wales, Corsica, and Alto Adige, will be carefully evaluated in the future.

(iii) Tax Payments

One of the first signs of the economic disruption of relations is the cessation of tax payments by the seceding region. With the stoppage of revenue flows to the center, the seceding region withdraws its contribution to the central budget. This action will provoke, albeit maybe with a lag, the cessation of tax revenue flows in the opposite direction. The timing of the playing of this tax card may depend on the goals of the secessionist region: sometimes it merely wants to make a statement, such as in the case of Slovenia and the cessation of its contribution to the central Federal Fund long before its declaration of independence. Alternatively, a region may be well into the secessionist process by the time it alters its tax status, such as was the case in Biafra, when the regional government ordered all tax revenues paid in its territory to go directly to its budget.[15]

(iv) Banking System and Monetary Affairs

As in the case of divorce, after the initial euphoria of "freedom" wears off, monetary issues arising from secession are the first to demand attention. These include the disentanglement of two economies intricately tied by a series of economic relationships, and the setting up of new institutions to take over where the old ones left off. These two processes have been occurring simultaneously in the successful secessionist cases of 1991-92, since there can be no time lag between the cessation of one system and the establishment of another. Indeed, a country cannot be without a currency while plans are made for a new one. As part of the first group of questions to be addressed is the following: how are reserves of money and foreign currency to be divided? As part of the second set of questions is: how does one set up a new monetary system? Gradually or rapidly, the seceding region's new banks will take over new roles, as the state banking system loses its jurisdiction and the region's monetary policy supercedes the state's monetary policy. However, the primary step is money creation, since, given the importance of money in modern societies, the creation of an independent monetary system underlies further functioning of the economy.

The first step in the creation of a new monetary system is the creation of a new currency, which will also require a central bank and the setting up of foreign bank accounts to eliminate the role of the central bank in the ex-state.[16] A new currency has the effect of providing a psychological boost to the population insofar as it has tremendous symbolic value. But more important is the need of the secessionist region to extricate itself from the ex-state and its monetary problems. The clearest economic advantage is the isolation of the currency of that region from that of the remaining state so that monetary oscillations, such as changes in the money supply, interest rates, and inflation, are not transmitted to the region. In the absence of an independent banking system, dependence on the center remains for capital inflows such as consumer and business credit, interest rates are not controllable, and inflation rates are transmitted intraregionally. Indeed, the creation of a new currency in Slovenia shielded it from sharing in the inflation in other parts of the country, which in some places have reached 35,000 percent annually.[17] Another reason why it is important for the seceding region to have its own currency is to avoid being blackmailed or suffocated economically by the center. The case of Biafra provides an example of this blackmail by the center: in 1968, the Central Bank of Nigeria announced the introduction of new currency notes, thus invalidating the currency in use in Biafra with the aim of preventing the region from buying foreign arms and financing external propaganda. If Biafra had had its own currency in place before, it would have been impervious to such a move by the central bank. Lastly, after a separate currency and its corresponding banking system has been established, an independent monetary policy can be pursued, giving economic independence to the seceding region.

However, the introduction of a new currency is not an easy task. There are minor logistical problems to be solved, such as the choice of the currency. Indeed, Slovenia went through two phases in this:[18] First, in 1990, it introduced the lipa, trading at one lipa per $4.[19] Then, in 1991, it introduced the tolar, which cannot be traded anywhere outside of Slovenia, and, as banks told customers, are not really bank notes, but coupons to be redeemed when the real money is printed.[20] Another minor logistical problem is the determination of the location for the printing of the currency. This is an issue as long as the region is still part of the state. Indeed, Estonia printed its kroons abroad, while Ukraine chose Canada for the printing of its coupons.[21] But these are minor considerations in comparison with some long-term problems raised by introducing a new currency. Among these, the biggest are that the seceding region has the disadvantage of little backing for its currency, it has little experience in dealing with monetary matters (except in the case of high decentralization, such as in Slovenia), and it is faced with the lack of acceptance of that currency in the global economy. The introduction of a new currency entails the establishment of the value of the new currency, the pegging of it usually to another (or the choice that it will freely fluctuate), and the determination of convertibility. In addition, there is the problem of the macroeconomic effects of withdrawing the old currency from circulation. The negative effects of this spill over into the state, as was evident when

Slovenia dumped its dinar holdings and thereby further aggravated inflation in dinar regions.

There is wide variation in the monetary efforts of the secessionist region of the former Soviet Union. Indeed, while Ukraine's parliament voted in March 1992 to completely replace the ruble with the local currency (coupon) on April 1, regions such as Kazakhstan have chosen, at least as of the spring of 1992, to remain within the ruble zone. In the case of the latter, its leader, Nazarbaev, has opted not to create a separate currency, and therefore to continue the old pattern of trade while introducing local monetary institutions that are not available through the Commonwealth. The critical problem faced by the former Soviet republics, including Russia, has to do with the difficulties involved in the creation of new banking systems.[22] None of the republics has experience in handling their own spending. The central state bank, which ceased to exist as of January 1, 1992, collected the republics' revenues and then gave out funds in return. This system is in the process of being replaced by a series of banks with western-style banking relations, in which the republican banks will be required to operate their own system of debits and credits, and use balance sheets. The enormity of the problem is understood by the fact that balance sheets are studied by first-year economics students in western countries, whereas they have been until recently entirely foreign to the leaders of the banking world in some seceding regions.

There is popular debate on the introduction of new currencies even if a seceding region chooses to remain within the union. The example of Quebec shows that if the population were to decide not to undertake secession but instead to increase autonomy, they might also choose an independence currency. Indeed, Quebec is in the process of determining the nature of its money and banking orientation. If it chose to continue using the Canadian dollar, how would it be related to the Canadian central bank? The current feeling, unlike that of the nationalists of the 1970s, is that Quebec should remain within the monetary union, but only the referendum at the end of 1992 will tell.

(v) Interrepublic Investments

States with industrial policies tend to channel investment capital into regions in which the returns are greatest. They follow the principle of comparative advantage in order to maximize returns. Even the private sector is not immune to government's incentives for the development of a predetermined location. Industrial policy, coupled with regional policy aimed at aiding the less developed regions, has resulted in a set of intricate interregional investment patterns linking regions within a union. At the time of secession, how are these links to be disentangled? If the seceding region is the recipient of investment, it may simply unilaterally retain the assets on its territory, and cease loan repayments. Alternatively, if it is the seceding region that has made the investments, it may try to reap its assets and call in its loans. The difficulty of finding a solution that goes beyond "finders-keepers" is exemplified by the exchange of remarks between the Soviet center and Lithuania: When Gorbachev presented Lithuania with a bill for the investment over the past few decades, Lithuania responded by threatening to present a bill for decades of socialist mismanagement and inefficiency.

If interregional investments are not interrupted, but as a result of economic reasoning on both sides are deemed to continue, the fact that one is dealing with international arrangements, rather than internal domestic ones, will raise a new series of questions. Among the issues to be determined is the question of the repatriation of profits: If the seceding region is the lender, should it be allowed to take out its profits from its former state? Furthermore, what currency is to be used in these transactions? If the seceding region has adopted a new currency, will that one be acceptable in the state, or should the seceding region use its holdings of the old currency? The determination of a legal framework within which investments are to occur is a serious obstacle to the continuation of interregional investments. While, before secession, a single set of laws was in effect, in the aftermath of secession not only are there two sets of legal systems but they will both be relatively new, and thus unfamiliar. If secession has been particularly bloody or abrupt, there will be a legal void, similar to a legal anarchy, that is likely to affect interregional investments negatively. Finally, with secession, taxation practices will change in at least the seceding region, raising the necessity to reevaluate the economic grounds upon which the initial investment was made.

(vi) Adjustment to Cessation of Subsidies

As was evident from Table 4.1, most of the states under study intervene in the pricing mechanism and engage in some form of trade protection. This translates into subsidies for the production of some goods. The nature of those goods and the location of their production is determined by regional and development policy of the state. In the aftermath of secession, the newly independent region has to face the unpleasant adjustment period associated with the loss of subsidies. This often entails shortages and higher prices. In Estonia, for example, the price of heating oil, imported from the former

Soviet Union, went from 83 rubles a ton to 12,000 rubles following independence.[23] Another example of an uncomfortable adjustment is that incurred by the industrial sector in Slovakia, which has for decades enjoyed the advantages of subsidies from the center. Presently, the hardships associated with the withdrawal of these subsidies has become a focal point of the Slovak nationalist movement.[24]

(vii) Labor Force and Human Capital

Secession has an effect on the labor force insofar as it alters the market for workers and labor productivity and raises some important questions with respect to the redistribution of human capital. Secession prompts migration, which has at least short-run disruptive effects on the labor market and productivity.

Secession tends to alter the composition of ethnic groups within a region, as well as change the majority ethnic group, thereby also changing the dominant language. This puts some members of a labor force at a disadvantage. Those outside the dominant ethnic group that chose not to learn the new lingua franca may migrate out of the newly independent region, either voluntarily or as a result of nationalist pressure in the seceding region[25] (such were the choices put before the Russian workers in Moldova when, in 1990, the new government passed a regulation requiring the use of Moldavian within five years). Irrespective of the cause of migration, the uprooting of labor has various economic consequences. In the seceding region, it may leave a gap that the indigenous labor force may not be able to fill, resulting in a labor shortage and subsequent wage increase if the market is functioning properly. A labor shortage may have a detrimental effect on a nascent economy. The example of Estonia is a case in point: the population of the area's three major industrial cities is 90 percent non-Estonian. These people are mostly factory workers that provide the labor, have the skills, and are probably unhappy with the recent events.[26] If some of these leave the region, do Estonians have sufficient local population to fill those jobs without hurting production?

In some cases, the vacancy created by the departing workers is exactly what is needed for the economy. The case of Eritrea exemplifies this: for decades, numerous Ethiopians have been employed in Eritrea. In 1992, in the aftermath of the fallen Mengitsu government, they are being expelled from the region. The economic reason for this has to do with oversupply of labor in the form of the male population that has been fighting the war for two decades, and now is in need of employment.[27] This trend is reminiscent of the withdrawal of females from the labor force in the United States when the men returned from fighting in the World War II.

At the same time, the migration of dislocated workers into the remaining state will cause a labor surplus in that labor market resulting in competition, displacement, and suppressed wages. In addition, migration will put pressure on the government to create jobs, as well as on the housing industry, and education, health, public transport, and other services.

However, workers are often constrained by institutional ties and cannot easily migrate. Often reasons such as intermarriages, or simply a housing shortage, are enough to discourage migration. Indeed, Russians in various seceding republics have found themselves in a position of nowhere to go because they belong nowhere: ethnically they are Russians, but they are born or have lived outside of Russia for decades.

Another question that arises in the period of redefinition is how is the labor force to be divided. If workers may be treated as tangible assets, then one response may be that they simply belong to the region where they are from (this argument becomes more complicated if workers reside and work in a place that is not their home). However, such a simple division of the labor force upon secession begs the issue of the central contribution to the creation of the human capital. If one draws an analogy with physical investments funded by the center in the seceding region, it is possible to view skilled labor as an asset that has been molded by central investments. The key issue then is to identify whether workers were trained at government expense and then to identify which level of government and whose funding was responsible for the training. If training and education of the seceding population was funded at the central level, then some claims may be made on that population, and the settlement of those claims may entail compensation for costs incurred. This is the economic argument underlying the occurrence of brain drain, which has been invoked not only in secession cases but also in numerous less developed countries in which public education and training are funded from the central budget, and people acquire skills and expertise at the expense of the center, and then migrate in search of better employment opportunities. In the case of secession, the trained population begins to contribute solely to the economy of the seceding region, thus the region that bore the costs and the region that gains the benefits are not the same. The more skilled the labor force is, the more this investment in human capital is an issue at the time of regional redefinition. There are exceptions—for example, in Slovenia and Corsica. In the former, human capital is a minor issue, because the decentralization of the educational system implied payment for education and training out of regional funds.[28] In the latter, it is not an issue, despite the centralized nature of the educational funding system, due to the relatively low level of expertise of the regional population, which would thus not cause a brain drain effect for France nor pose a major economic imbalance in the labor force.

(viii) Responsibility for Externalities

During the period of redefinition, responsibility needs to be allocated for externalities, both positive and negative, that are experienced across regional borders. The entanglement of economies, coupled with the continuous geographical space prior to secession has given rise to numerous positive and negative externalities, including the benefits to Serbia from a dam in Bosnia-Hercegovina, or the costs to Belarus from the spillout at Chernobyl in Ukraine. Presently the seceding regions tend to focus on the negative externalities that they have experienced from the center, from which they expect compensation, while the center tends to focus on the positive externalities that seceding regions have benefited from, and demand compensation for those. The most prominent externality issue that has recently been debated and most negotiated is pollution.

Given that the proliferation of regulation pertaining to the protection of the environment from industrial production is, in most cases, a phenomenon concentrated in the more developed, western states, most of the regions undergoing secession were not subject to environmental restraints. In the absence of regulations restraining pollution, significant damage to the environment occurred. This is especially acute in the communist countries, where there was both outdated technology as well as limited exposure of the problem. In Slovakia's secessionist efforts, the Slovaks blame the Czechs for environmental damage due to industrial production, the Bougainvillians blame the Papua New Guineans for the wreckage of their natural habitat by the exploitation of the mines, the Karen blame the Burmese for the deforestation of their traditional homeland, and the Quebecois Indians blame the Quebecois for the exploitation of the northern woods. The Kazakhstanis have another concern, namely the radiation-induced illnesses that hundreds of thousands of people seem to be suffering from.[29] This is due to the testing of nuclear weapons, as well as chemical and biological testing, whose effects, it is estimated, will take decades to clean up. Who should be responsible for the clean-up expenses? Is it just the center, or should the responsibility be shared by the newly independent regions? In the case of Kazakhstan, there is no center to bear the costs, but are there regions that will be making use of the nuclear weapons in their defense strategy, such as Ukraine?

Although these are all valid concerns, very little progress has been made in the allocation of a price to these externalities in order for compensation to be determined. This is because externalities are ranked low among the issues to be resolved. Indeed, it is difficult enough trying to unwind relationships that are more pressing, and divide assets that are tangible; the division of responsibility of intangibles such as pollution is bound to wait or go unresolved.

(ix) Internal Territorial Disputes

In rare cases, the boundaries of the seceding territory are not in dispute, whether for historical or cultural reasons. However, in most cases, delving into history far enough will reveal a variation of existing boundaries. Whether that fact is then exploited in the secessionist effort or not depends upon the outcome of a cost-benefit analysis that the region is bound to perform. For example, although Belarus is claiming some Lithuanian land (on the basis of historical boundaries), it has chosen not to press the point at this time. Similarly, the Slovenes have questioned their boundary with Croatia on the peninsula of Istra, but have chosen not to pursue the matter further at this point. However, in most cases, the territorial dispute is not mute.

The question of internal territorial boundaries entails ethnic, economic, and geopolitical considerations. The ethnic component is easiest to understand: the seceding region wants to extend the boundaries of its domain to include territory inhabited by people of the same ethnic group. The view is that if they are to secede, they would like to take with them their ethnic kin. Underlying this is the desire to change demographic factors so that the majority is united under one flag. Examples of this abound: the ex-Soviet republic of Armenia would like to unite with the ethnically similar ex-Soviet autonomous region of Nagorno-Karabakh, which is located within the ex-Soviet republic of Azerbaijan. Although the Armenian parliament has formally dropped its claims to unification (in early 1992), and the conflict in Nagorno-Karabakh has changed to an independence drive, the elements of a unification on the grounds of ethnicity are clear.

Territorial disputes may have a strong economic component to them. The area in dispute may be of particular economic use to the state, in which case the resistance to secession will be high. Alternatively, the claims that the seceding region makes on territory outside its boundary may be economically important, and therefore the chances of it being relinquished peacefully are small. Two examples of this exist in the present civil war in Yugoslavia.

First, Slavonia, one of the areas of Croatia where the fighting was most intense, is among the most fertile areas in Yugoslavia, forming part of the agricultural belt that continues into Vojvodina. Its loss to Croatia implies the loss of self-sufficiency in agriculture, no small consideration for a region contemplating independence. Second, in early 1992, a segment of the population in Dubrovnik explored the possibility of establishing a duty-free city state.[30] All means were used to dissuade this sentiment from taking hold, since the economic benefit of Dubrovnik, with respect to tourism, is invaluable to Croatia. Another example of economic territorial disputes of seceding regions takes us across the Atlantic, to the border between Newfoundland and Quebec. If internal borders become international borders in this area, then their location will be more carefully determined since Hydro-Quebec, the sole source of electricity in Quebec, buys 20 percent of its power, at bargain rates, from Newfoundland's Labrador.

Territorial disputes have their political dimension also. For strategic reasons, or out of a desire to ensure a balance of power, borders may be in dispute because the seceding region holds territory important to the center, or the center holds territory important to the region. The example of Punjab is relevant here. Punjab has been perceived in Indian foreign policy as a buffer between India and Pakistan. Punjab's demands for territory from the Indian state of Haryana would decrease this buffer by placing more territory into the hands of a region with unclear alliances.[31]

The source of the underlying boundary dispute is crucial insofar as it determines its resolution. Clearly, those territorial disputes that are ethnic in origin will warrant different solutions than those that are economic in origin: the question of the power prices between Quebec and Newfoundland can be resolved differently from that of the Armenians living encircled by Azerbaijanis. A secession involving the change of boundaries on the basis of ethnicity will have to involve population swaps or ethnic tolerance, both discussed in chapter 8. A secession involving economic resources will have to involve compensation, while political issues in boundaries warrant new alliances and international assurances. The calculation of the economic compensation that is necessary or acceptable is fraught with problems similar to those of determination of price of public assets, with the difference that natural resources are an integral part of the seceding region. However, if those resources have been exploited with the aid of central technology, investment, and manpower, then some central demands on them is understandable. An example of this is the development of mines in Katanga and Bougainville with outside capital and technology, raising the question of compensation at the time of secession.

(x) Social Security, Pensions, Medical Insurance

The social security system tends to be centralized in most of the countries under study. This is true even in some relatively decentralized states, such as Belgium and Canada, where the devolution of the social security system, although under discussion, is perceived as the beginning of the unraveling of the state. Secession raises questions pertaining to the ownership of all social funds and creates problems in the dissemination of these funds. Who owns the funds, the administrations at the regional levels, or the populations that made payments? When a region secedes, what happens to unemployment or pension payments to the workers that come from the center? Should a proportion of the fund be handed over to the seceding region in order to assure no interruption of pension payments or medical care?

In highly decentralized regions, such as those of Yugoslavia, pension funds, social security, and medical insurance have been administered at the republic level for decades. Consequently, the problem of dismemberment by region does not arise. However, the lack of agreement as to the boundaries of the seceding regions of Croatia and Bosnia-Hercegovina have led to the following two problems. First, decentralization of social security, health, and pension systems is not done on a county basis, therefore social funds of the population of Krajina, presently under Serbian control, are centralized in Zagreb. Second, given the large interregional displacement of workers due to the civil war, it is unclear which central administration is to pay for the refugees' social benefits. For example, the Serbian refugees from Slavonia that have relocated to Serbia have ceased to receive their pensions from Zagreb. Which new state is responsible for these payments, the secessionist region of Croatia, which has received their workers' contribution, or the receiving region, to which this labor force ethnically belongs?

(xi) Division of the Army and Military Arsenal

One of the unifying forces of each country is the existence of a common army. An army draws population and monetary contributions from all regions of the state, and thus is truly a state service. With secession of one region, or the unraveling of the entire state, the question of dismantling the army, as well as that of ownership of military assets, gains prominence.[32]

Indeed, probably the most pressing aspect of the negotiations between Russia, Ukraine, and Kazakhstan during early 1992 is the division of the army and the nuclear arsenal. For several weeks in early 1992, the world trembled as the possession of the nuclear weapons was unclear. The fear was somewhat dispersed following an agreement that control would remain in the central hands and that it was only the conventional forces that would become decentralized. The creation of new regional armies tends to be popular among supporters of independence, since it is perceived as a national symbol. Indeed, according to the defence minister of Ukraine, "When the talk is of creating an army, everyone applauds. But when economists speak of the problems of 'going it alone,' nobody listens."[33]

In the case of the former Soviet Union, the division of the army may prove to be the problem that tears the new Commonwealth of Independent States apart. Among the CIS members, eight decided in February 1992 that they would retain their armed forces under one central control: six agreed to a single command of conventional forces for a few years, while Belarus and Uzbekistan agreed but with great reservations.[34] Ukraine, Azerbaijan, and Moldavia will set up their own armies. In March 1992, President Yeltsin began moves to create a Russian army. This raises the question of which military assets would go to these republics. There are several approaches to this resolution: the formula preferred by the three republics is that they will take control of everything located on their soil, with exception of strategic weapons. This was done in the case of Moldova, when President Snegur simply announced the takeover of former Soviet military property in the republic in March 1992.[35] This type of takeover is perceived as unfair by the Russians, who claim that a disproportionate quantity of the arsenal was located in Belarus and Ukraine since these were border republics heavily manned for defense purposes. Therefore, the formula for division should be based on territory, population, and the length of borders. Such a formula would yield very different results. For example, the formula proposed by Ukraine and Belarus would give Ukraine 4,000 tanks, Belarus 2,400, and Russia 6,000, while the formula proposed by Russia would give Ukraine 2,900, Belarus 900 and Russia 7,100.[36] A similar discussion is presently under way in former Yugoslavia with respect to the federal army arsenal across the country. Most of the Yugoslav army's forces, including an estimated 100,000 troops, are concentrated in Bosnia-Hercegovina. Furthermore, the republic is also the site of most of the army's weapons factories. One proposal is that the troops simply be divided by ethnic lines, so that the Yugoslav army as such ceases to exist in the region, while the paramilitary Croat, Serb, and Muslim forces each absorb their fellow men.[37] This has *de facto* happened in the beginning of May 1992.

(xii) Choice of Symbols

Normally, the choice of symbols that a seceding region chooses to distinguish itself from the state it left is of minor consequence and of interest to few other than the regional population. The new paint on airplanes with national names, the issuance of visas at the border to those that until yesterday were not even aware of regional borders, and the hurried printing of stamps (even in regions that have yet to have their independence referendum[38]) are but some of the indications that people are part of a new state. Such symbols adopted by the seceding regions would not be included in this list of issues to be resolved if it were not for two symbols that have caused furor in the present secessionist climate: the particular choice of a name and the choice of a flag. Both are examples from former Yugoslavia.

The southern most republic of Yugoslavia carried the name Macedonia. It was composed ethnically of Serbs, Kosovars, Bulgarians, and Greeks. It has declared its independence from Yugoslavia and is demanding recognition by the world community. This recognition is blocked by Greece on the grounds that only Greek Macedonia has the historical right to that name and that Macedonian national identity was artificially created by Tito after World War II, so the region has no rights to the name on ethnic grounds.[39] Furthermore, Greece claims that Yugoslav Macedonia has territorial aspirations south of its borders. The question of names has arisen in another aspect of the Yugoslav conflict. The secessionist regions of Slovenia and Croatia have claimed that the remaining regions do not have the right to call themselves Yugoslavia, since that name represents another entity now defunct. However, this argumentation cannot but remind us of another example in history, that of Pakistan. When West Pakistan seceded from East Pakistan, it changed its name but had no claims to that of the remaining regions. This is true despite the fact that the name Pakistan is an acronym for the regions that were united in that country. The loss of one of those regions did not negate the right of the remaining state to use the name and all associated with it. Similarly, Yugoslavia means south Slavs, those that remain in the federation that was proclaimed in April 1992, whatever its composition, still are south Slavs, with the exception of the non-Slavic populations of Kosovars and Bosnian Muslims, and have the right to inherit the name and all its connotations.

The questions of flags is also one that is centered in Yugoslavia. After independence, the nationalist government of Croatia unfurled new flags that carried the checkerboard pattern. Although this motif was based in the region's history, with its roots in the association with the Austro-Hungarian

Empire, it was also the pattern that was used by the fascist regime of independent Croatia during World War II. As such, it was the flag under which Serbs, Jews, and gypsies were slaughtered and persecuted. Consequently, the choice of that flag raised serious concerns among Serbs and Jews residing in Croatia, and indeed, as much as that flag symbolized independence for the Croatians, it also symbolized persecution for others. The slogan of the Serbs in Croatia became that never again will they live under that flag.

The example of the symbolic value of names and flags serves to underline the necessity of keeping cool heads in such passionate disputes as secession. It is clear that much bloodshed and violence could have been avoided if Croatia had refrained from using a symbol so tied to its World War II history. Similarly, a slight modification of the name of Macedonia would have shown appreciation of the sensitivity of the issue for Greece and thus aided in the international recognition that Macedonia could greatly benefit from.[40]

EXTERNAL ISSUES

(i) International Economic Relations

A newly seceded region will establish economic relations with the international economy and, albeit with a lag, with its ex-state. In the case of the former, international economic relations rarely need to be established and negotiated from scratch. Among the steps that newly independent states must take in establishing themselves in the international arena are the taking over of their borders and customs. They will also want to open embassies and send representatives abroad. Included in the representatives are often those to international economic organizations whose participation is sought. Indeed, among the regions that have declared sovereignty in the course of 1990-91, most of them have attempted entry in the EEC, the OECD, and the World Bank. Moreover, in April 1992, former Soviet republics were accepted into the IMF, while former Yugoslav republics became members of the Conference on Security and Cooperation in Europe.[41]

Acceptance into all these international organizations is dependent upon how the existing organizations perceive themselves. The World Bank and the United Nations will most easily accept newcomers because of the nature of their mandates. However, for the EEC, such a potentially wide membership raises numerous questions as to how big can the association get before diseconomies of scale start setting in. Furthermore, if it is a union of European states, where exactly does Europe end? If the Baltic states are to be included in Europe, and similarly Belarus and Ukraine, then what about

Russia? Does that also not raise the question of Turkey, which is geographically closer in proximity to the European nucleus than Ukraine?[42] The rejection of Turkey implies that issues other than geography are determining membership. Moreover, how is the EEC to decide the principles by which the southern borders of Europe are to be ascertained? Opinion in Western Europe varies. There are those that are in favor of opening up to the east and embracing as many new states as possible, subject to certain conditions. This enlargement drive comes about from several motivations. First, accepting these states into the community of nations might improve the economic status of their populations, and thereby achieve several results, including the curbing of migration into Western Europe. Second, an improvement in the economies would imply the opening up of new markets that the Western states would have preferential access to. Third, the political might of an enlarged Europe might fill the gap in the world of superpowers that was vacated by the exit of the Soviet Union.

The seceding region will need to establish some ties with its ex-state. Pragmatic reasons such as geography and economics often dictate these ties. Unlike husband and wife, who, following divorce, can move away from each other, regions seceding from continuous land cannot change their locations. Even when secession occurs under conditions of war, the healing process postpones relations somewhat, but some of the ties that bind regions in the first place prevail. Indeed, in the case of Bangladesh, political and economic ties were reestablished with Pakistan shortly after secession, and trade links were at their prewar levels within one year of the conflict.

The nature of ties between a secessionist region and ex-state can take numerous forms. At one end of the spectrum, the seceding region and ex-state may have no formal political ties, and the cessation of trade may have left economic relations to a mere dwindling of preexisting relations. At the other end of the spectrum, the two political entities may decide to share in numerous activities, while retaining sovereignty in others. Various forms of integration, commonwealth, and confederation arrangements have been proposed and have sprung up in the past two years. For example, in the Soviet Union, the Commonwealth of Independent States has come to replace the political links between 11 of the former 15 Soviet republics.[43] In former Yugoslavia, various organizational forms have been suggested to replace the federation established by the constitution of 1974: Croatia and Slovenia proposed a confederal agreement that gave virtually no power to the center,[44] the EEC suggested a Swiss type of confederation composed of ethnically based cantons for the solution of the Bosnian and Hercegovinian crisis, while before the 1992 war broke out, a solution involving an asymmetrical federation among the republics was discussed.

(ii) Trade

Upon secession, the nature of trade undergoes a transformation. Both trade in the global markets as well as trade with the ex-state are altered due to the new status of sovereignty. Although even trade with the ex-state becomes international trade, it is treated separately here since it entails a different set of concerns. With respect to trade with the global economy, a newly seceded region is likely to try to solidify and expand the preexisting ties. The benefits to it of a speedy integration into the global system include foreign currency, access to manufacturing inputs and raw materials, and consumer goods. These are often all essential to the regional economy if it is simultaneously adjusting to the loss of state markets or to the elevated prices that trade with the ex-state entails in the absence of central subsidies. However, the seceding region is faced with numerous obstacles in its attempt to break into international trading networks. These often include the lack of experience in trade, especially in regions where foreign trade was channeled through a central trading unit (such as in the Soviet Union, Senegal, India, etc.). Also, the lack of hard currency with which to import is a problem for the seceding region. If the region has its own currency, then the issue of convertibility of that currency must be resolved before it becomes an acceptable currency for trade. Indeed, the new Russian republic is planning to make the ruble convertible in August 1992, but only after it has enabled its rate to be supported by a $6 billion fund.[45] Such support mechanisms are not available to most newly seceding regions, so convertibility is not easy to achieve. Another obstacle to be overcome in international trade has to do with the (often) low quality of goods put up for export that previously were not subject to international competition. It has been a rude awakening to many East European producers to find that some shabby goods that were successfully traded in less developed countries and other Eastern states do not fare well in hard currency markets. Another obstacle arises when the seceding region had enjoyed the advantages of subsidized central prices. The loss of these subsidies and the entry into world markets tends to produce an inflationary shock to the economy.

As a result of all these obstacles, it may be wise for the seceding region (and often also for the ex-state) to encourage the continuation of trade relations in the aftermath of secession. Indeed, profitable exchanges can still benefit both sides: For example, independent Estonia has continued to ship

90 percent of its industrial goods to the former Soviet Union, and many of its factories buy 80 percent of their inputs from there. The degree to which such trade relations occur depends on several factors. First, the relative dependency of the seceding region on the ex-state (or the dependency of the ex-state on the seceding region) will determine the magnitude of the loss of each others' markets. Even Slovenia, which has been highly insulated from the markets of Yugoslavia, has continued to engage in trade with Serbia, despite Serbian attempts to encourage a boycott of Slovenian goods. Second, the relative prices of goods must be renegotiated. In many cases, internal trade occurred with prices set by a central price commission, in order to pursue central policy. This implied biases that hurt or aided regions. With secession, new prices need to be determined, and these will reflect supply and demand in the global markets. This may prove to be a rude shock to both trading partners. Third, it must be determined what currency trade will take place in. If the seceding region has not introduced a new currency, trade can proceed with payments in the familiar currency, as is happening in trade between Russia and Kazakhstan. However, if a new currency is introduced, then that currency should be made convertible as soon as possible to ensure proper and fair valuation of goods, such as the trade between the Russian ruble and the Ukrainian hrivyn. Fourth, secession implies that the newly independent states have the right to enter into new forms of protection in their trade arrangements. This in fact is a big hurdle to the progress of trade between regions since protection may be perceived as a way of rectifying old wrongs. The higher the degree of dependency between regions, the greater the disruption to trade caused by such protective practices. This led Aslund to say that, in the case of the former Soviet Union, "everything should be done to maintain the existing economic links."[46]

However, the potential for trade disruption is great in the cases of seceding regions. To minimize this, Havrylyshyn and Williamson have made three concrete suggestions.[47] First, the regions should have a commitment to ban any restrictions to interregional trade. Second, regions should guarantee the same treatment to firms from other regions as in their own. And third, regions should agree to adopt common industrial standards, subject to either central or international authority. By adopting these guidelines, regions might avoid the recessionary pitfalls associated with abrupt decrease in trade.

(iii) Foreign Investment and Capital Flows

As with trade, international and interregional financial flows become altered in the aftermath of secession. A secessionist region will try to maintain and enlarge financial links with the world economy while at the same time establish new links with its ex-state. It will try to ensure the inflow of foreign capital, investments and loans, grants and aid, technical assistance, et cetera. There are several simultaneous processes that warrant consideration during the period of redefinition with respect to financial flows: the disengagement from those foreign commitments that are deemed unbeneficial, the division of foreign commitments among seceding region and ex-state, and the encouragement of new financial ties.

With respect to the severing of old ties, the problem is the following: The seceding region, in most cases, is the recipient of international inflows that have gone through the center. Therefore, they were negotiated, contracted, and executed by way of the ex-state. Upon secession, the future of those contracts is uncertain. Utter confusion results from competing demands of the ex-state and the seceding region, both of which attempt to use the international partner as an arbitrator. This confusion is amplified by the introduction of new tax and foreign currency laws as well as new legal systems in both the seceding region and the ex-state. This confusion was quite evident in Yugoslavia, where, at the time of Slovenia's secession, some 8,000 international agreements made with Yugoslavia had to be renegotiated or terminated.

With respect to setting up new international arrangements, the seceding region has the task of providing potential investors with the following: First, it must convince them that there is a valid reason for their investments. This reason is usually economic, such as the likelihood of a high rate of return. However, sometimes political and cultural influence is enough of a reason, as in the case of some German financial involvements in Croatia. Second, the seceding region must provide an atmosphere conducive to the inflow of capital. This entails a clear taxation policy, a coherent legal framework, a commitment to the establishment of an infrastructure where it is not already in place, and so forth. Third, the seceding region must have undisputable rights over the territory that is involved in the international agreements. The example of Sakhalin, an oil-producing province in Russia, has served to intensify apprehensions of foreign investors in regions where the locus of power is under dispute.[48]

Despite the clear need of secessionist regions for the inflow of capital, neither private investors nor government organizations have been forthcoming with capital in the regions of the former Soviet bloc. With the exception of possibly Germany, Western Europe and the United States have been slow in responding to economic pleas.[49] Estonia has been the most successful of the Baltic republics in attracting foreign investment, but even that has amounted to merely 3 percent of gross national product. Some 1,200 foreign companies have moved in since 1991.[50] Acceptance of the former Soviet states to the IMF will provide an impetus for financial assistance. However, this assistance does not come cheap. Upon acceptance to the IMF, the stake of the former Soviet republics would amount to 4.25 percent of the IMF, translating into about $5.1 billion that would have to be put up at the time of entry. One-quarter of this would have to be in hard currency, the rest in rubles.[51] The hard currency would have to come from other countries, since the republics do not have such foreign currency reserves. After entry, the republics can ask for assistance, which can be on the order of three to four times the size of the original input of capital, but the conditions for that assistance are based on very stringent adherence to rules pertaining to reform.

SECESSION AND TRANSITION TO A MARKET ECONOMY

Some of the regions under study are undergoing two difficult processes simultaneously: they are becoming divorced from their political and economic unions, and they are transforming their economies from centrally planned to market economies. The former Soviet republics, as well as those of Yugoslavia and Czechoslovakia, are examples of this "double-bang," and are all faced with few guidelines on how to survive these simultaneous changes. Rarely in history have two such large forces coincided in one region. Indeed, the present experience might be compared to that of Tibet during 1959, as described by Peissel:

> Thus the Lhasa Rebellion became more than a general opposition to the Chinese invasion. Simultaneously, as never before in history, a nation stood up to oppose both feudalism and communism . . . It was a double revolution: first, the long overdue revolution against aristocratic privilege and the religious tyranny of the great abbots, and also against the equally dismal tyranny of imperialistic Chinese communism: the Hungarian and French Revolution combined.[52]

As there are no guidelines for states and regions to follow during secession, there is similarly little knowledge about the transition from socialism to capitalism. Recently, universities have produced some theoretical deliberations: Indeed, by 1990, studies by Kornai, Hines, and Williamson presented complete analyses of transitional problems.[53] Even in the Soviet Union, the plans for future and reform all deviate along the same path, be they the Shatalin 500-Day Plan of 1990 or the "Grand Bargain" of 1991 devised by Allison and Yavlinsky.[54] However, all these efforts to describe and design the transition from plan to market are not based in experience.

Although societies have moved across various types of economic systems, such as the feudal and the slave economies and from capitalism to socialism, never has there been a large-scale transformation from a planned economy to a market economy. There have been small-scale efforts, often limited to several sectors of the economy, in more developed western states. These differ from the present efforts in the former Soviet bloc not only in scope but also in speed. Indeed, Britain took over a decade to move its economy from its form of socialism to a more market-oriented economy. And that was under the best of conditions, with institutions fully developed and a high level of income, coupled with the unifying force and energy provided by the ideology of Margaret Thatcher. Why is it expected that the imposition of rapid changes on the economies of Eastern Europe and the Soviet republics, which have none of the beneficial conditions of Britain, should work in the course of several years?[55]

This "shock therapy" that is being administered to the reforming regions of the former Soviet bloc means different things to different governments, as they choose which changes to focus on and when. According to Collins and Rodrick, there are three principal elements of a transition to a market economy. These include: macroeconomic stabilization (monetary and fiscal policies and competitive exchange rate), price reform (price liberalization, trade liberalization, and currency convertibility), and structural and institutional reforms (legal system including property rights, privatization, reform of banking system and financial intermediaries, hard budget constraints for firm, expansion of capital infrastructure, and the development of a social safety net).[56] In addition, some societal changes are warranted in the transition, such as the increase of the savings rate, the stimulation of innovative spirit and risk-taking, and the altering of the attitude toward work that has been associated with communism. Any one of several issues—currency convertibility, elimination of subsidies, decontrolling prices, and the elimination of restrictions on imports—are bound to put the economy in a tailspin. But when they occur at once, in conjunction, the effects may be devastating. Indeed, the results from Poland and Czechoslovakia, where the reforms have been in place longest, show a dramatic decrease in the standards of living, a decrease in industrial output, an increase in the unemployment and inflation rates, decreases in domestic demand, and a decrease in the gross domestic product.[57]

Thus, the seceding *and remaining* regions of Yugoslavia and the Soviet Union must contend with the dual impact on their economies of disassociation and transition. This deadly combination is bound to create short-run havoc even in the most advantaged of countries, let alone in those where national and foreign debts are high, local capital accumulation is limited, foreign currency is scarce, the legal system is often powerless and corrupt, and underemployment is rampant. However, it might be argued that secession and transition together in fact ease the pain of either of the processes. That is not to say that those regions undergoing secession will have better success than others, creating an invitation for further breaking up, but rather that there is much overlap between the tasks at hand in the aftermath of secession, and the tasks involved in the transition. A smaller region that is committed to independence and in the throes of public support for the government that brought about such changes may have better conditions to bring about the tremendous changes that are required. It has a smaller bureaucracy to contend with and it has less cumbersome institutions. The seceding region is starting from scratch in many areas, so it has the power to set matters up according to its goals and capacities. In addition, whatever problems arise and whatever costs are incurred associated with the application of economic shock therapy reforms, it is useful to have a target for the blame, such as the ex-state. Indeed, this transferral of responsibility for problems and hardships associated with both secession and transition has been popular among the leaders in the former Soviet bloc. Thus far, it was not a successful tool in Estonia, where the government responsible for bringing about independence was pressured into resigning in January 1992 due to the crisis of the economy.[58]

CONCLUSIONS

Although the legal aspects of achieving sovereignty might take a few weeks (if all parties have come to agreement), the logistical aspects take much longer and may stretch the process of achieving true sovereignty for as long as five to ten years. Indeed, to untangle economies under the best of circumstances takes years, let alone under the worst: the Malaysian and Singapore governments, at the time of their separation in 1965, chose December 1989 as the final date for "delisting" of Malaysian companies from the Singapore stock exchange.[59] The secessionist regions of countries that are unravelling, such as the Soviet Union and Yugoslavia, are not in a hurry to negotiate certain economic details because, with time, the central entity is diminishing in power. An Estonian authority recently said that if the wait is long enough, there might not be any negotiating partner left with whom to discuss these matters.

At the end of this partial list of issues that need resolution in peaceful secession, it does seem like the process is a frustrating obstacle course and perhaps could more simply be resolved by force. Besides the moral objections to such a solution, on economic grounds the use of force is bound to have a detrimental effect, at least in the short run, on both the seceding region and the ex-state. As such, it affects the viability of both regions, as discussed in the next chapter.

7

Post-Secession Economic Viability

It was fundamentally a matter of recognizing reality . . . It made no sense to
antagonize the Indonesians . . . East Timor was not a viable entity.

> —Brent Scowcroft, President Ford's national security adviser, when asked
> why the Ford administration did not warn the Indonesians against invading
> East Timor[1]

I am absolutely convinced that a confederation is a . . . liberal illusion that can
lead either to a federation or to war.

> —Gennady Burbulis, Russian government official discussing the future of
> relations among the independent states of the former Soviet Union in 1992[2]

The period of reequilibration is characterized by precarious adjustments in
the political, social, and economic spheres. Post-secessionist regions will
vary in their ability to tide over the hurdles that will present themselves after
severance of ties with the center. With respect to the economic adjustment,
its smoothness will depend upon several economic characteristics that are
embodied in the term *viability*. Economic viability is a concept often used
and rarely defined. A simple working definition adopted here is the following: viability of a region implies the ability to sustain growth in the aftermath
of secession at the preindependence levels. In adopting this definition, a
distinction must be made between the short run and the long run, since most
regions are capable of economic survival in the long run after forging new
relationships with the international economy and the nation from which they
seceded. With secession, regions strive to at least continue (if not improve)
their level of economic performance. The concept of an economic status quo
in the aftermath of secession has been addressed by Buchanon, who points
out that, from a philosophical perspective, there is no reason to assume that
a region has a right to an economic status quo. Indeed, according to Buchanon,

"this dubious principle of entitlement to the status quo" is simply not justified in either secession or divorce.[3] It is nevertheless a useful tool used in hypothesizing about post-secessionist viability.

Economic viability does not imply self-sufficiency. A region that is viable does not necessarily satisfy all its consumer and industrial demand with its local output. Although some may do this, that ability is determined by geography and access to technology, and usually excludes small regions with limited resources. Even in the sphere of food self-sufficiency, which is among the primary goals of states, viability is not to be confused with the political desire for food self-sufficiency. Instead, viability is more concerned with specialization, comparative advantage, and trade. For this reason, viability assessments pay a lot of attention to the trade patterns of regions, as is done below.

Of the 30 cases under study, at first glance it is clear that they will not all have the same resource advantages, the same international support, and the same ability to manage their economies independently. Indeed, there is a wide range of economic potential of the regions, which transcends their present level of economic development. In chapter 2, four variables were presented that were hypothesized to have an effect on viability: the level of economic development, trade dependency, net flows, and the degree of regional decentralization. These variables in turn encompass other characteristics. For example, the level of economic development conveys information on the degree of industrialization, business-mindedness, level of education, and nature of the infrastructure, since it tends to be positively related to these. Trade dependency has implications pertaining to the hard-currency earning capacity of industrial, agricultural, or raw materials output of the region.

These four variables together with their concomitant characteristics are by no means the only economic considerations in the determination of viability. Indeed, various other factors of lesser importance contribute to economic viability. Although these were described in chapter 2, they are briefly included below: First, the method by which secession was achieved has an effect on the economy (if independence is achieved through peaceful means, then the new region is not encumbered with reconstruction costs, as it might be when the economy is devastated by outbursts of violence in response to secessionary demands). Second, homogeneity of the population is important for the economy in the aftermath of secession, because it may minimize disruption of the labor force. Minorities within the seceding region might be threatened by secession, as their rights tend to be reevaluated, leading to the disruption of economic activity. Third, the degree of national price deviation from international prices is important in determining the facility with which a region can integrate itself into the global economy (a region accustomed to price intervention in its purchases from the national markets will undergo a costly adjustment following independence).

However, as noted in chapter 2, estimates of viability are rarely taken into account in the reevaluation phase of secession because the drive for secession is most often an emotional response to a perceived threat and, as such, is not subject to rational dissuasion. The hysteria associated with independence often blinds people to economic realities, which sink in only with time. This is very clear in the case of numerous former republics of the Soviet Union that were not prepared to heed warnings of economic hardship before secession (although some, like Estonia, experienced the downfall of the government associated with independence as a result of an economic crisis during the reequilibration period).[4]

VIABILITY OF THE SECEDING REGION

This chapter will discuss the viability of the seceding region, the viability of the remaining region, and viability under conditions of violence. With respect to the first two, it was proposed in chapter 2 that a positive relationship exists between viability and economic development, net outflows, and decentralization, while a negative relationship exists between viability and trade dependency. Yet, the ensuing discussion groups the cases under study by their levels of economic development only. This is not because of its supreme importance among the variables, but rather because it is the economic variable for which the data are most reliable.

With respect to economic development, there is wide variation among the regions, ranging from some of the most developed in the world (Lombardy) to some of the least developed (East Timor). The issue of economic development is also complicated by the fact that some regions have the potential for more development than they have actually achieved, usually as a result of the possession of lucrative assets, such as in the case of Bougainville, Katanga, Russia, and so on. The potential of this group of secessionist regions places them in a different category from less developed secessionist regions that have few resources to count on upon independence, and is therefore discussed separately below.

With respect to interregional flows, it is recalled that the movement of resources across regional borders usually refers to the allocation of funds from the central budget that flow into the regions and the outflow of tax revenue from the states to the central budget. The experience of the secessionist regions varies: In Slovenia, the net value of resource flows is negative. In other words, the center sends to Slovenia less than it receives, implying that the costs to the regions of federal demands are lower than the benefits. The fragmentary evidence on the subject seems to point to similar net flows in Lombardy, Bougainville, Biafra, and Katanga. In Lombardy, the net transfer out of the region, both with respect to capital as well as to goods and services, exceeds the inflow. The regions wealthy in resources, such as Bougainville, Biafra, and Katanga, are the principal income contributors in their nations, and as such do not benefit from the center in central budgetary allocations. In these five cases, the net outflow of resources has contributed to aggravating pre-secession perceptions of injustice—whether it is called a tax revolt (as in Lombardy) or the "milking of the cow" (as in Biafra)—as well as the perception that with secession those funds will be available for local use. With respect to Punjab, Quebec, and the Baltic republics of the former Soviet Union, the evidence is inconclusive, since some data support the contention that the region is a net recipient of central funds, while other data indicated it is a net loser.

Although generalizations are made to enable the division of regions into two categories of center-state relations, decentralized and centralized, there are clearly many varieties and distinctions within each category. The regions classified as decentralized, including Slovenia, Quebec, Punjab, and Bougainville, enjoy extensive regional powers with respect to economic decisions and processes. The regions are ranked in descending order with respect to the degree of decentralization that they enjoy and are discussed below in detail. There is a similar type of diversity among the regions that are part of centralized nations, such as Lombardy, Katanga, and Biafra, and the former Soviet republics.

Trade dependency on the nation varies widely among the cases under study. As discussed in chapter 2, although trade may be destined for markets at three spatial locations (regional, national, and international), only dependency on national markets is relevant for this study because it sheds light on economic viability of regions in the absence of ties to the center. In Bougainville, Katanga, and Biafra, the extraction of copper, petroleum, and other natural resources occurred principally for the international markets. In these cases, the technology, the know-how, and supportive materials for the production process were provided by foreign companies with little input from the national level. Prior to the breakup of Yugoslavia, the national trading system had increasingly become so fragmented that Slovenia was more integrated into the international markets than those of Yugoslavia.[5] Punjab also has a low trade dependency on the nation since it was remarkably successful in creating an economic self-sufficiency with respect to the principal inputs for its production.[6] Although it does depend on national markets for the sale of its output, this can be attributed to the national food policy that prohibited Punjab from trading its primary products in the international markets.[7] Lombardy also has a low trade dependency: it no longer depends on southern Italy for cheap labor, it has been purchasing other resources from the more expensive international markets, and it has harbored extensive ties with northern European nations such that a large proportion of its output is exported. The evidence with respect to regional dependency in Quebec is inconclusive. In Quebec, recent reports of the domesticity of the local labor force indicate that the Quebecois are increasingly taking on positions that previously were in the hands of outsiders (namely, the Anglos).[8] Further, recent reports indicating that the loss of the Ontario markets would not significantly impact on the region (as long as the U.S. markets remained open)[9] imply that regional dependency is low. In the former Soviet republics, the evidence seems to indicate that trade dependency is high in all regions with the exception of Russia.

(i) Viability of High-Income Regions with High Levels of Development

The evidence seems to indicate that secessionist regions of Lombardy, Slovenia, Quebec, Ukraine, and Catalonia are all viable entities that could, with little adjustment, sustain their pre-independence economic status. First, they are all developed regions, and development is positively related to viability. Second, the net flows from these regions are difficult to assess: Lombardy and Catalonia have experienced definite net outflows, while in Slovenia, they are likely. The evidence for Quebec and Ukraine is inconclusive. The greater the net outflows, the greater the viability when those outflows are stopped. Third, with respect to trade dependency, Ukraine and Catalonia are most dependent on their state economies. Quebec, Lombardy, and Slovenia, although making use of the domestic markets, have large trade ties with the international economy. The lower the trade dependency, the greater the viability. Finally, decentralization has been most prevalent in the case of Slovenia, followed by Quebec and Catalonia. Lombardy and Ukraine (while part of the Soviet Union), have highly centralized economic and political systems. Despite the fact that some of these regions do not have all the variables pointing in the direction proposed for viability to occur, they are considered viable because of the overwhelming importance of their high development levels. The particulars of some of these cases are discussed below.

Lombardy

Given that Lombardy, like Catalonia, is demanding increased autonomy rather than secession, the appropriate question is how the region would tolerate additional autonomy. The economy of Lombardy is among the strongest of those studied: it has sustained high rates of economic growth over decades. Although its economy is largely based in services and manufacturing, it has not neglected agriculture, and the fertile Po Valley could certainly provide sufficient agricultural and food products if necessary.

Lombardy is perfectly situated to participate in the developed part of Europe through trade, foreign investment, and diffusion of technology, given its central location and consequently low transportation costs. With respect to "mentality," the labor force has more in common with the Germanic population than with the southern Italians, so that the average worker in Lombardy produces 34 percent more than the average Italian.[10] Under conditions of increased autonomy, it is likely that Lombardy would intensify its orientation toward the north, probably changing its links with the less productive south. The less developed Italian south (the Mezzogiorno) is largely responsible for the Italian budget deficit since it absorbs spending and subsidies aimed at increasing employment and fostering industrial development. Without these transfers, the center might be able to balance its budget. For Lombardy, an increase in autonomy would probably imply a severance or severe alteration of economic ties with the south, which in turn implies that more funds would be available at the regional level. Indeed, Lombardy pays for 25 percent of the national taxes, and a change in the transfers would imply more at the regional level.[11]

Unlike regions such as Slovenia and Ukraine, Lombardy has already broken into the international markets, and its products are highly competitive. It also has ample experience in international trade and investments. But its link with the international world would not be the sole link that Lombardy would foster: indeed, it is presently in the midst of an effort to create an economic union with other north Italian, highly developed regions. Local parties have emerged in the Piedmont, Liguria, and Veneto, all of which have similar platforms as the Lega Lombarda, the leading party for autonomy in Lombardy. Together they have set up a "Lega Nord" that gives them a greater electoral base and stands for unification of their efforts, mainly aimed against the south. Therefore, the efforts of the region are not only to separate themselves from the Italian center, but to develop new links with regions on the basis of economic and cultural similarities.

Ukraine

With the independence that Ukraine achieved in December 1991, the second largest European state was created. Size and its concomitant resource diversity are just two of the prerequisites for adequate rates of growth that make Ukraine the envy of most of the developing world as it enters statehood. With respect to infrastructure, Ukraine has a well-developed system of rail and roads, it has access to water and well-established ports, and it has navigable riverways. With respect to the labor force, it has a relatively homogenous population (74 percent Ukrainian) that has an above-average educational level. With respect to agricultural production, it contains some of the most fertile soils of the former Soviet Union. It produced 46 percent of the total agricultural output of the Soviet Union in 1985, and it is a net exporter of foodstuffs.[12] With respect to industry, the region is highly industrialized, outranked only by the Baltic republics. According to the viability estimates of the Deutsche Bank, Ukraine has the highest potential of all the former republics, achieving a score of 83 out of 100. The only indicator on which it ranks low is business-mindedness. The indicators chosen in this study show a somewhat less optimistic picture. Although the region is obviously viable in the long run, in the short run the existence of trade dependency and the lack of decentralization are likely to make their influence felt. With respect to dependency, the Ukrainian economy is highly interrelated with the Soviet economy, as evident from Table 4.2. With respect to decentralization, the Ukrainian economy was highly integrated with the former Soviet Union with respect to decision-making and control in economic matters. Despite this high level of dependency and low level of decentralization, the region is deemed viable because of the following: First, the newly created Commonwealth of Independent States functions as an intermediate step between full interregional trade and full independence in trade. Although the trade links among CIS members and the global economy may in fact turn out to be the same as during the time of Soviet centrally planned trade, they will have been established out of self-interest rather than central directive.[13] Second, the existence of the CIS offers regions the time to adjust and prepare for genuine entry into the international economy as well as to gain experience in the running of internal affairs.

The biggest impediment to the viability of Ukraine is the lack of energy sources. Despite the fact that Ukraine has coal and natural gas (indeed, some 60 percent of the former Soviet citumen and anthracite coal reserves are in Ukraine), its economy has for decades relied on cheap oil from Russia. By March 1992 oil supplies from Russia had sharply declined, so that gasoline was sold on the black market for 15 times its price at the pumps (which are empty). Natural gas supplies from Turkmenistan, the major supplier to Ukrainian industry, have been halted over a price disagreement. In its efforts to decrease its dependency on Russian oil, Ukraine has agreed tentatively to build a pipeline from Iran. However, it is unlikely that this move would serve its purpose since that pipeline would run through not only Russia but some of the most unstable regions of the former union: Azerbaijan and Chechen-Ingushetia. Adjusting the Ukrainian economy to international prices of oil is the biggest obstacle confronting the state.

Quebec

During the 1970s and early 1980s, Quebec's viability was questioned. At this time, renewed interest in secession had coincided with a general recession and economic downturn, so that independence for the region was closely tied to economic performance. Secession was perceived by many as further hurting the economy insofar as it implied the loss of financial support from Ottawa and immediate doubling of the unemployment rate due to the loss of trade with Canada: according to Snyder, "Unemployment, already severe, would double overnight because at least a third of Quebec's manufacturing jobs depended on sales to the rest of Canada."[14]

Today, no longer restrained by a weak economy, Quebec is a viable economic entity. It is a developed region that has little dependency on the nation. This lack of dependency is clear in several ways: First, with respect to international trade, the region has been a large trader with the outside world, especially with the United States. The nature of the goods that it is exporting has changed to reflect its changing economic base, which during the past two decades has shifted from dying industries, such as textiles, and modernized its industrial and technological sectors. Second, in the past decade, the Quebecois took greater control of their resources, and the ethnic composition of the economic and business leaders has changed, serving as an indication that the economic matters of the region are best served with greater independence from the center. In addition, the evidence from various economic studies, discussed in chapter 4, showing that the outflow from the region is roughly equal to what it gets from the center, leads many to the conclusion that Quebec could do quite well on its own. This, coupled with the existence of separate institutions such as its own stock exchange, universities, and so forth, leads to Galbraith's statement that the economic viability of Quebec is no longer questioned.[15] Despite the setback that the region may experience from the cancellation of the sale to New York of power from

Hydro-Quebec utility company, and the consequent possible cancellation of the expansion project, Quebec's economy is sufficiently diversified that such a loss would not imperil its viability.[16]

Slovenia

There are at least two reasons why Slovenia is likely to be a viable economic entity. First, the Slovenian economy is based on industrial production, which includes the production of machinery and tools that are essential for further production. If indeed the prerequisite for self-sufficiency is the local production of inputs, then Slovenia certainly has satisfied that condition. Moreover, the vertical integration of its key industries further contributes to its self-sufficiency.

A second reason why Slovenia is likely to succeed as an autonomous economy is unrelated to the nature of its economic base. Slovenia has acquired a high level of expertise in foreign trade that results from years of experience in competing in foreign markets. Its reputation as a quality producer and reliable supplier can be traced to the time of the Austro-Hungarian Empire, when its role as a manufacturing center was established. Slovenia's current international reputation and expertise are reinforced by a local infrastructure that includes highly developed services (such as banking, transport, and insurance) that facilitate international interactions.

Despite these advantages, the Slovenian economy has been in pain in the early months of its independence. There is evidence that the economic crisis is felt deeply in Slovenia, manifested by a decrease in production and the bankruptcy of many leading firms. The loss of markets in Serbia, due partially to the boycott of Slovenian goods (the so-called "trade war") and partially to the lack of resources due to the general economic decline in light of the civil war, has affected the Slovenian economy more than expected. Moreover, the commitment of the western leaders to the support of the newly independent state has been overshadowed by the quest for a solution to the more pressing Serb-Croat civil war raging in the heart of Europe.

(ii) Viability of Relatively High-Income Regions with Development Potential

Bougainville

Bougainville is a region with great income potential, much of which is already realized. It is responsible for a large share of the world's copper production, and it produces 45 percent of the Papua New Guinean revenues (see Table 4.1). With independence, these financial assets would be retained domestically. Despite the region's obvious potential, arguments for and against the viability of Bougainville as an independent nation have been made by Griffin and are described here. Some points against the viability of the region are: the "lack of economies of scale, lack of defense facilities, the competitiveness of marketing primary produce, the lack of resources once copper is exhausted, and the boredom and lack of opportunity that would ensue."[17] Griffin argues against the importance of these on several grounds. First, the benefits of the economies of scale might not sustain themselves if animosity between the regions results in civil war or coercive policies. Second, the costs of law and order need not be so great if the region is able to harness traditional social controls to work with a modern police force. Third, trade agreements for agricultural products with neighboring regions, including Papua New Guinea, could be beneficial to all and reduce the competitiveness that the island would encounter in the global markets. Fourth, although copper will not last forever, the capital generated from it can be invested in a diverse range of economic activities that can sustain economic growth once copper ceases to contribute to the state income. Thus, Griffin concludes that Bougainville is a viable economic entity.

Punjab

For decades, Punjab has been the highest income region within the Indian union, surpassing the industrial states of Maharashtra and West Bengal. Of all the states of India, Punjab has the most viability as an independent region. Not only has it achieved the highest rates of growth, but it is also self-sufficient in agriculture, and it is a net exporter of foodstuffs. Moreover, its economic growth has diffused into nonagricultural sectors so that its industrialization is geared to increasing the capacity of its own economy.[18] Although the level of development, by world standards, is not high in Punjab, there is ample potential in the region for significant economic development. Indeed, there are numerous Asian countries that are independent with much less potential than Punjab. There are some characteristics of the Punjabi economy that do not auger well for viability. For example, the relatively centralized nature of the Indian union has translated into a lack of experience in controlling local economic affairs. This is especially true in the case of trade, all of which has been subject to central control of licensing, pricing, and choice of destination.

Katanga

Katanga was the wealthiest region of the Belgian Congo, and by some estimates, one of the wealthiest in Africa. Although landlocked, with inadequate transportation systems and infrastructure, the region was viable as an independent entity for two reasons. First, the economic potential of the region was so vast that it could have sustained the region in the immediate aftermath of the secession and paved the way for the structural transformation of the economy. In the period immediately before attempted secession, 1950-57, its real rate of growth averaged 6.7 percent.[19] The wealth of the mines, measured at 8 percent of the world's copper and most of the world's cobalt and industrial diamonds, was already beginning to diffuse itself into other sectors of the economy, such as the manufacturing sector, the local production of consumer and producer goods, and a relatively efficient agricultural sector.[20] The control of its resources by a Katangan government, and the subsequent retention of the outflow of money to Leopoldville (which is estimated at close to 50 percent of the total resources of the former Belgian Congo[21]), would have enhanced the economic position of the region after independence.

The second reason why Katanga was viable as an entity independent from the rest of the Congo was due to the foreign interests that would have continued to invest (some might say exploit) the region. There was a concentration of immense capital in the hands of a single expatriate enterprise, the Union Minière du Haut-Katanga, which was not likely to voluntarily drop the development of the mines because of a change in government.

(iii) Viability of Low-Income Regions with Low Development Potential

Kosovo, Tadzhikistan, Western Sahara, and East Timor are regions that seem inviable as independent entities. However, it is with reservation that one dismisses them as such because regions with even fewer apparent possibilities have sustained their independence over long periods of time.

All four regions share characteristics that contribute to making them less developed in the first place. Their natural characteristics are infertile soil (Western Sahara, Tadzhikistan), lack of access to water (Kosovo, Tadzhikistan), lack of big cities as centers of commerce and trade, and poor transportation systems. The labor force is characterized by below-average education and skill levels, and the regions are not self-sufficient in foodstuffs.

Only Kosovo is rich in mineral deposits, many of which are not properly mined for lack of investment and infrastructure. Furthermore, only Kosovo has the potential to be self-sufficient in foodstuffs. However, Kosovo has interethnic population problems that greatly imperil the functioning of its labor markets, as well as the training of its future labor force. Tadzhikistan is likely to have similar interethnic problems. With respect to the Deutsch Bank assessment of viability, Tadzhikistan ranks the lowest of the former Soviet republics, with a total score of 18 out of a possible 100.[22] The highest scores were achieved for the location of mineral resources and the hard-currency earning capacity of these raw materials. However, even this should be taken with a grain of salt since almost one-half of the territory houses the Gorno-Badakhshan Autonomous Region. This separate administrative unit is mostly inhabited by the Ismaili Muslims, who differ from the Sunni Muslims, who are the Tadzhiks, and therefore the two groups are likely to experience an increase in problems rather than a harmonious alliance. To count on this autonomous territory as part of the Tadzhikistani wealth is erroneous in this time of lack of central control and cohesion, when most former Soviet autonomous regions are pursuing independence from their republics.

VIABILITY OF THE REMAINING REGION

In this study of viability, the focus is on the survival of the seceding region. However, after secession the viability of the remaining region often comes into question. There are cases in which the secession of a high-income region would make economic survival of the ex-country very difficult. This would impact on the response that the center would give to secession. According to Buchanon, "secession may be forcibly resisted if it would undermine the economic viability of the remainder state, even if the continued independent existence of the remainder state is not at risk."[23]

Despite the connotations of strength implied by the acronym ROC (rest of Canada), secession of regions in numerous cases raises serious questions for the viability of the remaining state on several levels. First, there is the possible inviability because of the economic strain experienced by the remaining region. This is especially true when the seceding region is relatively more developed, so that the remaining state must contend with the loss of capital, infrastructure, and other factors that made the region more developed. Such problems are presently encountered by the less developed former Soviet republics: indeed, the viability of Tadzhikistan and Kirghizia is endangered by the withdrawal of the Russian republic, and is only buffered by the existence of the CIS. Second, the viability of remaining regions is endangered because of the economic factors involved in the secession process. There are numerous manifestations of this, and in the case of secession during war, the economic strain may be high. This is best exemplified by the case of Serbia in the aftermath of the civil war. The war provoked by the secession of Slovenia and Croatia has cost Serbia dearly. Not the least of this is the need to support the war, which resulted in an annual inflation rate of 25,000 percent in March 1992.[24] Another example of an economic cost to the remaining region is associated with the introduction of a new currency in the secessionist region and the subsequent havoc caused by the dumping of the old currency. Indeed, Russia so fears the influx of rubles that is likely when Ukraine gets rid of its superfluous rubles that it is pressing Ukraine to sign a Commonwealth bank union agreement obliging states to return all their rubles to the Russian authorities.[25] Third, another economic factor involved in the viability of the remaining regions has to do with the ability to secure credit and aid in the aftermath of secession by its parts. This may be due to political reasons, such as the support of the secessionist regions by the international community or the bilateral granting partners. Otherwise, it simply may reflect the drying up of funds, such as occurred during 1991-92: At this time, numerous newly independent regions depend on foreign capital in order to survive secession. However, given the collapse of the Soviet economy and the demands made by it and Eastern Europe on western aid, there are already signs of a capital shortage. In addition, the Third World is also drawing on the fund of western capital in excess of what the West is capable of generating. Not only do numerous states have their own pressures and competing ends for capital, but they are reluctant to invest in regions in which the center has been unable to hold together the state. Germany will be less forthcoming with its surplus because of its needs for the reconstruction of former East Germany. Japan is in the process of becoming more selective about the destination of its surplus yen. However, all of these factors may not necessarily be an issue. In the case of Papua New Guinea, in which the general sentiment both among policymakers and academics was that the state would suffer from the loss associated with the closing of the mines in Bougainville, the state has begun aggressively exploiting other minerals such as oil and gold.[26]

A fifth aspect of the viability question has to do with geography and therefore indirectly with economics. The possible secession of Quebec raises serious concerns for the viability of the remaining provinces of Canada on the grounds of territory. Quebec is the second largest province with respect to area. Its territory spans from the United States to the Hudson Bay, dividing the rest of Canada.[27] Its secession raises questions similar to those raised by other noncontinuous territories, such as the Russian republic divided by Lithuania, Pakistan divided by India, and so forth. If Quebec secedes, what is the future of the Maritime Provinces? Can they survive as Canadian entities separated from the federal center by Quebec as well as the sea? Perhaps an alignment of those regions with the United States, in whose proximity they are located, might occur, altering the present balance of size and power between the United States and Canada.[28]

VIABILITY AND VIOLENCE

With respect to the degree of violence that accompanies secession, the regions are divided into two categories. Peaceful interregional conflicts, often taking place through parliamentary means, characterize Quebec, Lombardy, Slovenia, Catalonia, the Basque Provinces, and most of the republics of the former Soviet Union. In Quebec, the question of secession was placed before the population in a referendum in the late 1970s (at which time the prevailing sentiment was against secession) and will be repeated in the fall of 1992 in view of the resurgence in secessionist aspirations resulting from the events surrounding the controversial Meech Lake Accord. In Lombardy, a regional party, the Lega Lombarda, has captured public sentiment and rests its platform on alleged economic injustices. This party is steadily rising in popularity, and its ties to other northern regional parties with similar concerns is lending it a significant popular base.[29] In Slovenia as well as the Baltic states, elections in 1990 placed in power parties whose platforms were based on secessionist issues. The Slovenian government furthermore amended its constitution to give itself the right to secede and proceeded to do so in June 1991.[30] In the Baltic states, the new regional governments put the independence issue to the voters, in line with demands from Moscow of a referendum prior to further discussion of separation.[31]

Violence characterized the secessionary movements of Punjab, Bougainville, Sudan, Eritrea, Katanga, and Biafra, among others. In Punjab, secessionist goals of setting up an independent nation (Khalistan) were first approached through terrorist activities (starting in the 1970s and culminating in the murder of Indira Gandhi). In Bougainville, the battle between the rebels and government troops has resulted in the closing of the principal copper mine, which is costing the national government $1,000 per minute in foregone revenue.[32] The magnitude of economic impact of this rebel activity is so high that it has resulted in the escalation of violence by the central government. The secessions of Katanga and Biafra caused civil wars with significant loss of lives and extensive economic disruption to both the regions and the states. The efforts at secession of East Timor and the Karen region were equally bloody, with an estimated one-third of the population decimated in the former. Presently, the most violent cases of secession-related violence are those in Croatia and in Nagorno-Karabakh. In the case of the former, it is estimated that, by March 1992, some 6,000 to 10,000 people had been killed, and hundreds of thousands of refugees displaced from their homes. The damage to property has been great, with entire villages decimated and hospitals, schools, and industries rendered nonfunctional. The violent conflict of the Serbs with Croats in Croatia and with Muslims in Bosnia-Hercegovina has numerous similarities with that of the Armenians and Azeris. In both cases, the violence reflects centuries of intolerance with roots in ethnic distrust, religious differences, and historical injustices. The Armenians, not forgetting the genocide by the Turks of 1915 and the protection provided by the Soviets, are fearful of the withdrawal of the Soviet army and support from the area.

How does violence influence the viability of a seceding region? Most important, the regions that undergo greater violence have less capacity to reconstruct. Clearly the Timorese, if and when they become independent, will have one-third less population in their labor force. Similarly, the Karen have lost some of their most committed fighters, who might have also performed well in the labor force. With respect to property and infrastructure destruction, areas of Croatia and Southern Sudan will need large inputs of capital to reconstruct, as did parts of the Congo and Nigeria. The violence has done great damage to production: although no estimates are known to the author, it is likely that the terror of the Sikh militants has decreased the motivation to invest in agriculture and has decreased the productivity of the population that lives in fear. Similarly, the disruption of the war in Croatia has resulted in a dramatic decrease in production of agricultural goods in Slavonia, resulting in food insufficiencies. Also, the violence associated with the war in the tourist areas has had a detrimental effect on regional income, since the population that largely lives from tourist industry has now experienced two years of inactivity in that sector.[33]

Is the world witnessing more violence in the redrawing of national boundaries than we have in the past? What happened to the peaceful methods such as the referendum that determined the secession of Norway from Sweden in 1905? Presently, there seems to be a tendency to fill the vacuum created by exiting authoritarian leaders (Tito, central Soviet government) with violent intergroup interaction. Peter Reddaway puts the present violence in the Soviet Union in historical perspective by comparing the Soviet empire to that of the Portuguese and tsarist Russia:

> Among the empires that have ended in recent decades, some, like the British and the French, have drawn to a close with a considerable amount of planning, dignity, and provision for postimperial cooperation . . . By contrast, alas, the Soviet Empire seems to belong with the empires of the Portuguese, who abruptly withdrew from Africa in the mid-1970s, and the tsarist Russians, who did not prepare for the end, but resisted it until it came for both the empire and the tsarist autocracy in 1917 . . . In consequence, both Portuguese and tsarist empires left a legacy which led directly to civil wars, chaos, and extreme authoritarianism. The danger is acute that the Soviet Empire will leave a similar trail in its wake.[34]

8

Secession and Self-determination in the Late 20th Century

National independence in the modern world requires the intervention of the world system of states.

—Rosa Luxemburg

The redefinition of borders and the realignment of regional economies have taken place throughout history. While in the past reevaluations of center-region relationships have consisted of cost-benefit analyses based largely on religion, language and military power, in the present, economic factors seem to have taken on a new importance. Indeed, this study has shown that all 37 contemporary secessionist regions have clearly identifiable economic components that serve to increase the secessionist drive.[1] In only six could one say that economics played an insignificant role.[2] It furthermore seems likely that issues in regional economics will play an ever larger role in the revaluation of center-region relations in the years to come. This is true for several reasons. First, communications technologies have served to promote western lifestyles and thus create a demand for the concomitants of economic development. Given the widespread realization of what is attainable, pressure is exerted on regional leaders to maximize economic development. This drive for economic growth will tend to focus attention on economic elements of the relationship between regions and the center. Second, competition for scarce resources has increased as environmental pressures have restrained methods of production and population growth has put pressure on educational, health, and employment systems. This competitive environment is further intensified by the end of the cold war, which has decreased the availability of politically motivated aid and investment, causing regional leaders in potentially secessionist regions to become resentful of the dissipation of regional resources, and thus regionally introverted with respect to policy and goals. Moreover, given this scarcity in the supply of capital, donors will become more selective in their targeting of recipients and will pay more attention to economic factors that will benefit rather than harm their own economies. Together, the increased demand for economic growth and the decreased supply of the means to attain it have placed new pressures on the region to maximize its ability to attain economic goals. Hence the cries for decreased capital outflows from Lombardy and Slovenia and the call for the populations to reign inward their economic might. Even in less developed Punjab and Singapore, the perception that economic development was impeded by membership in a large union led to the desire to create a smaller economic unit in which assets could be more easily controlled and managed.

The increased importance of economic factors in secessionist activity is not the sole new aspect of secessions in the late 20th century: despite the war in Yugoslavia, there have been a large number of *peaceful secessions* in the early years of the 1990s. At the time of writing, the 15 former Soviet republics have become independent without significant violence *with the center* with the exception of the central incursions into Baku and the Vilnius massacres when Gorbachev used force to attempt to preserve party control.[3] In addition, the secession of Slovenia was relatively peaceful as it was limited to several days of half-hearted fighting. It is likely that Eritrea, emerging from two decades of violence with the center, will achieve independence with little resistance now that the center is no longer what it was. This is not to argue that there is no violence in the present efforts to redraw national boundaries: obviously the wars in Croatia and Bosnia-Hercegovina, as well as those between the Armenians and Azeris, indicate the passion with which populations perceive territorial issues. However, these are not violent efforts at seceding *from a center,* rather they are violent manifestations of interregional conflicts. Indeed, the crucial reason for the war in Yugoslavia is not the secession of Croatia or Bosnia-Hercegovina but rather the resolution of the issue of the Serbian population in those areas. Similarly, the independence of Azerbaijan is not the cause of the violence but rather the question of the Armenian population that has for generations resided on the territory presently under Azeri control.

This lack of violence with the center during secession is different from the past, when regions broke off from states in the aftermath of wars and disintegration of empires. Indeed, the past few redrawings of the map of Central Europe occurred during the two world wars and a series of Balkan wars.[4] Unlike in the past, the present peaceful alteration of borders has most often been preceded by referendums, so that 1991-92 may be called the years of the referendum. Indeed, during that time, all former Soviet republics and many autonomous republics carried out referendums, as did the republics of Yugoslavia, while referendums are pending for the upcoming year in places as diverse as Western Sahara, Scotland, Krajina, Quebec, and Ethiopia.

PLUS ÇA CHANGE, PLUS C'EST LA MÊME CHOSE

Despite some ways in which the current secessionist activity represents a break with the past, numerous other aspects of secession in the late 20th century have remained similar to those throughout history.

There is no doubt that the institutional and structural changes that shook the world in the years preceding 1992 were broad and deep. The demise of communism, the spread of the capitalist ideology, the opening-up of borders, the increase in refugees and employment seekers all over the world, the increased importance of the United Nations in its role of arbitrator, are some of these changes. Indeed, on a global level, the bipolar political balance of power has been altered so that the United States alone remains a military superpower, while economic superpower status is shared by the United States, Western Europe, and Japan. On a state level, nationalism has emerged as a potent force that pits national groups against each other in a frenzy of intolerance. On a micro level, the individual has emerged as a focus of economic activity, as the pursuit of personal profit replaces the group as an ideological concept. Although these changes were concentrated in the Western and socialist world, their ripple-through effects permeated Third World states.

The alteration of state borders is simultaneously both a ramification and a concomitant of these changes. Therefore, that the map of the world is changing to accommodate the numerous aspects of global change should be of no surprise. Indeed, the unification of Yemen and Southern Yemen and East and West Germany, as well as the breakup of the Soviet Union and Yugoslavia, are in all likelihood only the beginning of additional work for cartographers. The secessionist fever that gripped the world in 1990 shows no signs of abating.

However, irrespective of the breadth and depth of the current border alterations, a long-term historical perspective indicates that borders are not written in stone and have often been altered in response to various pressures. Indeed, Central Europe looked very different in 1815, 1871, 1904, and 1919,[5] and even centuries of existing borders do not imply their acceptance by the population. In addition to border changes, an analysis of the global changes of the early 1990s indicates that there are some ways in which the present does not differ from other periods of history. Some of these similarities are listed below.

(i) Religious Intolerance

In the quest for the redefinition of nations and states, we seem to be witnessing inter-regional violence motivated by religious intolerance among religious groups. The demand for an independent Palestinian state, as well as the demand for "liberation" of Northern Ireland are both undoubtedly religious in orientation. Indeed, virtually all the movements for secession that we have studied from an economic point of view can also be expressed in religious terms, with the exception of those in Italy and Spain. The civil war in Yugoslavia is a clear case of religious intolerance, between the Catholics and the Eastern Orthodox, as is the violence in Kashmir, in which Hindus are pitted against the Moslems. The Buddhists are fighting the Hindus in Sri Lanka and the Christians in Myanmar, the Muslims and Christians are fighting each other in Sudan, Bosnia, and Nagorno-Karabakh. It seems that the principle of *cuius regio, eius religio* (he who controls the area, controls the religion) is applied in reverse, so that he who controls the religion in an area, controls the area.

These religious wars for control of people and territory are reminiscent of recent and not-so-recent history. The crusades represented Christian efforts against the Muslims, the fourth crusade pitted Christian against Christian, the Thirty Years' War engaged the Catholics against the Protestants, and so forth. In more recent times, despite professed secularization of politics in at least western states, instances of a close relationship between religion and politics abound. World War II witnessed the association of the Catholic church with the fascist rule in both Italy as well as Croatia.[6] And in the early 1980s, Pope John Paul II, together with the U.S. administration under President Reagan, worked to undermine the Polish government.[7]

A special feature of the late 20th century is the attempt by religious groups to fill the void that is left behind by the departing ideology of communism. Fundamentalist Muslims are ready to redeem their subjects in the formerly Soviet Muslim republics, and the Catholic church is busy embracing the Catholic inhabitants of formerly communist states. However, problems arise today, as they did in the past, when the expansionist efforts of religions collide upon a people: the clearest example of this today is the attempted penetration by Catholics into parts of Eastern Europe that have traditionally been Christian Orthodox.[8]

Indeed, in the past as well as today, O'Conner's characterization of wars with religious motivations is to the point. He said, describing in particular Northern Ireland, "of course, this is not a purely religious war; no religious war was ever pure."[9]

(ii) Old Alliances

In the redrawing of European boundaries, are we seeing a reemergence of old alliances? The most significant case of this presently revolves around Germany, which for the third time since 1870 is emerging as a major power. Not a few scholars, politicians, and common folk have questioned the possible significance, and desirability, of the unification of Germany in 1989. There are those who perceive the subsequent emerging strength of Germany within the world, especially Europe, as part of the trend that has vacillated through time but may be traced to the Holy Roman Empire. Indeed, the alliance between the Vatican and its northern neighbors, including Italy and Germany, has persisted and intensified in the 20th century through two world wars. Today, this alliance seems most evident in the case of former Yugoslavia: The Catholic population of Slovenia and Croatia, traditionally Germanic in orientation, is supported by Germany, Austria, and Italy in its efforts against the Eastern Orthodox Serbs.[10]

The post-Maastricht era is colored by two moves on the part of the Germans that drew attention to their renewed might in Europe: first, their refusal to decrease interest rates to satisfy the demands of the EEC, and second, their assertion of an independent path in foreign policy with their hurried recognition of Croatia. This show of might sent tremors throughout Eastern Europe, which presently finds itself faced with an economic giant that may be friend or foe, as was the case some 50 years ago. Poles and Czechs are resentful and are fearful of Germany's intentions.[11] Indeed, domestic critics are becoming more vocal in their concern over Germany's economic expansion in the East: what it did not succeed in accomplishing by political means, it is now achieving by economic means.

(iii) Territorial Disputes

There is potential land grab in the air. Territorial disputes that lingered below the surface for decades are reemerging in a period in which even minor gripes are voiced. In this era, which in numerous warring or transitional states is characterized by the lack of a legal framework, a free-for-all atmosphere has permeated interstate relations. In societies in which some 150 political parties can become registered in the course of several months, such as has occurred in parts of Eastern Europe, a whole variety of demands are made by a wide variety of groups whose legitimacy with respect to claims is questionable.

This tendency for land grab is evident in remarks by politicians, couched in expressions of sentiment of peaceful resolution. Examples of these pleasant efforts at redressing perceived territorial grievances include the Belarussian claim to Lithuanian territory, made in February 1992,[12] as well as claims made on Moldavian territory by Romania, Ukrainian territory by Russia, and so forth. But the most compelling evidence of potential land grab is witnessed among the neighboring states of Yugoslavia, reminding the world of the Balkan Wars of 1912-13, as well as the World Wars I and II.[13] Albania has clear intentions on the Kosovo region, as memories of Greater Albania that existed during World War II linger. Greece would probably not refuse the opportunity of restoring its past borders into what is today the Yugoslav republic of Macedonia, and Bulgaria has laid its claim to western parts of Yugoslav Macedonia. Romania would be happy to come to the aid of its population in the Banat region of Serbia, and Hungary is readily awaiting its chance to repossess parts of Vojvodina, dating its claims to its 15th century empire. Austria has debated the inclusion of Croatia into its federation as its 10th republic. Italians are ready to turn to the regions historically under their tutelage, namely parts of the Dalmatian coast, Montenegro, and Albania. They are furthermore under pressure by Italian citizens that were expelled from Croatia in the aftermath of World War II and are waiting for Italy to redeem past wrongs.

If one were to superimpose maps of the Balkans drawn by aspiring states mentioned in the land grab above, it would be clear that the region would have to be enlarged some tenfold in order to accommodate everyone's demands. It is still too early to tell whether the European states will make use of this opportunity to fish in troubled waters, or whether they will use diplomatic means to protect their interests and achieve their ends.

(iv) Double Standard

The events of the past few years have brought to the surface the clear double standard that has characterized political decisions, especially with respect to (i) the treatment by states of their minorities, and (ii) the international recognition of independence declarations.

With respect to the status of minorities, Lendvai described the situation in Central Europe one century ago, and indeed, neither the play, nor the actors, have changed significantly in one hundred years: "What Hungary wanted of Vienna, it refused to Croatia, then its ally in a common kingdom. What Croatia demanded from Hungary it, in turn, refused to the Serbs living within its borders. And this double standard in dealing with the rights of one's own nation and those of alien minorities has remained a dominant feature in the family of new states that emerged from the disintegration of the great empires."[14] One hundred years later, in the Yugoslav conflict, Croatian President Tudjman is willing to fight strenuously for Croatia's independence, but is unwilling to recognize the desires for independence of the Serbs in Krajina and Slavonia. Even with respect to the crisis in Bosnia-Hercegovina, Tudjman is quoted as saying that "Croatia must be firm in ensuring the national rights and wishes of the Croatian people in Bosnia-Hercegovina."[15] In other words, he will ensure the freedom of choice of the Croats and Muslims for independence but will refuse to apply the same principles to the Serb population of the republic. A similar case of double standard is in effect in Italy. In January 1992, after Italy immediately followed Germany in the recognition of Croatia, President Cossiga was the first foreign leader to travel to Zagreb, and the state's airports were the first to deny landing rights to the Yugoslav airline. However, in February of the same year, the Italian government refused the demand of the leading party of Alto Adige (a formerly Austrian region attached to Italy at the end of World War II) to have a periodic international review of the relations between Rome and this Germanic state on the grounds that center-state relations are an *internal matter,* not subject to international scrutiny.[16] Why are their center-state relations an internal matter, but not Yugoslavia's? Would Rome's reaction to secessionist attempts in Alto Adige differ so dramatically from those of Belgrade?

The double standard is also evident when it comes to international recognition of secessionist movements, and the policy of the United States has been a good example of this. In theory, the United States has supported self-determination; in practice, this policy has only been applied selectively. This selectivity in what is often a knee-jerk response to self-determination pressures belittles U.S. sincerity and raises many cries of injustice around the world. For example, while the U.S. government had advance knowledge that the Indonesian army was planning to invade East Timor and thereby deny the Timorese peoples the right of self-determination, it did not take steps to prevent the invasion, and indeed limited itself to a slight reprimand of the Indonesian government at the time of the invasion. In the war with Iraq in 1991, the U.S. administration made no mention of the fact that there is a way that, historically, Iraq can make claims on Kuwait territory. Hence, if one wants to intervene on the side of justice, these claims must be looked into. Indeed, it is unclear even now where the border with Kuwait actually is. Furthermore, why were nearly a half million Kurds killed before the United States and the U.N. decided to help them, and why was that help in the form of the establishment of refugee camps rather than autonomy status? Why is the Armenian mistreatment in Azerbaijan disregarded today, along the same lines of the denial of the Armenian genocide of 1915?[17] Further, why was the United States so willing to rectify the wrongs done by the communist government against the Baltic republics 50 years ago, but so unwilling to do the same to rectify wrongs done to Serbia by the communist government of Tito with respect to the carving of the autonomous region of Kosovo from its territory? Why does Croatia merit international recognition while Macedonia, which has been more successful in providing mutual tolerance among its ethnic groups, is shunned? And, perhaps most poignantly, given the present bloodshed in Eastern Europe, why does the West uphold the principle of self-determination for the Croats, Slovenes, and Muslims, but not for the Serbs, who account for one-third of the population in Bosnia-Hercegovina? It points to very odd, inconsistent, and unprincipled behavior on the part of western states, and the United States and Germany in particular.

One other aspect of the double standard at play in international responses to self-determination has to do with the fact that there is often a discrepancy between acceptable internal and external resolutions to issues. To once again take the United States as an example, it is clear that while the United States is supporting, albeit selectively, movements for self-determination across the world, it also supported the efforts of Abraham Lincoln and the federalists in their fight against the secessionist South. Indeed, both George Washington, who struggled for self-determination, and Lincoln, who suppressed it, are admired. Self-determination and the proposal for confederacy by the southern states were strenuously rejected, and the Articles of Confederation, providing for a loose linkage of the 13 colonies, were scrapped in favor of the Constitution, which offered a centralized solution. Is it that political philosophy and morality have evolved over the past century so that mores and values differ, and that such a shift in policy and principles is acceptable? Is the Western world in the 1990s more accepting of secessionist movements than the world was in the 19th century? Unfortunately, that there is selectivity and hypocrisy in politics should come as no surprise to scholars of current events, nor should it come as a surprise that superpowers are not moral forces as well as economic and political forces.

The policy of recognition and acceptance of secessionist regions in the United States and Western Europe seems to be greatly influenced by the socioeconomic system of the secessionist region. Actually, the West seems more accepting of secession in states that were previously under communist rule, such as Eritrea, the Baltics, Slovenia, and so forth. We do not witness such support in the case of East Timor, Bougainville, or Western Sahara. We certainly did not recall much enthusiasm in the case of Bangladesh. It cannot be argued that Estonia is receiving more support than Bougainville because its population and territory are so much more significant in scale. Nor can it be argued that Estonia is receiving so much support because it is western, and therefore culturally and ethnically closer to the western epicenter, because that raises the question of why Corsicans and Catalonians have not received more attention. It is likely that the support that the former Soviet bloc republics are receiving from the West has to do with the desire to end the cold war by eradicating all vestiges of communism. The efforts of Eritrea are in fact aided because they represent an affront on the communist government of Mengitsu, but East Timor, Southern Sudan, Bougainville, Casamance, and the Tamils of Sri Lanka are not supported.

(v) The Use of Enemies

It is very useful to have a state enemy, as it has been throughout history. The existence of an enemy at the state level serves the function of providing unifying cohesion among the population. It also diverts attention from other concerns. For lack of an enemy, states turn their attention inward and focus on domestic issues. Communism was perceived by many people, both in the East and the West, as the enemy: indeed, it may be credited with having provided the populations in numerous regions of the globe with a focus of hate. The seceding regions of the Soviet Union have had the privilege of hating communism, or the center in Moscow, for decades. Now, with the demise of that unifying emotion, they are forced to address their internal issues. In Georgia, the most pressing internal issue has to do with the interethnic relations involving the Ossetians, while in Ukraine, economic and cultural differences between the western, eastern, and southern regions are the focus.[18] The Czechs and Slovaks have an interesting experience: The Czechs have hated communism, so when given the chance, they enthusiastically embraced capitalism. The Slovaks, on the other hand, hated the Czechs more than communism, and therefore today are less inclined to give up all elements of communism.

(vi) Triggering Events

Scholars have often claimed that some event must occur to trigger or spark secessionist or nationalist activity. In the late 20th century, the demise of communism may certainly be viewed as a triggering event, not only in the states where it was replaced as a form of government but also in those that were indirectly affected by the rising nationalism in Central Europe. The recent nationalist tendencies of the Scots fall into this category. As a nationalist candidate for a local council seat recently noted: "I see all these other countries in Europe getting their independence and I can't help but say, 'Hey, we want a bit of that too!'"[19] When secessionist activity in Scotland surfaced some two decades ago it was triggered by the discovery of the North Sea oil, and the subsequent dreams of Scotland's wealth if full control of those resources were retained in Edinburgh. Economic factors such as this triggered secessionist activity in Bougainville, Punjab, and Lombardy.

These triggering mechanisms have existed throughout history. One example is from the beginning of recorded history: The secession of the ten northern tribes of Israel was economic in nature: it was triggered by the coming to power of Rehoboam, son of Solomon (in 930 B.C.), who increased taxes upon taking power. The population, dissatisfied with the high rates of taxation that they were forced to pay, declared their secession.[20] Moreover, Birch cites the Holocaust as the triggering event in the Zionist movement, while for the Quebecois, it was the arrival of non-French immigrants that threatened French culture.[21]

QUESTIONS OF NATIONHOOD AND SELF-DETERMINATION

This present period, characterized by the birth of new nations, compels scholars and policymakers to think about what defines a state. This is especially true in light of the lack of such thought at the government level, as indicated by the premature recognition of seceding republics of Yugoslavia.[22] The question of what defines a nation and a minority within that nation was not answered by western policymakers, leading directly to interethnic wars in Croatia and Bosnia-Hercegovina.

The abundant academic literature on this topic is presently in the process of further enlargement as questions of nationhood and self-determination are being reevaluated under the new conditions of the late 20th century. In the determination of what defines a state, several considerations are relevant. Geography may define a state: there are mountain chains, bodies of water, and shorelines that form natural demarcations. However, states have only rarely followed these geographical rules. For example, why does the Iberian peninsula contain two states (three, counting Andorra), while the Italian peninsula contains only one? Further basis of states may be race, ethnicity, language, and religion. Despite numerous attempts to make countries pure in one or more of these respects, the majority of states are highly heterogeneous. Oftentimes a shared historical experience binds peoples together, and habit keeps borders intact. Size is also a consideration in the determination of states, although its importance has been decreasing in the modern world. At present, numerous microstates dot the globe, 55 with populations under 1 million: indeed, tiny Luxemburg, San Marino, Bahrain, and Malta have not only survived but thrived.[23] In the modern world it is no longer a necessity to be a part of a large unit for both political and economic reasons. With respect to the former, the international community has devised methods to protect the sovereignty of states, so that territorial expansion is not acceptable. This is indicated clearly by the United Nations' action in the Iraqi invasion of Kuwait, as well as legal measures such as the Helsinki Final Act of 1975, which confirmed the inviolability of the postwar borders. With respect to economics, sufficient economic integration has occurred in the global economy that states no longer constitute separate economic entities. Self-sufficiency is rare, and increasing interdependence among regions is clear in trade, investment, and other flows of goods and services. This global system enables small states, such as Hong Kong and Singapore, to participate in the international division of labor and not suffer a handicap because of the limited size of their domestic markets. Thus, in addition to economic and political arguments in favor of small states, some have argued that size is inversely related to peace prospects: in fact, it was argued some 50 years ago that the world would be better off with the proliferation of small states, along the lines of the Swiss cantons, and thus that peace could be better maintained.[24] Moreover, the benefits of small states have been discussed also by psychologist Simenton, who claims that small states tend to produce more creative individuals because their creativity is not suppressed by centralized expansions.[25]

Presently, attention to human rights, political participation, and political expression permeates the western democracies. However, nonwestern political traditions are not immune to the pressure to follow this trend. Not only has general internationalization, due to increased communications and travel, had the effect of showing Asian, African, and Latin American populations some of the political concomitants of democracy, but also the international community is less tolerant of human rights abuses than it was in the past. Given this sentiment, self-expression of peoples the world over is encouraged as a sign of democracy. It might even be argued that the right to self-determination is the ultimate step in democratic achievement. The present time resuscitates the debate on the right to self-determination that raged at the time of John Stuart Mill and the breakup of the multinational empires at the end of World War I.

If we accept the link between self-determination and democracy both in theory and in practice, then we must address the consequences. One of these is that there could be ethnic groups, ad infinitum, that contend for independence, raising the question of just how much self-determination should there be, and where should it end. Since each minority has a minority residing among it, and there are independence movements within independence movements, the world from South Africa to Sweden and from Angola to Indonesia could become a series of microstates. To take this trend to its logical conclusion, however absurd, might imply a world of thousands upon thousands of sovereign states.

What are the drawbacks of a proliferation of microstates? In addition to the obvious problems of duplication of services, political inefficiency, and so forth, perhaps the most compelling problem is that created by the quest for ethnic purity. The trend in many of the seceding regions of the world has been to draw support for their cause on the grounds of ethnic injustice. If states are to be defined by the ethnic characteristics of their populations, in other words if they are nation-states, that by definition presupposes a certain degree of intolerance for those who do not belong. Given that the world is an ethnic mosaic, the mere logistics entailed in the population regroupings that would be necessary are mindboggling. The example of the population movements at the time of partition in India and Pakistan, the exodus of the Tartars, the Sudetan Germans, et cetera, remind us of the pain and expense involved in that type of solution. In the absence of population movements, the world might witness genocides and atrocities such as those presently common among the Serbs, Bosnian Muslims, and the Croats. Harris has identified what he calls "perverse national liberations," defined as cases of national liberation (in the creation of a new state) "that imposes subordination on the inhabitants of a territory, not emancipation."[26] Indeed, he describes cases in which "the hideous oppression of one minority is translated into the hideous oppression of another." This includes, according to Harris, the Boers, who were mistreated by the British and later went on to mistreat the South Africans, British convicts that mistreated Australian aborigines, et cetera. Cases of such ethnic subordination are emerging in the newly independent states of Estonia, for example, which has a proposed bill pending that would grant immediate citizenship (with the right to own property) only to those who can prove their citizenship before 1940, or their direct descendants, thus excluding the almost 40 percent Russian population of newcomers.[27]

Opinion differs as to whether large-scale ethnic bloodbaths due to such changes in minority/majority status of ethnic groups is really a possibility. Gorbachev argued in favor of the maintenance of a union among the former Soviet republics as late as December 1991; without this, he warned, there would be a movement towards wars between republics and extensive human-rights violations.[28] On the other hand, Fukuyama argued that although there have been skirmishes due to the rise of intolerant nationalism, they are limited to a few areas, such as the Nagorno-Karabakh region in Azerbaijan and the Fergana Valley in Uzbekistan, while the majority of the population, notably that residing in Russia and Ukraine, have experienced only moderate nationalism.[29] Hence, he does not believe that it follows that this interethnic violence presents a worldwide threat. Pierre Trudeau, speaking in general without limiting himself to a single state, claimed that whenever political boundaries coincided with ethnic ones, chauvinism, xenophobia, and racism inevitably threatened liberty.[30]

It is argued here that self-determination as a principle to adhere to under all circumstances is simply flawed. It is based upon the belief that people of different ethnic backgrounds and different religions are incapable of coexistence, and therefore encourages intolerance among individuals. The objective should not be to give all nationalities a right to live in an ethnically pure region, but rather to create an environment in which diverse peoples can live together in harmony, and in which religion, ethnicity, race, and language are not the basis for discrimination. This harmony is not a theoretical possibility, since in the ethnic mosaic that characterizes Central Europe, Africa and Asia, ethnic groups have coexisted for centuries. Although they may have experienced deep hatred and passion against other groups in principle, they have managed to coexist and produce and function with the exception of short periods of release, namely wars. A recent survey in Slovakia indicates this point plainly. In the regions where Hungarians and Slovaks live in close proximity, only 20 percent of the Slovaks feel threatened by Hungarians, while in regions where Slovaks have no exposure to Hungarians, 71 percent feel threatened.[31] People who, for economic or emotional reasons or simply from inertia, are destined to reside and work side by side with those of another ethnic group or religion have managed to evolve a strategy for dealing with it. There is a realization that people simply cannot leave and take their land with them. As Lincoln pointed out in his first inaugural: "A husband and wife may be divorced and go out of the presence and beyond the reach of each other; but the different parts of our country cannot do this. They cannot but remain face to face; and intercourse, either amicable or hostile, must continue between them."[32]

If states are to be composed of diverse groups of people, what is to hold them together? There must be more to the glue than what Baxter described as holding West and East Pakistan together: Islam, India, and Pakistani International Airlines.[33] Europe has a wide range of different political systems that reflect different solutions to the question of how to keep unity among diverse peoples. France, probably the most centralized, has a unitary system and represents one end of the pole. Britain is less centralized, as its constituent regions have some forms of independence, such as a separate legal code in Scotland. Germany is a federation, with numerous powers decentralized to the republics. And, examples of the most decentralized systems are Switzerland, with its 600 years of confederation, and the Yugoslav system of rotating leadership that drew to a close in 1991. Yugoslavia under Tito also sustained a common political culture, while at the same time giving minorities a sense of cultural self-determination. The Austro-Hungarian Empire achieved political uniformity among a small number of groups, while at the same time ensuring them cultural nationalistic satisfaction. They had uniformity in politics and economics over its territory, while tolerating cultural differences.

How does one achieve interethnic, interreligious, and interracial tolerance, so that these issues are not the driving force behind border changes? There is a short-run and a long-run consideration. They both involve politics and economics and the establishment of a culture of tolerance. In the short run, the seceding regions must be granted their independence, however small the unit that strives for it. A necessary precondition for future economic or political association of seceding republics of the presently unraveling countries is the taste for sovereignty. Indeed, the president of Singapore stated after independence that in the future there may yet be a reunification between Singapore and the Malaysian federation, since "absence makes the heart grow fonder."[34] If that implies the creation of a sovereign Croatian region within the Serbian enclave in Croatia, however absurd that may be, it should be encouraged and supported. Such a delineation will in all likelihood not last long. Indeed, in the long run, when political maturity is achieved, self-interest will probably cause a different orientation than self-determination, which will fade in importance. It may happen that, once national identities have been securely established, nationalist passions will subside. This will give way to forces clamoring for further unity of some kind. Common economic interests and cost/benefit analyses may indicate, as they have in the case of Western Europe and the persistence of the United States of America, that some economic interest is served by unity in diversity. This is the long-term trend, one even clear to the Canadians, many of whom believe that within 50 years all of North America will be one state.[35] But the world must have patience. This current phase is most likely transitional, not only in the former Soviet bloc, but in all the secessionist activity.

Only sovereignty, with its concomitant right of choice, will enable the future regrouping of seceding entities according to their inclinations at the time. Just like the Slovenes and Croatians chose the union with Serbia after World War I because that seemed the best among choices, they now want the power to make a new choice and to regroup with Western Europe. According to the Ukrainian minister for defense, "What we need today is a chance to breathe some freedom, to really feel some sovereignty. Then maybe in five years or so we start talking of uniting or some association."[36]

In speaking about interaction among regions, Lincoln said, "Is it possible then to make that intercourse more advantageous, or more satisfactory, after separation than before? Can aliens make treaties easier than friends can make laws? Can treaties be more faithfully enforced between aliens than laws can among friends?" Secessionist regions today do not doubt the importance of both political and economic alliances. Indeed, new nations of Europe are taking numbers in the waiting line for membership to the EEC, in what seems like a contradictory effort to give up some of their new sovereignty. Surely, the Slovenian peoples have more in common ethnically and linguistically with the Serbs than with the French. However, those ties seem to be irrelevant, and the new desires reflect the desire for choice, in so far as nations want to reassess with whom they will be paired up. Therefore, in the new alliances, those ethnic issues that are perceived by some as being critical in numerous secessions cease to be an issue in the choice of new alliances. Indeed, the new alliances have more to do with economics than with ethnic orientation—regions tend to want to be paired up with those more developed nations that will have two economic effects on them. First, they will act as a motivator and example, and thereby pull the new state up to their level. Second, they will provide a cushion in case financial flows are necessary. In this sense, the old theme expressed in the popular Peter Sellers movie, "The Mouse that Roared," has reemerged.

Therefore, the key dilemma faced by the present world is how to go beyond the small group and look at the larger grouping, such as that composed of a set of ethnic groups. Such a state consciousness is part of a culture of tolerance in which questions of ethnicity, religion, and race are secondary. Despite Rusinow's argument that ethnicity questions will not fade away, it is likely that under the right conditions, over time these questions will recede in importance.[37] The road to this culture of tolerance entails the achievement of political maturity, and is fraught with problems. Achieving it entails the following: First, in the short run, ethnic minorities may suffer as independence changes the actors of the minority/majority social mix, and this may perhaps be accompanied by efforts to rectify past injustices. To minimize this perverse liberation, international bodies such as the United Nations, the Helsinki Act Organization, and the European Council should monitor whether countries are complying with the Universal Declaration of Human Rights. Second, allowance must be made for the fact that different states achieve political maturity at different times. Sovereignty is a key element of political maturity and is deemed a necessary step for states to go through before they consider new associations. Third, on the road to a culture of tolerance, there may be a pressure to adopt an authoritarian regime. This may come about from those who are threatened by the changes associated with sovereignty, those who are sceptical of the "new democracy" associated with sovereignty,[38] or those who tend to favor certain religious structures, such as Islamic fundamentalism. In many of the recently seceded states of the former Soviet bloc, the early 1990s have brought about not a power vacuum, but an authority vacuum. Indeed, to speak of a power vacuum created by the fall of communism is not correct, since regions have elected their presidents and parliaments, each with their own instruments of government. Instead, there is a lack of a strong hand. However, despite Berlin's argument that universalism and the perverse totalitarianism that emerged from the political philosophies of the 18th century philosophers are on the demise in the Western world, while individuality is on the rise,[39] a reversal to a "strong arm" in politics in some regions is likely.

The fourth and perhaps major obstacle on the road to a culture of tolerance is economics. Economic depravation, decreasing standards of living, and increasing poverty have characterized the lives of an increasing number of people across the world. At the same time, those who have more are also reacting by wanting to keep more for themselves—ranging from tax revolt in Italy to the rejection of Haitian immigrants by the United States, all in an effort to control the dissipation of money to outsiders. The situation in the former Soviet Union is a clear example of a regression in the standard of living, as a state that ranked as a superpower just a few years ago is asking for food aid to enable it to feed its population. The lack of economic development is likely to reverse the trend towards democratization as it has done on numerous occasions in the past.[40] This does not imply that economic development means the cessation of secessionist trends. Indeed, the occurrence of these in Western Europe is clear indication that despite economic growth, nationalism due to economics or ethnicity thrives. Despite the flow of human resources across borders in response to industrial and service manpower demands, despite the internalization of technology and cyclical economic fluctuations, groups identify with local and regional interests.

Thus, not only is economics a key element underlying secessionist efforts, but economic development is a necessary but not sufficient condition to achieving a tolerant society upon which to base future cohabitation of ethnic groups within political boundaries. That it is not sufficient has been clearly shown by the proliferation of numerous secessionist efforts in places such as Scotland, Wales, Spain, and so forth, indicating that economically developed regions ruled by democratic parliamentary governments are not immune to secessionist trends. While it had been believed some decades ago that politicized ethnicity in the West was a trend that would not emerge again, its reemergence necessitates novel and effective ways of addressing the centrifugal and centripetal forces exerted by a multitude of interests coexisting within a political boundary.[41] Such trends should not evoke romantic reminiscences about how successful the Austro-Hungarian and Soviet empires were in holding together disparate economic and ethnic entities, nor should we put too much hope on a supranational ideology that would unify people. Indeed, Marxism was to play that role, as well as materialistic individualism, insofar as their adherents should have shed all vestiges of association with a small interest group. Neither of these succeeded, and no other supranational force is in the making. Therefore, given that a culture of tolerance has not yet evolved in the numerous regions of the world that could benefit from it and that secessions continue to cause hardship and injustice in many cases, it is necessary for the international community to identify some concrete steps to take to minimize the pain associated with the redrawing of boundaries.[42] Among these, I would argue the need for a consistent and principled approach to secession so that the same rules are applied to all players. As noted above, on this score, the western governments failed dismally in the Yugoslav crisis. In addition, the international community need not be too hasty in preventing secession if the demand for it exists, because that demand will be repressed only to arise again in the future, until sovereignty is tasted and political maturity allows further associations along new lines. Lastly, there should be the creation of an international body to review secessionist claims. It needs to be specialized in all aspects of secession, and for this reason the international court is not appropriate, although it was turned to on various occasions (including the question of self-determination of Western Sahara).[43]

NOTES

Notes to Chapter 1

1. Chazan has identified four waves of such movements: the first was during the delineation of the European states of Italy and Germany, the second was after World War I with the redrawing of boundaries following the defeat of the Austro-Hungarian and Ottoman Empires, the third was after World War II and the boundary problems arising from decolonization, and the fourth is occurring presently (Naomi Chazan, "Irredentism, Separatism, and Nationalism," in Naomi Chazan, ed., *Irredentism and International Politics,* Boulder: Lynne Rienner, 1991, pp. 142-143).

2. Numerous books and papers have been published in the recent years about the subject of Soviet nationalities in general, including the systematic analysis of the relations between the regions and the center by Bohdan Nahaylo and Victor Swoboda (*Soviet Disunion: A History of the Nationalities Problem in the USSR,* New York: The Free Press, 1990) and Nadia Diuk and Adrian Karatnycky (*The People Challenge the Soviet Union,* New York: William Morrow, 1990).

3. The Romanian government in November 1991 said that if Ukraine becomes independent, then it must negotiate the fate of the disputed territories of northern Bukovina, Herta, Hotin, and southern Bessarabia, lands that Moscow took from Romania in 1940 and incorporated into Ukraine. *New York Times,* November 30, 1991.

4. William Morris, ed., *The American Heritage Dictionary of the English Language,* Boston: Houghton Mifflin, 1969, p. 1171-2.

5. In the academic literature, the definition of secession varies in emphasis according to author. Secessionist movements tend to have the following characteristics, as defined by Premdas: There is an organized struggle, a demand for territorial self-government, common language, religion or ethnicity, a perception of self-determination as a right, and the desire to be a state in the international organization (Ralph R. Premdas "Secessionist Movements in Comparative Perspective," in Ralph R. Premdas, S.W.R. de A. Samarasinghe and Alan B. Anderson, *Secessionist Movements in Comparative Perspective,* New York: St. Martin's Press, 1990, pp. 15-16).

6. Donald Horowitz, "Irredentas and Secessions: Adjacent Phenomena, Neglected Connections," Chazan, ed., *Irredentism,* pp. 9-10.

7. Ibid., p. 12-13.

8. Robert J. Thompson and Joseph R. Rudolph, Jr., "The Ebb and Flow of Ethnoterritorial Politics in the Western World," in Joseph R. Rudolph Jr. and Robert J. Thompson, eds., *Ethnoterritorial Politics, Policy and the Western World,* Boulder: Lynne Rienner, 1989, p. 2.

9. Allen Buchanan, *Secession,* Boulder: Westview Press, 1991, p. 9.

10. In Switzerland, the constitution of 1975 allows cantons to split into half cantons while denying them the right to secede from the confederation.

11. The Soviet Union was divided into four levels of regional, ethnically based administrative units: there were 15 union republics, followed in descending order by 20 autonomous republics, 8 autonomous regions (*oblast*) and 10 autonomous areas (*okrug*).

12. This vote was met with a statement from the Ukrainian government that such an attempt would be put down by force. *The New Republic,* December 24, 1990, p. 5.

13. *The New York Times,* November 30, 1991.

14. Although some scholars, such as Barnett, have argued to the contrary, this remains a controversial theoretical possibility of limited applicability to real world events, and hence will not be included in this study (Randy Barnett, Liberty Fund Symposium on Liberalism, Federalism and the Question of Secession, Tucson, Arizona, December 1990, quoted in Buchanan, p. 24).

15. Buchanan, p. 14.

16. For a list of countries and their territorial disputes, see Fredrich Kratochwil, Paul Rorlich, and Harpreet Mahajan, *Peace and Disputed Sovereignty: Reflections on Conflict over Territory,* Columbia University Institute of War and Pease Studies, Lanham: University Press of America, 1985, Appendix 1.

17. This attempted secession in Australia was diluted by concessions from the center that resulted in the rectifying of the economic injustice perceived by the population of Western Australia, which voted in the referendum to secede. See Anthony Birch, *Nationalism and National Integration,* London: Unwin Hyman, 1989, pp. 187-188.

18. Nathan Gardels, "Two Concepts of Nationalism: An Interview with Isaiah Berlin," *The New York Review of Books,* November 21, 1991, p. 21.

19. *The New York Times,* March 29, 1992.

20. Frederick L. Shiels, ed., *Ethnic Separatism and World Politics,* Lanham: University Press of America, 1984, and Walter Connor "Politics of Ethnonationalism," *Journal of International Affairs,* 27, no. 1, 1973, pp. 1-21.

21. This and several others were presented in *The Economist* (October 26, 1991) as the results of a contest to rename the former Soviet Union. Others include RELICS (Republics Left in Chaos by Socialism), PITS (Post-Imperial Total Shambles), and COMA (Confederation of Mutual Antagonism).

22. Milan Andrejevich, Roundtable on Yugoslav Political and Constitutional Issues 1990-91, at the meetings of the American Association for the Advancement of Slavic Studies, Miami, November 23, 1991.

23. See, for example, Richard L. Rudolph and David F. Good, eds., *Nationalism and Empire: The Habsburg Monarchy and the Soviet Union*, New York: St. Martin's Press, 1992.

24. The practice of referendums, as a solution to this problem, has been studied by Robert Thompson ("Referendums and Ethnoterritorial Movements: The Policy Consequences and Political Ramification" in Rudolph and Thompson, eds., pp. 181-220) and David Butler and Austin Ranney, eds., *Referendums: A Comparative Study of Practice and Theory*, Washington: American Enterprise Institute for Public Policy Research, 1978.

25. Vladimir Lenin, *Collected Works* vol. 20, quoted in Bohdan Nahaylo and Victor Swoboda, *Soviet Disunion*, New York: The Free Press, 1989, p. 15.

26. *The New York Times*, January 1, 1992.

27. *The Economist*, November 2, 1991.

28. Thomas Land, cited in Peter Russel and Storrs McCall, "Can Secession Be Justified? The Case of the Southern Sudan," in Dunstan M. Wai, ed., *The Southern Sudan: The Problem of National Integration*, London: Frank Cass, 1973, p. 119.

29. The present conflict between the Serbs and the Croats in the Krajina region has a tradition of religious intolerance on the part of the Catholic religion in that area. A clear example of this is the Catholic efforts to convert the Eastern Orthodox population, which were identified as early as the mid-1700s, with forcible conversions. See Gunther E. Rothenberg, *The Military Border in Croatia 1740-1881*, Chicago: University of Chicago Press, 1966, p. 29.

30. Sri Lanka, House of Representatives, Parliamentary Debates (Hansard), vol. 48, col. 1313, September 3, 1962, quoted in Robert Kearney, "Ethnic Conflict and the Tamil Separatist Movement in Sri Lanka," *Asian Survey* 25, no. 9, September 1985. p. 903.

31. *Webster's Dictionary*, New York: Warner Books, 1979.

32. J. L. Talmon, *The Myth of the Nation and the Vision of Revolution*, London: Secker and Warburg, 1981, p. 544-5.

33. See Gregory Gleason, *Federalism and Nationalism: The Struggle for Republican Rights in the USSR*, Boulder: Westview Press, 1990, p. 19.

34. Among the abundant literature on this subject, see, for example, Paul Henze, "The Spectre and Implications of Internal Nationalist Dissent: Historical and Functional Comparisons," in *Soviet Nationalities in Strategic Perspective*, London: Croom Helm, 1985; Roman Szporluk, *Communism and Nationalism*, New York: Oxford University Press, 1988; Robert Conquest, ed., *The Last Empire: Nationality and the Soviet Future*, Stanford: Hoover Institution Press, 1986; Nahaylo and Swoboda, *Soviet Disunion*, among others.

35. Gardels, p. 19.

36. Connor Cruise O'Brien, "Nationalists and Democrats," *The New York Review of Books*, August 15, 1991, p. 31.

37. Eric Hobsbawm, "Some Reflections on the Break-Up of Britain," *New Left Review* 105, September-October 1977.

38. E. J. Hobsbawm, *Nations and Nationalism Since 1780,* Cambridge: Cambridge University Press, 1990, p. 171.

39. Horowitz, p. 21.

40. See, for example, Jaroslav Krejci and Vitezslav Velimsky, *Ethnic and Political Nations in Europe,* New York: St. Martin's Press, 1981, among others.

41. Walter Conner, "Nation-Building or Nation-Destroying?" *World Politics* 24, 1972, p. 320.

42. See A. I. Asiwaju, ed., *Partitioned Africans,* New York: St. Martin's Press, 1985.

43. Indeed, Russia's Academy of Sciences has identified 76 border disputes. *The Economist,* July 13, 1991, p. 22.

44. That the Indians of Canada won the right to their territory in January 1992 and will redraw the map of Canada is as much due to the nature of the Canadian democratic government as to their perseverance, a condition that is lacking in the continent of South America.

45. O'Brien, p. 31.

46. Chazan, *Irredentism,* p. 143.

47. On December 19, 1991, the Republic of Serbian Krajina was declared in parts of Croatia.

48. The status of Krajina lies at the core of the Serb-Croat civil war, and Tatarstan is capable of gravely undermining the Russian Federal Treaty and may be to Russia what the Baltic republics were to the former Soviet Union.

49. For example, Dobrudja on the Black Sea is divided between Bulgaria and Romania and the Bulgarian minority in Romania is becoming restive. Further, the border between Romania and the Soviet Union has been redrawn several times, and it is unclear what its future is. See Daniel Nelson "Europe's Unstable East," *Foreign Policy* 82, Spring 1991, pp. 137-158.

50. A. Przeworski and Henry Teune, *The Logic of Comparative Social Inquiry,* New York: John Wiley, 1970.

51. A federation is defined as a state in which executive and legislative powers are shared between central and subcentral governments, while in a unitary state only the center holds these powers. A confederation is a set of states that are unified for specific purposes while retaining their sovereignty. According to Davis, there are 44 types of definitions of federations currently in use by scholars (Rufus Davis, *The Federal Principle: A Journey Through Time in Quest of Meaning,* Berkeley: University of California Press, 1978, p. 204).

52. Robin Jeffrey, *What's Happening to India: Punjab, Ethnic Conflict, Mrs. Gandhi's Death and the Test for Federalism,* Basingstoke: Macmillan Press, 1986, p. 69.

53. This distinction between "we want in" and "we want out" in regional demands is taken from Peter Leslie, "Ethnonationalism in a Federal State: The Case of Canada," in Rudolph and Thompson, eds., p. 47.

54. See B. H. Shafruddin, *The Federal Factor in the Government and Politics of Peninsular Malaysia,* Singapore: Oxford University Press, 1987, p. 26.

55. According to Van Walt van Praag, classical international theory of law recognizes five modes of acquiring legal title to territory: accretion, prescription,

conquest, cession and "occupatio" (Michael C. Van Walt van Praag, *The Status of Tibet: History, Rights and Prospects in International Law,* Boulder: Westview Press, 1987, p. 178).

56. Claude Phillips, "Nigeria and Biafra," in Shiels, ed., p. 194.

57. Peter Woodward, *Sudan, 1898-1989: The Unstable State,* Boulder: Lynne Rienner, 1990, p. 223.

58. Bougainville is an island some 500 miles off the eastern coast of Papua New Guinea, only six miles from the northwestern Solomon Islands. The entire district of Bougainville comprises Bougainville and Buka, together with two Melanesian and three Polynesian outliers. The distance from the mainland creates a natural barrier between center and region, and dilutes the power that the center can exert on the island.

59. Bougainville was granted a semiautonomous status, the only of its kind in the nation, to appease the irredentists that demanded a separate nation at the time when Papua New Guinea won independence from Australia in 1975. This status gave it more decentralization than the remaining regions.

60. The inhabitants of Bougainville have darker skins than people of the mainland, whom they refer to as "redskins." However, there are about 20 language groups on the island, so the homogeneity does not extend to language. Population statistics of this region are imprecise. The first measure of the population was taken in 1966, and entailed a 10 percent sample of the population. Later estimates varied widely in their results (L. P. Mair, *Australia in New Guinea,* Carlton: Melbourne University Press, 1970).

61. The Tibet Autonomous Region is the territory invaded by China in 1950. There is another territory that is inhabited by the Tibetans, namely regions of today's Quinghai Province, that fell under Chinese rule in the 18th century. There has been significant in-migration of the Han Chinese in this province so that the Tibetans presently constitute only 20 percent of the population (*The New York Times,* September 9, 1991).

62. Tibet holds the title of Tibet Autonomous Region, and thus has a status shared by numerous other regions within China.

63. Tibetans make up 2.12 million, and there are 79,000 Han Chinese also (*The New York Times,* October 7, 1990). Although population censuses were held in Tibet from 653 A.D. onwards, they were all highly inaccurate and the estimation of populations has been very difficult. Grunfeld contains a survey of both Tibetan and Han population estimates until 1979 (Grunfeld, pp. 218-222).

64. Sri Lanka is a unitary state, characterized by what has been called Sinhalese Political Buddhism (see A. Jeyaratnam Wilson, *The Break-up of Sri Lanka: The Sinhalese-Tamil Conflict,* Honolulu: University of Hawaii Press, 1988, chapters 1-2). Following the Tamil challenges to that kind of unitary rule, a special status was awarded to the Northern and Eastern Provinces in which the Tamils are the majority of the population (this special status is discussed in greater detail in chapter 4).

65. Although the Sri Lanka Tamils account for 12.6 percent of the population of the entire island, within the four northern districts, where they are a majority,

they range from 50.6 to 95.3 percent of the population (derived from Department of Census and Statistics, *Census of Population and Housing,* Sri Lanka, 1981, Preliminary Release No. 1, Colombo: Department of Census and Statistics, 1981). The Sri Lanka Tamils are to be distinguished from Indian Tamils, who are descendants of migrants from India of the past century. They tend to stay out of the conflict.

66. East Timor became Indonesia's 27 province in 1976. It has been maintained as a special and "closed" province. As such, it implies security and personnel from the center, as well as separate political and economic regulations.

67. Before the annexation of East Timor, the entire population was Timorese. Presently, 20 percent of the population consists of inflows from other regions of Muslims in a highly Catholic region (*The New York Times,* October 21, 1990).

68. Punjab has a special status within India insofar as it, along with Kashmir and Assam, is under president's rule, implying that their local governments are suspended and they are ruled directly from the center.

69. The Indian population statistics in this table are all taken from Government of India, *Statistical Abstract of India, 1984,* New Delhi: Central Statistical Organization, p. 3.

70. Although the Akali Dal was set up in 1944, it was not until the time of Indian Independence that it started agitating for autonomy. In 1960 it was clear that no agreement could be reached, and the leader of the party, Tara Singh, called for a campaign of civil disobedience.

71. As with Punjab and Kashmir, Assam is also ruled directly from the center under presidential Rule.

72. The violence in Assam caused the dropping of the state from the 1991 census, although projections are that the Assamese may in fact have become a minority within their state (*The New York Times,* February 11, 1991). This has occurred due to the high rates of in-migration of bordering Bengali-speaking Hindus and Muslims.

73. Most of the statistics pertaining to Kashmir are given for the entire territory of Jammu and Kashmir. A breakdown of the data was not always possible.

74. As Assam and Punjab, Kashmir has been ruled directly from the center.

75. The region of Kashmir had been divided between Pakistan, India, and China. There are indications that an independent Indian Kashmir would favor unification with the other regions.

76. There is no information pertaining to the percent of Karens in what was formerly Karen state. The Karen are ethnically different from the majority of Myanmar's population, and they are Christian in religious orientation, setting them apart from the Buddhists and Muslims to the west.

77. Southern Sudan consists of the following regions: Bahr el Ghazal, Equatoria, and the Upper Nile.

78. In 1991, the military government decreed a federal system, dividing Sudan into nine states, each of which is to be responsible for local administration and tax collection. (*The Wall Street Journal,* February 6, 1991).

79. The southerners make up 30 percent of the population (Russel and McCall, p. 111). The principal of these is the Dinka ethnic group, which is distinguished from the northern groups by race and religion: the northerners are brown Africans, while the southerners are black Africans; the northerners are Muslim, while the southerners are Christian and animistic.

80. In 1952, the United Nations helped create a federation agreement according to which Eritrea was to have some measure of independence from 1952 onwards when the British withdrew. However, that agreement was cancelled in 1962.

81. Eritrea contains nine nationalities that have developed an Eritrean culture partially as a result of their shared history and experience. The Tigrinya speakers, encompassing approximately 1.5 million people, are the largest group (see Okbazghi Yohannes, *Eritrea, A Pawn in World Politics,* Gainesville: University of Florida Press, 1991, pp. 6-8).

82. After independence, no special status was accorded to Cabinda, although in effect, it was not continuous with the Angolan territory and was a source of great foreign income, and therefore needed special attention. In 1977 a revolutionary movement announced the liberation of Cabinda and the establishment of a provisional government. However, this movement was so weak that it did not pose a serious threat to Luanda, and the effort petered out. See Lawerence Henderson, *Angola, Five Centuries of Conflict,* Ithaca: Cornell University Press, pp. 27, 262.

83. The principal ethnic group of Cabinda, the Bakongo, are linked to the population of southwestern Zaire and have little in common with the ethnic groups of Angola. Their exact numbers are unknown, due to migrations, however, it is estimated that during the mid-1960s, the figure was 400,000, dispersed over three countries (Douglas L. Wheeler and Rene Pelissier, *Angola,* New York: Praeger, 1971, pp. 6-8).

84. Historically, Portugal, rather than France, was the colonial power of the region. It was only integrated with Senegal in 1866, and the capital was taken by France two decades later. Then, the north converted to Islam by the turn of the century, whereas the Casamancese retained their animist religious beliefs.

85. The Diola, the dominant ethnic group of the region, does not speak Wolof, the country's main language. A study by Geller claims that various smaller ethnic groups, including the Diola, Mandinka, and others have been developing a strong regional Casamancian identity (Sheldon Gellar, *Senegal, An African National Between Islam and the West,* Boulder: Westview Press, 1982, p. 99).

86. Kurds inhabit territories of present-day Iraq, Iran, Turkey, Syria, and the former Soviet Union. The greatest proportion of the territory and the population (ten million) lies within Turkey, but the wealthiest territory, with oil fields, is in Iraq.

87. Iraq is a unitary state. In 1970, the Kurds signed an agreement that gave them an autonomous Kurdish region and allowed Kurdish language to be taught in schools. But the agreement collapsed and instead produced the Kurdish rebellion of 1974. After the allied war against Iraq in 1991, and the subsequent weakening of the government of Saddam Hussein, the Kurds have demanded

full autonomy for the traditional Kurdish lands. See Edmund Ghareeb, *The Kurdish Question in Iraq,* Syracuse: Syracuse University Press, 1981.

88. Kurds are Muslims of Indo-European stock (Turkik), while the majority of Iraqis are Arabs. See Christine Moss Helms, *Iraq: Eastern Flank of the Arab World,* Washington: Brookings Institution, 1984, chapter 1. Moreover, the use of the Kurdish language in schools is illegal in Turkey. Kurds can vote, but cannot have their own political parties or media. They are not officially recognized as a minority (they are "mountain Turks") although the much smaller Greeks, Jews, and Armenians are. The mention of the word Kurdistan is illegal, so newspapers print "..." in place of it. (*The Wall Street Journal,* December 3, 1990).

89. The first settlers from Europe to the region were French, followed by the British only in 1760. The governors of the new British colony were conciliatory toward the French population, giving them the right to their own institutions in many spheres. It was not until 1839 that a policy of assimilation was attempted. However, this became obsolete by the time the confederation of four provinces took place (1867) and Quebec gained autonomy in the process. (The Canadian state was created by the British North America Act. The remaining provinces were added at a later date, between 1870 and 1949).

90. Peter Leslie, "Ethnonationalism in a Federal State: The Case of Canada" in Rudolph and Thompson, eds., *Ethnoterritorial Politics,* p. 48

91. Puerto Rico was a Spanish colony until 1898, when Spain ceded the island to the United States. The United States granted it commonwealth status.

92. Puerto Rico has, since 1952, commonwealth status according to which it is not an integral part of the United States as a state, but it has some autonomy that differentiates it from a colony.

93. The statistics for the Soviet republics presented in this column and the subsequent two are all taken from various tables and pages of Deutsche Bank, *The Soviet Union at the Crossroads: Facts and Figures on the Soviet Republics,* Frankfurt: Deutsche Bank AG, 1990.

94. Tadzhiks are Sunni Muslims who speak a Persian dialect.

95. The Tatar Autonomous Region was a lower-level regional administrative unit than a republic. However, in 1992, it voted not to even be part of the Russian federation, becoming one of two of the 20 subregions that did not sign the treaty in March 1992 defining their role in the new post-Soviet Russia.

96. This number refers to the Moslems of the region, mostly of the Tatar ethnic group.

97. Given the present war in Croatia, one cannot but draw parallels with the independence efforts during World War II. At that time, Hitler installed a puppet regime under the presidency of Ante Pavelic, and the ustashas (extreme right wing) committed atrocities against the Serbs (and Jews and gypsies) on their territories in order to create an ethnically pure Croatia. Croatia was the only German satellite region except for Romania that had its own "final solution." According to the Wiesenthal center, the concentration camps in Croatia were the fiercest outside of Germany, and it is estimated that around 500,000 Serbs perished at the hands of the Croats. There is much controversy

over this number, a discussion of which is contained in the article by Kaplan, which also discusses how the Croatian post-independence president, Franjo Tudjman claims, as late as 1991, that the Holocaust never happened and that what little deaths occurred were because the Jews killed the Serbs. (A discussion of the book reissued in 1991 by President Tudjman, a historian, is contained in an article by Robert Kaplan "Croatianism: The Latest Balkan Ugliness" *The New Republic,* November 25, 1991. Tudjman claims that the numbers killed in Croatia were significantly lower than those accepted by both the Yugoslav government and international organizations. Moreover, he goes on to say that the three groups the ustashas killed—Serbs, gypsies and Jews—actually killed each other: "According to Tudjman, the mass murder of Serbs by Croats during World War II is not an issue, since not all that many Serbs were killed in the first place, and those who were slaughtered were mainly done in by the Jews. Case closed" [p. 18].)

98. The Serbian Autonomous Region of Krajina, with headquarters in Knin, consists of 12 communes in Dalmatia, Lika, Banija, Dordun, and Slavonia. It covers an area of some 7,900 square kilometers and has a population of 268,400. It was set up on April 30, 1991, complete with its own legislative, administrative, and executive bodies.

99. Within Tito's federation, Krajina had no special status within the republic of Croatia. It never enjoyed the status of autonomous region that was granted to Vojvodina, which had a significantly lower percent of minority population. Then, in 1991 it declared itself an autonomous region, and then a republic. However, it did have a special status during the Austro-Hungarian rule. At this time, Krajina was called Vojna Krajina (military Krajina) and it served an important function for the Austrian Empire. It was populated over the centuries by Serbs evading the Ottoman empire, and in exchange for land, they agreed to defend the empire, and thereby Europe, from Turkish invasion. As such, Vojna Krajina was a separate administrative-political territorial unit, ruled directly by Vienna, and did not come under the jurisdiction of the Croatian parliament until 1881. See Gunther E. Rothenberg, *The Military Border in Croatia 1740-1881,* Chicago: University of Chicago Press, 1966.

100. The average proportion of Serbs in Krajina is 62%. There is a great variety among the communes, ranging among the following highs and lows: Donji Lapac 91.1%; Vojnic 88.6%; Dvor 80.9%; Pakrac 38.4%; Kostanjica 55.5%; and Obrovac 60.1%. (These numbers are taken from the 1981 census, as published in Savezni Zavod Za Statistiku, *Statisticki Godisnjak 1983,* Belgrade, and Jovan Ilic, "Characteristics and Importance of Some Ethno-National and Political-Geographic Factors Relevant for the Possible Political-Legal Disintegration of Yugoslavia," in Stanoje Ivanovic, ed., *The Creation and Changes of the Internal Borders of Yugoslavia,* Belgrade: Srbostampa, 1992, Table 6, p. 89.)

101. The present problems in the region, although deeply rooted in historical relationships, started brewing following the election of President Tudjman in June 1990. Among the first changes that his new government instituted was to decrease the rights of the Serbian population in the following ways: 1) Serbs

were relegated to the status of a minority, whereas before they were an equal peoples with the Croatians, thus enjoying the recognition of their history on that territory (indeed, whereas the Declaration of the Basic Rights of Nations and Citizens of Democratic Croatia, passed in 1944, gave the Croats and Serbs equality under law, the new constitution of Croatia, adopted in December 1990, relegated the Serbs to a minority [*Narodne Novine* 59, 1990]). This was perceived as insulting to an ethnic group that had inhabited that region since the 13th century. 2) Their cultural rights were denied insofar as they lost the right to use the cyrillic alphabet in the schools and the media. 3) Serbs were fired from positions in the police force and the administration (See David Martin, "Croatia's Borders: Over the Edge," The New York Times, November 22, 1991). At the same time, a law was passed according to which Serbian property owners but nonresidents of Croatia were forced to pay higher real-estate taxes on property held in Croatia, simply on the basis of their ethnic origin.

102. Given Kosovo status as an autonomous region within the republic of Serbia, it was unclear whether to make its reference point in this study Serbia or Yugoslavia. It was decided to use Yugoslavia because Kosovo wants to secede from Yugoslavia, not only Serbia. This is different from Krajina, which wants to secede from Croatia, not Yugoslavia.

103. Within the federation as it existed until 1989, Kosovo was an autonomous region within the republic of Serbia. This special status was dropped following the all-Serbia referendum on internal borders, and the original status (pre-Tito) of the region was restored.

104. The question of ethnic composition of Kosovo lies at the heart of the present crisis. According to the census of 1981, the population is predominantly Kosovar (77.5% of the region) although there is some doubt as to the validity of those statistics. Nevertheless, that number must be considered in historical context. There was a time when the region was predominantly inhabited by Serbs (indeed, according to the bookkeepers of the invading Ottoman Empire, the region was populated by Serbs). Then, during World War II, much of the region was annexed to Albania under Italian rule, to form Greater Albania. Since the war, various factors contributed to altering the demographics of the region, including: illegal border crossings from low-income and repressive Albania, high fertility rates among the Albanian population (the highest in Europe, over 2.5% per year), terror against Serbs with the aim of large-scale evacuations, and Tito's policy of relocating Serbs from Kosovo to Vojvodina (see Alex N. Dragnich and Slavko Todorovich, *The Saga of Kosovo*, Boulder: East European Monographs, 1984, chapters 12-14).

105. In 1990, the parliament approved a Slovak motion to return the hyphen to the official spelling of Czechoslovakia, making it the Czech and Slovak Republic. For details on this motion, see Stanislav J. Kirschbaum, "Slovakia in the Post-Communist Constitutional Process," paper presented to the 23rd Annual Convention of the American Association for the Advancement of Slavic Studies, Miami, November 23, 1991.

106. Czechoslovakia became a federation in 1969.

107. There are 4.5 million Slovaks out of a population of 5.3 million in Slovakia. There are also 566,000 Hungarians, 80,000 gypsies, and 17,000 Russians.

108. This region, in the foothills of the Carpathian Mountains, has gone back and forth between Romania and Hungary four times in the last century and is regarded by each as national ground. It was last ceded to Romania by the Treaty of Trianon in 1920.

109. In 1952, the "Autonomous Hungarian Region" was established which gave the population little more than bilingual street signs. During the Hungarian uprising in 1956 against the Soviets, the Hungarian population in Transylvania also became agitated, provoking anti-Hungarian measures. In 1960 the autonomy and special status of the region ceased to exist, since an administrative reorganization of the region resulted in the taking of some Hungarian villages and the addition of non-Hungarian villages in order to change the demographic character of the region (John F. Cadzow, Andrew Ludanyi, and Louis J. Elteto, "Chronology of Transylvanian History," in *Transylvania, The Roots of Ethnic Conflict,* Kent: Kent State University Press, 1983, pp. 31-33).

110. The population of Transylvania is around seven million, of which some three-fifths are Romanian and the rest is Hungarian (two million) with 400,000 Germans and some Serbs and Ukrainians (George Schopflin, "Transylvania: Hungarians Under Romanian Rule," in Stephen Borsody, ed., *The Hungarians: A Divided Nation,* New Haven: Yale Center for International and Area Studies, 1988, p. 130). Although Romanians are the strict majority in this region, some pockets are mostly Hungarian, such as the county of Harghita, where they make up 85 percent of the population (*The New York Times,* November 12, 1990).

111. In 1921, the island of Ireland was partitioned so that two states would inhabit the island.

112. One is hard-pressed to call the United Kingdom a completely unitary state. In the words of Birch, "The United Kingdom is a somewhat untidy state, neither federal nor completely unitary, that has no formal constitution and can only be understood in historical terms" (Anthony Birch, *Nationalism and National Integration,* London: Unwin Hyman 1989, p. 78).

113. The parliament of Northern Ireland was suspended in 1972, and since then the region has been ruled directly from Westminster.

114. Ethnically, the population in the United Kingdom, Ireland, and the six counties of Northern Ireland is homogeneous. The crucial distinction in this case is the religion of the population. Although the majority of the island is Catholic, within the six counties of Northern Ireland, Protestants constitute a majority.

115. Scotland has a special status within the British union insofar as it has its own legal system, educational system, and the Presbyterian Church of Scotland.

116. Louis XV bought Corsica from the city-state of Genoa in 1768.

117. Corsica was given special status in 1971, which implied a new legislature and assembly, consultative councils, and cultural identity. There would also be a separate employment agency, credit ban, agricultural development agency, and a regional company devoted to industrial, commercial, and tourist development. In addition, the Corsican language became compulsory in schools. See

Louis Snyder, *Global Mini-Nationalisms: Autonomy or Independence,* Westport: Greenwood Press, 1982, pp. 79-80.

118. The Basque Provinces include Alava, Guipuzcoa, Navarra, and Vizcaya.

119. The 1978 constitution of Spain accommodated Spain's regional groups by creating 17 autonomous regions so that all regions negotiate with the central government their rights and obligations. Thus, the Spanish state underwent a transformation from a unitary state into one based on 17 regional governments. Autonomy gave Basque Provinces, as well as Catalonia, the power to elect their own parliaments, to control taxation, education, and police, and to supervise broadcasting.

120. Robert Clark, "Spanish Democracy and Regional Autonomy: The Autonomous Community System and Self-Government for the Ethnic Homelands," in Rudolph and Thompson, eds., *Ethnoterritorial Politics,* p. 29.

121. The Catalan provinces include Barcelona, Tarragona, Gerona, and Lerida.

122. See note 119 for the political structure of Basque Provinces.

123. The leader of Catalonia for the past 12 years, Mr. Jordi Pujol, claims that anyone that lives and works in Catalonia is a Catalan. The Economist, March 21, 1992, p. 54.

124. At the time of the Biafra war, Nigeria was a federation consisting of four regions. After the civil war, new subdivisions were created.

125. The Belgian Congo, at the time of independence until the end of the war in 1963, was a unitary state with six provinces. However, it became a federation of 20 regions after the war with Katanga.

126. There are numerous ethnic groups residing within Katanga; however, the issue in the secession was not the intolerance between the regional minority and the national majority, but rather between the indigenous population and the newcomers. Various ethnic groups indigenous to Katanga became allied against these newcomers, who were perceived as immigrating to partake of Katanga's economic prosperity. Thus the conflict was seen more in terms of protection against the strangers, as in Lombardy presently, rather than against one specific ethnic group.

127. The Economist, *The World in Figures,* London: The Economist Newspaper, p. 162.

128. The special status of Singapore was established prior to federation. According to Turnbull, the region was to have greater autonomy than other regions of the union. Singapore would have a smaller representation in the federal government than its population, and would have its own executive state government (C. M. Turnbull, *A History of Singapore 1819-1988,* 2nd ed., Singapore: Oxford University Press, 1989, p. 272-73). In addition, Shaffrudin explains how Singapore was also given autonomy in education and labor, as well as a special status with respect to citizenship (Shafruddin, p. 23).

129. The Chinese, the dominant ethnic group, were followed by the Malays (13.6 percent) and Indians (9 percent). (Chiew Seen-Kong, "The Socio-Cultural Framework of Politics," in Jon S. T. Quah, Chan Heng Chee, and Seah Chee Meow, eds., *Government and Politics of Singapore,* Singapore: Oxford University Press, 1985, p. 49, Table 3.1).

130. Ethnically the population is closer to the Solomon Islands, a link that was further consolidated by the intermarriages and the extensive trade that took place.

131. In 1988, the Bougainville Revolutionary Army resurfaced after dormancy since 1975. Although the rebels only numbered about one hundred, they enjoyed much support among the population, unlike the separatism of the early 1970s, which was not supported by the northern island population. See James Griffin, "Movements for Separation and Secession," in Anthony Clunies Ross and John Langmore, eds., *Alternative Strategies for Papua New Guinea*, Melbourne: Oxford University Press, 1973, p. 120.

132. The revolt of 1959, when the Tibetans were crushed after demanding the withdrawal of the Chinese and the end to Han assimilation, was indeed violent. However, after that, resistance was peaceful. One of the reasons why the resistance to Beijing has been peaceful is because it was led by Buddhist monks that profess pacifism. However, the most important reason is the extreme suppression of political liberties that the central government and the communist party have exerted upon the Tibetans.

133. Since no direct measures of secessionist aspirations exist among the Tamils, Kearney has taken various local and national elections as indicators of popular support for the separatist movement. According to his study, the elections in 1977, 1979, and 1981 suggest popular endorsement (in latter elections, some boycott is evident). See Kearney, p. 909.

134. The Portuguese left their colony of 400 years and the East Timorese declared their independence on November 28, 1975. They were annexed to Indonesia nine days later. The official Indonesian version of events claims that the people of East Timor exercised their right to self-determination when their national assembly voted to integrate with Indonesia (communique by Embassy of Indonesia in Washington, printed in *The New York Times*, January 5, 1991).

135. The Fretilin (acronym for the Revolutionary Front for an Independent East Timor) have now been reduced significantly, to 200-400 (according to government estimates) or 5000 (according to Fretilin spokesmen). Their popularity is hard to gauge, but it is clear from the sporadic reports by foreigners that have been in the region after the 14-year ban on travel to the territory was lifted, support for the Indonesian government is very limited. Indeed, people have expressed that they felt more free under the Portuguese than the Indonesians (*The New York Times*, October 21, 1990).

136. In 1944, the leaders of the Akali Dal established a committee whose goal was to devise a scheme for the establishment of an independent Sikh state, in the case of the partition of the subcontinent. However, this never came to pass because, unlike Pakistan and India, the Sikhs were not a majority in any one region. Although the border changes of 1966 rectified, it was too late then for independence in the spirit of partition. See Jeffrey, *What's Happening to India*.

137. Although the Akali Dal is the party that throughout most of the time has been in favor of the establishment of an independent state, it is difficult to gauge the popularity of secession because of the center's suspension of the local political mechanism and the postponement of elections.

138. The United Liberation Front of Assam is the militant wing of the All Assam Students' Union, which gained recognition in 1979 as the leader in the pressure for secession and the champion of Assamese rights.

139. Under the terms of the British transfer of power in 1947, Kashmir was to chose between union with India or Pakistan. The Hindu mahjaraja chose to join the Indian union despite the predominantly Muslim population. U.N. resolutions of 1948 and 1957 guaranteed the population a vote for self-determination, but this was ignored by the Indian government. Thus, the legality of the incorporation with the Indian union is questionable.

140. The central government of Myanmar has recently suspended its military operations in the Karen areas and has proclaimed the desire to reach a negotiated solution. This is viewed with distrust, but is also perceived as an admission that the junta is unable to win the war against the rebels (*The New York Times,* April 29, 1992).

141. According to the Panglong Agreement signed in 1947 between Burma and the British, the ethnic groups within Burma were promised autonomy in the union of Burma, as well as the right to secession. With independence in 1948, political disputes began, and numerous ethnic groups took up arms against the central government. Further, the military takeover in Burma in 1962 occurred because ostensibly the civilian government of U Nu had endangered the Union by making unnecessary concessions to the demands for autonomy of the ethnic groups. The Karen were placed under direct military administration and thus lost all semblance of autonomy (*Link,* January 6, 1991)

142. The war is the result of an effort by the Arab north to eliminate non-Arab ethnic groups in their effort to create a pure Islamic state. In addition to military action, the center's efforts in the south have included starvation of the local population by the blockage of food inflows, and in the western part of the country, the burning of villages. The central government is said to be conducting this war by arming Arab ethnic groups and increasingly directly intervening on their behalf (see *The International Herald Tribune,* July 4, 1990).

143. In 1953 the Anglo-Egyptian Agreement for independence of Sudan was signed. At this time, no southern leaders were consulted. This was later cited as one of the reasons why the Southerners were not bound by the agreement that did not involve their participation (See Russel and McCall, pp. 116, 119).

144. The Sudanese People's Liberation Army, composed mostly of Dinkas, is the political entity presently controlling much of the southern countryside outside of Juba and some six smaller towns.

145. The Southern Sudan regions had a separate regional constitution prior to federation.

146. The Southern Sudanese have found themselves at a disadvantage after their patron, President Mengitsu of Ethiopia, was overthrown in 1991. Indeed, that marked the turning point for the Sudanese People's Liberation Army, since they lost their sanctuary, their communications base, and the necessary supplies and arms to sustain their fight. This has contributed to the near defeat of the rebels in May 1992, as well as the inflow of Chinese military hardware and

"dozens of Iranian military advisers" in the spring of 1992 (*The New York Times,* May 26, 1992).

147. The population of former Spanish Sahara, and its liberation movement, the Polisario, have been battling the armies of Morocco and Mauritania since the fall of 1975, following the Spanish withdrawal. Mauritania withdrew in 1979 and made peace with the Polisario nine days later, while Morocco is not relinquishing its historical claims to Greater Morocco.

148. At the time of the Tripartite Madrid accords on 1975, Spain had 103 days to withdraw from the territory that it ruled for one century. According to the accord, the northern two-thirds of the Western Sahara were allotted to Morocco, and the southern third to Mauritania. It explicitly denied the indigenous Sahrawi people the United Nations plebiscite they had been promised.

149. The Polisario is fighting for what they call the Sahrawi Arab Democratic Republic. A referendum will take place in 1992 to determine whether Western Sahara will be independent or will be a part of Morocco. This referendum, funded by the United Nations, will be problematic because of the high degree of illiteracy and nomad characteristic of the population, as well as the question of who should be allowed to vote (see text of chapter 1).

150. This region had a separate history from the remaining regions of Ethiopia most recently because it was an Italian colony in the 19th and early 20th century, and as such developed a distinct culture. Then, it was seized by the British during World War II, and subsequently handed over to Ethiopia in 1952. One decade later, Emperor Heile Selassie absorbed it into a unified Ethiopia.

151. A referendum is to be held within two years of May 1991, when the Eritrean People's Liberation Front drove the Ethiopian army out of its territory. The referendum will determine whether the region will stay aligned with Ethiopia or not.

152. The members of the separatist movement are engaged in some terrorist activities, although they so far have not attacked the oil installations. The central government has sent 15,000 troops and imposed a curfew to control the situation (*The New York Times,* March 24, 1992).

153. The territory in which the Cabinda population resides was delineated some 100 years ago on the basis of political and commercial considerations of Portugal and its colonial competitors. There was no regard for the boundaries of the populations, nor the pre-colonial histories. Therefore, it should not come as a surprise that Cabinda did not wish to remain within the territory of Angola upon the withdrawal of the Portuguese forces in 1975. See Henderson, p. 28.

154. The separatist movement is called the Front for the Liberation of the Enclave of Cabinda (FLEC). It is a movement composed of numerous factions that dates to the mid-1960s. According to a report in the *New York Times,* the Front gets little active help from the population, but rather benefits from "extensive passive support, based on the nations of Cabindan solidarity and distrust for the Luanda Government" (*The New York Times,* March 24, 1992). National elections are expected in mid- to late 1992, in which the impact of the recent joining of the separatists by two senior UNITA members (Fernandens and Nzanpuna) will be felt.

155. During the rule of the Portuguese, the status of the territory of Cabinda was ambiguous: the constitution listed it as a separate territory (rather than as part of Angola). However, administratively it was ruled from Luanda. After independence, the constitution did not treat it separately.

156. Self-rule for the region is being sought by the Movement for the Democratic Forces of Casamance.

157. The Kurds in Iraq are represented by two main groups both of which control guerilla forces; the Kurdish Democratic Party, and the Patriotic Union of Kurdistan. These two parties have tried to bury their differences in recent years and together with other smaller parties including the communist, socialist, and Marxist parties to form the Iraqi Kurdistan Front. It is noted that in 1946, with the help of the Soviets, a short-lived Kurdish Republic of Mahabad was set up in northern Iran (*The New York Times*, March 27, 1991).

158. In 1989, 60 percent of the population was in favor of some form of autonomy (*The Wall Street Journal*, May 25, 1990).

159. A poll taken in 1990 indicates a deeply divided population: 7 percent supported independence, while 48 supported statehood and 44 supported commonwealth status (*The New York Times*, October 11, 1990).

160. For a discussion of the incorporation of Latvia, Tadzhikistan, Georgia, Ukraine, and Tatarstan into the Soviet federation, see Nahaylo and Swoboda, *Soviet Disunion*.

161. The Soviet constitution did give its republics the right to self-determination and secession. This idea dates back to the "Declaration of the Rights of the Peoples of Russia," which proclaimed four principles, one of which is the right of the peoples of Russia to free self-determination, including secession (Nahaylo and Swoboda, p. 18). However, as in the case of Yugoslavia, no document explained the procedure that was to be followed in order to secede until 1990. At that time, the Supreme Soviet passed legislation entitled "On the Procedure for Deciding Questions Pertaining to the Secession of Union Republics from the Soviet Union" (for a discussion of this legislation, see Valery A. Tishkov, "The Soviet Empire Before and After Perestroika" in Rudolph and Good, eds., *Nationalism and Empire*.

162. Violent confrontation with the center was experienced when independence demonstrations in 1989 were suppressed, while violence in the region is ongoing in the struggle between the South Ossetians and the Georgians and their definitions of territory, borders, and sovereignty.

163. In 1782, in order to assure protection against invading Turkey and Iran, Irakly II asked for Russian protection of the Kartli-Kakhetia region (Georgian lands). The treaty of friendship between the two regions did not mean much, and in 1801, Alexander II annexed the region to the Russian Empire. The remaining lands were incorporated after the Russo-Turkish wars in 1811, 1829, and 1878.

164. See Nahaylo and Swoboda, p. 35.

165. In March 1992, 82 percent of eligible voters voted for separation from Russia and the establishment of a sovereign state. Sixty-one percent of the voters were in favor. (*The New York Times*, March 23, 1992).

166. Given that this is an autonomous region, therefore at a sub-republic level, the rights of self-determination laid out both in the constitution as well as the 1990 law of the Supreme Soviet pertaining to secession do not apply.
167. The secession of Slovenia was essentially peaceful, with the exception of a minor encounter with the federal army in July 1991, in the aftermath of its declaration of independence.
168. A coalition government was voted into power in the elections of 1990 with the platform of secession, or at least greater autonomy than existed in the federal organization of Yugoslavia during the last years of Tito's rule. Polls indicate that confederation had greater acceptance among the population than secession, at least prior to the military intervention of July 1991.
169. The Yugoslav constitution did allow for secession of its republics, although it did not spell out how this was to occur. In its preamble, it states, "The nations of Yugoslavia, proceeding from the right of every nation to self-determination, including the right to secession . . ." However, the constitution also stipulates that any alteration of borders associated with secession must be approved by all republics (see Milan Andrejevich, "Croatia and Slovenia Propose Separation of Yugoslav Republics," *Report on Eastern Europe* 2, no. 11, March 15, 1991, p. 27).
170. After World War II, Croatia voluntarily entered into the union with Serbia and Montenegro. It was on the losing side, and its options were assessed to be better as a part of the Kingdom of Serbs, Croats and Slovenes than a region within Austria.
171. The nationalist government of Tudjman was voted into power without the support of the majority of Croats (see *Danas,* May 1990). Nevertheless, when a referendum about independence was held in May 1991, over 90 percent of the population favored the dissolution of the present federal system and the establishment of a sovereign independent nation, linked in a loose confederation with Yugoslavia's other republics (*The New York Times,* May 20, 1991).
172. The Serbs of Krajina took offense at the anti-Serbian sentiment portrayed by the Tudjman government and refused to give up their arms during the summer of 1990; they barricaded their villages so as not to be accessible to the Croatian forces. Hostilities continued and intensified until the referendum of the Croats, at which time the Croats voted to secede from Yugoslavia. The Serbs of Krajina had no intention of seceding from Yugoslavia, and certainly not to once again live under a Croatian government similar to the one they experienced during World War II.
173. The Serbs of Krajina refused to be governed by a government that flew the same flag as the fascist government during World War II and consequently had its own referendum on May 12, 1991, to determine the population's desires pertaining to secession. It was clear that the sentiment was if Croatia secedes from Serbia, Krajina will secede from Croatia. Indeed, the overwhelming response of the population was in favor of joining the Republic of Serbia and remaining within Yugoslavia (on details of the referendum, see Jovan Ilic's essay in Ivanovic, *The Creation and Changes of the Internal Borders of Yugoslavia*). The war that broke out in June 1991 was not so much over the

right of Croatia to secede but rather the territory that they would be allowed to take with them. At the beginning of August 1991, the Croatian government drew up a plan offering its Serb minority key concessions it had sought, including home rule, control over the local police, and greater political power. However, it was too little and too late. The Krajina region has already set up its own government and proclaimed itself an autonomous region (*The New York Times*, August 1, 1991). The party that represents the Serbs in Croatia is the Serbian Democratic Party.

174. Although the Yugoslav constitution did allow for the secession of its republics, no such rights were shared with subrepublic units. This is very different from the Swiss constitution, for example, which allows for the secession at the subcanton level, but not for secession from Switzerland.

175. The validity of the Kosovar claim to independence rests on their political party and parliament. A document was signed in July 1990 by Kosovar delegates to the suspended parliament, declaring Kosovo a republic with "the same constitutional status as the other republics" (*The International Herald Tribune*, July 3, 1990). However, the Serbs claim that their parliament has no validity, since autonomy of the region was a false creation of Tito's aimed at decreasing the power of Serbia. Indeed, Serbia had a referendum in which the overwhelming majority voted to reincorporate Kosovo into Serbia and to reinstate the preexisting territorial and political structure. In June 1990 Serbia further passed a "special circumstances" law giving it power to take over from the regional authorities by suspending the Kosovo Assembly and Executive Council. Then, on May 25, 1992, the Kosovar population of Kosovo voted in a referendum on secession, and over 90 percent of the votes were in favor. The Serbian population did not partake in the vote (*The New York Times*, May 27, 1992).

176. As in the case of Krajina, subrepublic status did not warrant a region the right to secession.

177. There is no doubt that the Albanian government has provided moral support to the Kosovar cause in Kosovo, especially since Serbia has become involved in the war with Croatia and Bosnia. However, as of June 1992, the intervention has not been active.

178. During the Velvet Revolution, nationalist parties have emerged in Slovakia, including the Christian Democrats, the Public Against Violence, and the more radical Slovak Party of Freedom and National Party. The population is at present in favor of greater autonomy from the Czech lands, and the secessionary sentiment is on the rise: although a poll in late 1990 indicated that only 16 percent of the population supported full independence, events since March 1991 indicate support for secession is on the rise. (*The New York Times*, December 16, 1990, and March 15, 1991, and *The Wall Street Journal*, March 11, 1991).

179. The new constitution that is in the process of being formulated is going to have a provision for secession (for a discussion of the constitution under discussion, see Kirschbaum, "Slovakia in the Post-Communist Constitutional Process").

180. There have been clashes between the ethnic Hungarians and Romanians, as the former press for more autonomy, while the latter fear that these demands for autonomy would lead to a full-fledged separatist movement. This is feared because it is Romania's richest province.

181. The region of Transylvania was ceded to Romania in 1920 with the Treaty of Trianon, resulting in the giving to Romania of more territory than was left to Hungary (John F. Cadzow, Andrew Ludanyi, and Louis J. Elteto, p. 28).

182. The violence intensified after 1968.

183. Immediately at partition, it was clear that the division of support for this new administrative change would not be supported by some (see John Darby, "The Historical Background" in *Northern Ireland, The Background to the Conflict,* Belfast: Appletree Press, 1983).

184. The Sinn Fein party (the political arm of the Irish Republican Army), has the support of about 11 percent of the voters (*The New York Times,* April 28, 1991). Polls of the population indicate that the desire for independence is not wide-spread, even among the Catholic population; according to the Economic and Social Research Institute of Dublin, in 1979, 39 percent of Catholics in Northern Ireland favored unification, while 49 percent preferred to remain within the United Kingdom (C.C. O'Brien, *Neighbours,* London: Faber and Faber, 1980, p. 81).

185. Britain has no formal constitution.

186. Scotland was independent for several centuries before it was united voluntarily to England by the Act of Union of 1707. This was supported by a majority in the Scottish Parliament.

187. The Scottish National Party is the principal forum for independence. In 1991, they hold only 5 of the 72 parliamentary seats in Scotland; the parliament is dominated by the Labor Party, which has 48 seats. See Michael Keating "Territorial Management and the British State: The Case of Scotland and Wales," in Rudolph and Thompson, eds., *Ethnoterritorial Politics.*

188. Corsica was ruled as a colony by the Genoese Republic for four centuries until 1769, when it was annexed by France (this link was guaranteed in 1815 by the Treaty of Vienna).

189. The separatists have little backing among the population. Indeed, the Corsican Assembly elected in 1982 contained only seven autonomists, out of a total of 61 members. It is possible, however, that this low number may be attributed to the fact that some 42 percent of the Corsican voters boycotted the elections. See William Saffran, "The French State and Ethnic Minority Cultures: Policy Dimensions and Problems," in Rudolph and Thompson, eds., *Ethnoterritorial Politics,* p. 148.

190. It is estimated that the "autonomist" movements represent some 20 percent of the Corsican population. An opinion poll in 1990 indicated that 44 percent would like increased autonomy, while only 6 percent are in favor of full independence (*The Economist,* January 12, 1991).

191. The process of integration of the Basques Provinces took place over several centuries as a result of conquest, pact, and marriage (see Robert P. Clark, *The*

Basques: The Franco Years and Beyond, Reno: University of Nevada Press, 1979, chapter 1).

192. Opinion polls show that only one in four people favor independence of the Basque Provinces (*The New York Times,* January 28, 1990).

193. The present Spanish constitution forbids a referendum on secession.

194. Since the imposition of Castillian control over Catalonia, the two regions have not stopped feuding.

195. There are two leaders of Catalonia that are nationalist in orientation: Jordi Pujol, who has headed a coalition government (Convergence and Union Parties) for the past 12 years, is in favor of as much autonomy as possible within Spain, and Angel Colom, whose Republican Left Party wants outright independence. However, the separatist party received only 8 percent of the vote in 1992 (*The Economist,* March 21, 1992, p. 54).

196. In May 1967, the Eastern Region's assembly voted to secede from Nigeria. This amounted to the retention of all tax revenues paid in its territory, and the taking over of all federal services on its territory.

197. Katanga was part of the Belgian empire in Africa. As such, its union with its neighbors was involuntary. At the time of the Congolese independence from Belgium, little concern was paid to the aspirations of the Katanga population.

198. The Pakistani army was involved in the crisis. However, the war could have prolonged itself endlessly were it not for the entrance of India into the conflict, tipping the balance in favor of secession. See Nigel Harris, *National Liberation,* London: I. B. Tauris, 1990, pp. 199-209.

199. The union with West Pakistan was ardently supported by the Bengalis in 1945-46.

200. For a description of the party politics leading up to the secession of Bangladesh see Craig Baxter, "Pakistan and Bangladesh," in Shiels, ed., *Ethnic Separatism.*

201. The internal riots consisted of race riots between the ethnic Chinese, Malayas, and, to a lesser degree, the Indians.

202. The divorce between Malaysia and Singapore was initiated by the Malaysian government and consisted essentially of an expulsion. At the root of the dispute were two parties: the People's Action Party (PAP) was in power in Singapore, while the Alliance had control on the mainland. The two parties differed on many basic issues: the former was socialist, the latter conservative; the former wanted to protect all nationalities, the latter was a Malaysian party, and so on. See R. S. Milne and Diane K. Mauzy, *Singapore: The Legacy of Lee Kuan Yew,* Boulder: Westview Press, 1990, chapter 4.

203. The relations between Singapore and the Malaysian Federation deteriorated due to economic factors. Singapore had numerous economic grievances against the center that would have, in all likelihood, flowered into demands for secession over time. However, at the time of its expulsion from the federation, Singapore was concerned about its economic viability and thus did not actively consider secession (see chapter 5).

204. Although the Malaysian Federation did not provide for the secession of its constituent units, it did provide for the expulsion of its parts by a simple act of parliament. See B. H. Shafruddin, p. 26.

Notes to Chapter 2

1. Lee Buchheit, *Secession: The Legitimacy of Self-Determination*, New Haven: Yale University Press, 1978; Michael Burgess, ed., *Federalism and Federation in Western Europe*, London: Croom Helm, 1986; Donald Gelfand and Russell Lee, eds., *Ethnic Conflicts and Power: A Cross-National Perspective*, New York: John Wiley, 1973; Raymond Hall, *Ethnic Autonomy: Comparative Dynamics*, New York: Pergamon, 1979; Setin Rokkan and Derek Urwin, eds., *The Politics of Territorial Identity*, London: Sage Publications, 1982; Dov Ronen, *The Quest for Self-Determination*, New Haven: Yale University Press, 1979; Frederick Shiels, ed., *Ethnic Separatism and World Politics*, Lanham: University Press of America, 1984.

2. Naomi Chazan, ed., *Irredentism and International Politics*, Boulder: Lynne Rienner, 1991; Astri Suhrke and Lela Garner Noble, eds., *Ethnic Conflict in International Relations*, New York: Praeger, 1977; Judy Bartelsen, ed., *Nonstate Nations in International Politics: A Comparative System Analysis*, New York: Praeger, 1977; James Mayall, *Nationalism and International Society*, Cambridge: Cambridge University Press, 1990.

3. John Breuilly, *Nationalism and the State*, Chicago: Chicago University Press, 1985; Colin Williams, ed., *National Separatism*, Cardiff: University of Wales Press, 1982; Anthony Smith, *The Ethnic Revival*, London: Cambridge University Press, 1981; Leo Despres, ed., *Ethnicity and Resource Competition in Plural Societies*, The Hague: Mouton, 1975, among others.

4. Robert LeVine and Donald Campbell, *Ethnocentrism: Theories of Conflict, Ethnic Attitudes and Group Behavior*, New York: John Wiley 1972; Vanik Volkan, *Cypress—War and Adaptation: A Psychoanalytic History of Two Ethnic Groups in Conflict*, Charlottesville: University Press of Virginia, 1979.

5. Rupert Emerson, *From Empire to Nation: The Rise to Self-Assertion of Asian and African Peoples*, Cambridge, Mass.: Harvard University Press, 1960; Ali Mazrui, *Post-Imperial Fragmentation*, Denver: University of Denver (Center on International Race Relations), 1960; O. Jaszi, *The Dissolution of the Hapsburg Monarchy*, Chicago: University of Chicago Press, 1929; R. Hartshiorne "A Survey of the Boundary Problems of Europe" in C. C. Colby, ed., *Geographical Aspects of International Relations*, Port Washington, N.Y.: Kennikat Press, 1970; F. Czernin, *Versailles 1919*, New York: G. P. Putnam's Sons, 1964. Also, see the section on economic nationalism in the aftermath of the breakup of empires in Nigel Harris, *National Liberation*, London: I. B. Tauris, 1990, pp. 244-268.

6. Fredrik Barth, ed., *Ethnic Groups and Boundaries*, Boston: Little, Brown, 1979; Nathan Glazer and Daniel Moynihan, eds., *Ethnicity*, Cambridge: Harvard University Press, 1975.

7. Allen Buchanon, *Secession*, Boulder: Westview Press, 1991.

8. Mark McLaughlin, "Employee Secession: A Company's Rights When Staffers Leave and Clients Follow," *New England Business* 8, no. 19, November 17, 1986, pp. 58-59.

9. J. Anderson, "Nationalism and Geography" in *The Rise of the Modern State*, Brighton: Harvester Press, 1986; J. Agnew "Is there a Geography of Nationalism? The Case of Place and Nationalism in Scotland" in C. H. Williams and E. Kofman, eds., *Community Conflict, Partition and Nationalism*, London: Croom Helm, 1987; D. B. Knight, "Geographical Perspectives on Self- Determination," in P. Taylor and J. House, eds., *Political Geography: Recent Advances and Future Direction*, London: Croom Helm, 1984.

10. Walter Conner, "Nation Building or Nation Destroying?" *World Politics* 24, 1972, p. 342.

11. Frederick Shiels, "Introduction" in *Ethnic Separatism*.

12. See Smith, pp. 1-3.

13. This view is held by M. Hechter (*Internal Colonialism: The Celtic Fringe in British National Development, 1536-1966*, London: Routledge and Kegan Paul, 1975) and T. Nairn (*The Break-Up of Britain: Crisis and Neo-Nationalism*, London: New Left Books, 1977).

14. Miroslav Hroch, *Social Preconditions of National Revival in Europe*, Cambridge: Cambridge University Press, 1985; Beth Michneck, "Regional Autonomy, Territoriality, and the Economy" paper presented to the American Association for the Advancement of Slavic Studies, Washington, D.C., October 1990; Anthony Birch, *Nationalism and National Integration*, London: Unwin Hyman, 1989.

15. Christine Drake, *National Integration in Indonesia: Patterns and Policies*, Honolulu: University of Hawaii Press, 1989, p. 145.

16. E. J. Hobsbawm, *Nations and Nationalism Since 1780*, Cambridge: Cambridge University Press, 1990.

17. Immanuel Wallerstein, *Africa: The Politics of Independence*, New York: Vintage, 1961, p. 88.

18. Milica Zarkovic Bookman, *The Political Economy of Discontinuous Development*, New York: Praeger 1991.

19. James Buchanan and Roger L. Faith, "Secession and the Limits of Taxation: Toward a Theory of Internal Exit," *American Economic Review* 77, no. 5, December 1987.

20. John Wood, "Secession: A Comparative Analytic Framework," *Canadian Journal of Political Science* 14, no. 1, March 1981.

21. A. D. Smith, "Introduction: The Formation of Nationalist Movements," in *Nationalist Movements*, New York: Macmillan, 1976.

22. Peter Leslie, "Ethnonationalism in a Federal State: The Case of Canada," in Joseph Rudolph, Jr., and Robert J. Thompson, eds., *Ethnoterritorial Politics, Policy and the Western World*, Boulder: Lynne Rienner, 1989, p.47.

23. Ian Bremmer, "Fraternal Illusions: Nations and Politics in the USSR" paper presented to the American Association for the Advancement of Slavic Studies, Miami, 1991, p. 47; Albert O. Hirshman, *Exit, Voice and Loyalty*, Cambridge, Mass.: Harvard University Press, 1970.

24. Hobsbawm, p. 32.

25. The "Independence Criteria" include the following: degree of industrialization, degree of self-sufficiency, mineral resources, agricultural hard currency–earning potential, raw materials hard currency–earning potential, and business-mindedness. *The Soviet Union at the Crossroads: Facts and Figures on the Soviet Republics,* Deutsche Bank, Frankfurt, 1991.

26. Wei Ding, "Yugoslavia: Costs and Benefits of Union and Interdependence of Regional Economies," *Comparative Economic Studies* 33, no. 4, 1991.

27. C. M. Turnbull, *A History of Singapore 1819-1988,* Singapore: Oxford University Press, 1989, p. 288.

28. The distinction between the long run and the short run is relevant since most regions are able to survive in the long run after reconstruction and the formation of new economic relationships with the international economy and the ex-nation.

29. *The Wall Street Journal,* February 14, 1990.

30. A distinction is made between income and development: a region may be characterized by high income (often the result of a single lucrative resource) while, according to a variety of indicators, it is a less developed region.

31. The study by Ding uses the following eight variables in the estimation of viability among the Yugoslav republics: Gross Social Product (GSP), GSP per capita, population, imports as a proportion of GSP, external exports as a proportion of GSP, regional exports as a proportion of GSP, unemployment, and enterprise losses as a proportion of GSP.

32. In order to simplify measurement, wealth is assumed to be reflected in income per capita.

33. Tom Nairn, *The Break-Up of Britain,* London: New Left Books, 1977.

34. Milica Zarkovic Bookman, *The Political Economy of Discontinuous Development.*

35. William Beer, *The Unexpected Rebellion: Ethnic Activism in Contemporary France,* New York: New York University Press, 1980.

36. Michael Hechter, *Internal Colonialism: The Celtic Fringe in British National Development 1536-1966,* Berkeley: University of California Press, 1975.

37. Peter Alexis Gourevitch, "The Emergence of Peripheral Nationalisms: Some Comparative Speculations on the Spatial Distribution of Political Leadership and Economic Growth," *The Comparative Study of Society and History* 21, July 1979, p. 303-322.

38. Karl Deutsch, *Nationalism and Social Communication,* 2nd ed., New York: MIT Press, 1966, and *Nationalism and its Alternatives,* New York: Knopf, 1969; Samuel Huntington, *Political Order in Changing Societies,* New Haven: Yale University Press, 1968.

39. Connor, p. 344.

40. This view is attributed to Otto Bauer, and discussed in Alexander J. Motyl, "From Imperial Decay to Imperial Collapse: The Fall of the Soviet Empire in Comparative Perspective" in Richard L. Rudolph and David F. Good, eds.,

Nationalism and Empire: The Habsburg Empire and the Soviet Union, New York: St. Martin's Press, 1992, p. 28.

41. The word "usually" is used because the relationship between income per capita and education is not always positive, as was found by David Morawetz (*Twenty-five Years of Economic Development,* Baltimore: The Johns Hopkins University Press, 1977).

42. Development does not imply self-sufficiency in absolute terms, since the region might be linked to the international economy.

43. Few subnational regions seriously consider full autonomy, and instead their aim is the reintegration with other entities, so that the real question is how attractive they are to others that may wish to integrate with them.

44. The description of trade dependency by the author has appeared in "The Economic Basis of Regional Autarchy in Yugoslavia," *Soviet Studies* 42, no. 1, January 1990.

45. Oleh Havrylyshyn and John Williamson, "From Soviet Disunion to Eastern Economic Community?" *Policy Analyses in International Economics* 35, Washington: Institute for International Economics, 1991, p. 17.

46. The proposal was dropped when the state was offered better financial terms for federal grants. It is noteworthy that Western Australians had no culture of their own, nor were they a distinct ethnic group (see Birch, p. 65).

47. Clearly, this argument does not apply to private or unmandated flows (such as capital investment in low-income regions) since it is assumed those occur in pursuit of profit.

48. Frank Ley and Edwin M. Truman, "Toward a Rational Theory of Decentralization: Another View," *American Political Science Review* 65, March 1971, p. 88.

49. United Nations, *Decentralization for National and Local Development,* New York, 1962, p. 88, cited in Al-Agab Ahmed Al-Teraifi, "Regionalisation in the Sudan" in Peter Woodward, ed., *Sudan After Nimeiri,* London: Routledge, 1991, p. 92.

50. A discussion of deconcentration and devolution is not relevant in this study, but is contained in Al-Teraifi, pp. 92-93.

51. Frederick Pryor, *A Guidebook to the Comparative Study of Economic Systems,* Englewood Cliffs, N.J.: Prentice-Hall, 1985.

52. Havrylyshyn and Williamson, p. 8.

53. The problems associated with decentralization must be recognized, and they do in some cases outweigh the benefits. These include the fact that the local newly empowered bodies may begin to perpetuate local systems of oppression or that there may be increased inefficiencies and diseconomies. It may also, as will be discussed in chapter 8, lead to the alienation of minorities, as it fosters separatism by giving importance to the local units.

Notes to Chapter 3

1. The regional disparity in Papua New Guinea characterized by relative higher income of coastal regions, especially Bougainville, precedes the country's independence. The higher rates of growth are attributed to coastal export activity (K. Wilson, "Socio-economic Indicators Applied to PNG," *Yagl-Ambu* [Port Moresby] 2, no. 1, 1975).

2. The copper mine of Bougainville is responsible for 45 percent of the mainland's exports and 17 percent of the central government's revenue. *The Wall Street Journal,* January 3, 1990.

3. There are no statistics on the industrial classification of the labor force in Bougainville. As a result, the portion of the indigenous population that works in the organized sector for wages is used as a proxy, and this has been estimated to be 8.2 percent of the population. Moreover, according to government statistics, the Bougainville mines employ 4 percent of the total wage labor force of the country (Azeem Amarshi, Kenneth Good, and Rex Mortimer, *Development and Dependency: The Political Economy of Papua New Guinea,* Melbourne: Oxford University Press, 1979, pp. 133-4).

4. According to Griffin, Bougainvillians stand apart from the mainland insofar as they are significantly more educated than the average population, a fact attributed to the proliferation of missionary schools in the region. This has contributed to the positioning of Bougainvillians in all parts of the nation as well as in the important positions in administration, the army, and the police force (James Griffin, "Movements for Separation and Secession," in Anthony Clunies Ross and John Langmore, eds., *Alternative Strategies for Papua New Guinea,* Melbourne: Oxford University Press, 1973, p. 117).

5. Although according to some indicators, Tibet is better off than it was before the Chinese invasion (for example, health and education standards have risen), incomes have continued to lag behind those in the rest of China. *The New York Times,* October 7, 1990. Prior to Chinese investments and efforts to integrate the Tibetans, the region relied on herding, highland agriculture, and subsistence agriculture.

6. This refers to the value of output of agriculture and industry in 1984 and is the only number available (State Statistical Bureau, People's Republic of China, *Statistical Yearbook of China 1985*, Oxford University Press, 1985, p. 32).

7. Calculated by using gross value of output of agriculture and industry as value of total output (*Statistical Yearbook of China 1985,* p. 30).

8. This refers to 1984 (*Statistical Yearbook of China 1985,* p. 223).

9. The Chinese government built up a secular public-school network, and the region experienced a rapid growth in student enrollment (see George Ginsburg and Michael Mathos, *Communist China and Tibet: The First Dozen Years,* The Hague: Martinus Nijhoff, 1964). However, the instruction in the schools was in Han, replacing Tibetan as the educational language.

10. The principal economic activity, agriculture, is hampered by the geographical characteristics of the region. These contribute to naming the region the "Dry Zone," which is traditionally not as productive as the southern "Wet Zone" because of the nature of its monsoons.

11. In the Northern Province, the principal economic activity is agriculture, especially the cultivation of rice, onions, chilies, and tobacco. In the Eastern Province, agriculture is supplemented by extensive commercial activity in the coastal regions.

12. In 1977 the Northern and Eastern Provinces accounted for 7.6 percent of the entire manufacturing labor force, while they accounted for 13 percent of the total population (Chelvadurai Manogaran, *Ethnic Conflict and Reconciliation in Sri Lanka,* Honolulu: University of Hawaii Press, 1987, p. 136, Table 21).

13. This number is lower than the national average of 23.4 percent *illiteracy.* Manogaran, p. 123, Table 16.

14. The Economist, *The World in Figures 1981,* London: The Economist Newspaper, p. 190. In rupiahs, the local income per capita was Rp 141,000 in 1983 (M. Hadi Soesastro, "East Timor: Questions of Economic Viability," in Hal Hill, ed., *Unity and Diversity: Regional Economic Development in Indonesia Since 1970,* Singapore: Oxford University Press, 1989, p. 213) while that of the entire state is Rp 4,332,000 (Hall Hill and Anna Weidemann, "Regional Development in Indonesia: Patterns and Issues," in Hall Hill, ed., *Unity and Diversity,* p. 8, Table 1.1).

15. The Economist, p. 170.

16. Agriculture is the principal economic activity of the region. In addition to rice, the region also produces maize, and its principal export crop is coffee. It has no significant natural resources and is distant from centers of economic activity. However, the second largest sector of the economy, with respect to employment, is the government sector. See J. K. Metzner, *Man and Environment in Eastern Timor,* Canberra: Australian National University, Development Studies Center Monograph no. 8, 1977.

17. M. Hadi Soesastro, p. 213, Table 8.4.

18. Ibid., p. 217.

19. Christine Drake, *National Integration in Indonesia: Patterns and Policies,* Honolulu: University of Hawaii Press, 1989, Appendix I, p. 272. East Timor did not share the experience of some Asian regions, where extensive missionary activity resulted in high literacy rates (such as Kerala). Instead, significant strides were taken only after 1975, when 570 primary schools were built, along with 85 junior high schools and 29 high schools, a university, and a polytechnic institute (*The New York Times,* October 21, 1990). According to the World Bank, the Indonesian literacy rate was 74 percent in 1989 (The World Bank, *World Development Report 1991,* Oxford: Oxford University Press, Table 1).

20. The income data for the Indian states are taken from the Centre for Monitoring Indian Economy, reprinted in *The Economist,* May 4, 1991, p. 4 (survey). Similar relative incomes are observed for earlier years in The Reserve Bank of India, "Analysis of Estimates of State Domestic Product," in *Reserve Bank of India Bulletin,* September 1981.

21. V.K.R.V. Rao, *India's National Income 1950-1980*, New Delhi: Sage, 1983, p. 91, Table 7.1.
22. This refers to the average of 1976-78. During this time, the Indian average was 20.8 percent (Reserve Bank of India, p. 818).
23. This refers to 1971. Later statistics are not available since the subsequent census changed the classification of workers, thus preventing an estimation of the industrial sector. In 1981, for example, workers were classified into main and marginal, with large subdivisions in the agricultural sector.
24. This refers to 1981 (Government of Punjab, *Statistical Abstract of Punjab*, Chandigarh, 1984, Table 3.12).
25. V.K.R.V. Rao, *India's National Income*. Tea is one of India's principal exports, and Assam is responsible for the production of 60 percent of the nation's tea. It also produces 50 percent of the nation's total petroleum output and natural gas (Government of India, *India: A Reference Annual*, New Delhi: Ministry of Information and Broadcasting, 1983, pp. 476-77).
26. Government of India, *Statistical Abstract of India, 1972*, New Delhi: Central Statistical Organization, 1972.
27. No statistics are available for literacy in Assam since the census was prevented from occurring during the past two census years. The Indian literacy rate refers to 1989.
28. V.K.R.V. Rao, *India's National Income*.
29. Government of India, *Statistical Abstract of India, 1972*.
30. Government of India, *Statistical Abstract of India, 1984*, New Delhi: Department of Statistics, 1984, Table 225.
31. Smuggled items include agricultural, mineral, and forest products, as well as opium. The border ares where the Karen live are extremely rich in teak and are important to the Thai timber trade, which suffered disruption in the course of the insurgency.
32. The Karen rebels, along with several other ethnic peoples such as the Shan, Kachin, Mon, Arakanese, and others, control the smuggling trade that accounts for three billion dollars annually, or 40 percent of the state GNP (*Link* [New Delhi], January 6, 1991).
33. C. H. Harvie and J. C. Kleve, *The National Income of Sudan 1955/56*, Department of Statistics, Khartoum, 1959, p. 80.
34. Calculated from C. H. Harvie and J. C. Kleve, *National Income of Sudan*.
35. The regions of Southern Sudan, Equatoria, Upper Nile, and Bahr el-Ghazal have fertile land and oil deposits.
36. The education of the Southern Sudanese peoples was mostly done by the Christian missionaries; consequently, English was the principal language. Government education was sparse, even after independence, so that the north remains more highly educated than the south.
37. The Economist, p. 89.
38. This refers to Morocco, and is taken from the World Bank, Table 1.
39. The region contains few natural resources other than phosphates and aquifers. In addition, livestock is important in the economy.

40. Calculated from The Economist, pp. 83, 89.

41. This literacy rate refers to the Moroccan population.

42. Okbazghi Yohannes, *Eritrea: A Pawn in World Politics,* Gainesville: University of Florida Press, 1991, p. 268.

43. For the most part, Eritreans feel superior to the rest of Ethiopia. Much of this feeling stems from the benefits of colonization that they experienced in the forms of schools, industries, a press, political parties, et cetera. While Ethiopians are proud of the fact that they were never colonized, Eritreans in turn are proud of how they have benefited from the Italian presence.

44. The greatest source of income for this extremely impoverished agricultural land is the port of Massawa, the principal water gateway for Ethiopia. Trading and port facilities hold the greatest hope for this land, in which agriculture is highly underdeveloped both in the type of inputs as well as in the output. The was has also contributed to the low levels of agricultural production insofar as it has prevented the widespread distribution of high yielding varieties of seeds and has caused an erosion of top soil due to deforestation, since trees have been used for fuel.

45. Illiteracy in Ethiopia is 90 percent, although there are regional and ethnic variations. The most literate and educated portion of the population is the Amhara ethnic group, which accounts for 28 percent of the population while housing 40 percent of the student body. Following this group, the Eritreans are the most educated, largely because of the influence of the Italian colonial policy. In 1972 the Eritreans, who account for 7.1 percent of the population, contained 11.7 percent of the student enrollments (Edmond J. Keller, *Revolutionary Ethiopia,* Bloomington: Indiana University Press, 1988, p. 139).

46. Cabinda has little agriculture and virtually no manufacturing. However, its oil revenues make it a relatively high-income region, although, as in the case of Bougainville, how much the population actually benefits from this income is debatable. Wheeler and Pelissier discuss the "high standard of living" of Cabinda in Douglas Wheeler and Rene Pelissier, *Angola,* New York: Praeger, 1971, p. 221.

47. It might be inferred that the proportion of income from Cabinda is high because that is the principal source of oil in the state, and 45 percent of the state's exports consist of oil, thus indicating the economic importance of Cabinda in the state (The Economist, p. 56).

48. There are no data available, but given that there is virtually no manufacturing in the region, we may infer that the contribution of manufacturing to regional income is low.

49. See previous note. We may also infer that the employment in manufacturing is low.

50. The region has potential because it contains the most fertile soil in the country. However, it was not the recipient of government-sponsored agricultural investments for modernization and the development of cash crops, which were instead channeled into the north, where the dominant ethnic group, the Wolof, concentrated their power. Moreover, it was not the location of industrial or infrastructure development. If this seeming bias against the south were

eliminated, the fertility of the soil might create a basis for a lucrative agricultural sector.

51. There are no specific data available to the author. Secondary evidence may be used to infer that both industrial income and industrial employment in Casamance are low, since 85 percent of the country's industry is located in the area immediately surrounding Dakar (Rita Cruise O'Brien, "Introduction," in *The Political Economy Of Underdevelopment: Dependence in Senegal,* Beverly Hills: Sage, 1979, p. 20).

52. Ibid.

53. No breakdown of literacy by administrative region is available. According to Pfeffermann, rural illiteracy throughout all of Senegal is 95 percent. Casamance is mostly rural, with 57 percent of the population living in villages of less than 500 inhabitants (Guy Pfeffermann, *Industrial Labor in the Republic of Senegal,* New York: Praeger, 1968, p. 12). The literacy figure for Senegal (62 percent) takes into consideration the urban areas.

54. The Economist, p. 173.

55. During the 1970s, between 40 and 50 percent of Iraq's oil production was concentrated in the Kurdish regions, while during the Iraq-Iran war, this increased to 80 percent (Christina Moss Helms, *Iraq: Eastern Flank of the Arab World,* Washington: Brookings Institution, 1984, p. 15.

56. *The Economist,* February 10, 1990.

57. The Quebec economy rests on its diversified services, such as finance, real estate, insurance, retail and wholesale trade, construction, transportation, and telecommunications.

58. *The New York Times,* June 17, 1990.

59. Milica Zarkovic Bookman, *The Political Economy of Discontinuous Development,* New York: Praeger, 1991, p. 39.

60. Income statistics for Puerto Rico are taken from *The New York Times,* October 11, 1990.

61. As a result of the special status Puerto Rico enjoys, companies have relocated to the island to avoid paying taxes (and to take advantage of low wage labor). Hence the source of the island's prosperity, relative to other Caribbean nations, is this foreign investment. The tourist industry accounts for less than 10 percent of the island's income (while in Hawaii, it is close to 40 percent).

62. The Economist, p. 144.

63. This includes only manufacturing and construction (ibid., p. 143).

64. This was estimated on the basis of the World Bank estimate of Britain's income and the assessment of Birch, according to whom the gross domestic product per head in Northern Ireland was only 78 percent of that in the United Kingdom (Anthony Birch, *Nationalism and National Integration,* London: Unwin Hyman, 1989, p. 106).

65. Northern Ireland has a higher income per capita than the Republic of Ireland but a lower income per capita than England. Hence, its relative position depends upon what region it is compared with.

66. This refers to 1961 (Sabine Wichert, *Northern Ireland since 1945*, London: Longman, 1991, p. 57).

67. Ibid.

68. There is no pattern of regional specialization since there are no particular endowments of resources that give a regional comparative advantage, other than oil.

69. John Firn, "Industrial Policy," in Donald MacKay, ed., *Scotland 1980: The Economics of Self-Government*, Edinburgh: Q Press, 1977, p. 64.

70. This refers to 1974. Ibid., p. 65, Table 4.1.

71. Republique Française, Ministère de l'Economie, des Finances et de la Privatisation, *Annuaire Statistique de la France 1986*, Paris: Institute National de la Statistique et des Etudes Economiques, 1986, p. 340.

72. Basque Provinces and Catalonia together produce a large proportion of Spain's steel, textiles, and natural gas, and are thus considered the country's most valuable industrial areas (Louis Snyder, *Global Mini-Nationalisms: Autonomy or Independence?* Westport: Greenwood Press, 1982, p. 113).

73. According to Zirakzadeh, two-thirds of Spain's integrated steel plants are located on the Basque coast and one-third of Spain's shipyards, trawlers, and supertankers. Over half of all steel produced in Spain is made in the Basque Provinces, as are two-thirds of all machine tools (Cyrus Ernesto Zirakzadeh, *A Rebellious People*, Reno: University of Nevada, 1991, p. 21).

74. Generalitat de Catalunya, *Catalunya Endavant*, Barcelona, 1982, p. 110.

75. The source is the Generalitat de Catalunya, reprinted in *The Economist*, March 21, 1992, p. 54.

76. The Catalonian GNP per capita is 125 percent of the total Spanish GNP.

77. It produces 18 percent of the GNP with 15 percent of the population. *World Press Review* (reprinted from *Veja*, Brazil), April 1992, p. 24.

78. Generalitat de Catalunya, p. 101.

79. Ibid., p. 109.

80. Calculated from Table 3.2 and World Bank, Table 1.

81. World Bank, p. 205.

82. Servizio Stampa Della Giunta Regionale Della Lombardia, *La Lombardia Si Presenta: 2*, La Geografia Milan: Arti Grafiche Reina, 1980, p. 6.

83. Istituto Nazionale di Statistica, *Le Regioni in Cifre*, Roma: Istat, 1992, Table 7.2.

84. Income statistics for the former Soviet Union refer to 1989 and are taken from The World Bank, *Transition* 2, no. 2, February 1991, p. 5.

85. Statistics pertaining to regional share of total income refer to 1988 and are taken from The World Bank, *Transition* 3, no. 6, June 1992, p. 9.

86. Gertrude E. Schroeder, "Nationalities and the Soviet Economy," in Lubomyr Hajda and Mark Beissinger, eds., *The Nationalities Factor in Soviet Politics and Society*, Boulder: Westview Press, 1990, p. 48.

87. Ibid.

88. Ibid.

89. Ibid.

90. Wei Ding, "Yugoslavia: Costs and Benefits of Union and Interdependence of Regional Economies," *Comparative Economic Studies* 33, no. 4, 1991, p. 25.

91. This number from the World Bank refers to 1989. A comparison with the number provided from Ding may be inappropriate since taken from a different source, so the following data in dinars is provided. Slovenia: 30.391 billion dollars; Yugoslavia: 15.208 billion dinars (Savezni Zavod za Statistiku, *Statisticki Godisnjak Jugoslavije,* Beograd, 1985. The numbers refer to constant 1984 dinars).

92. Savezni Zavod za Statistiku, *Statisticki Godisnjak Jugoslavije,* Beograd, 1990, Table 201-1. The same source applies to Croatia and Kosovo below.

93. Ibid., Table 205-1. The same source applies to Croatia and Kosovo below.

94. Ibid., Table 203-9. The same source applies to Croatia and Kosovo below.

95. Ibid., Table 203-12. The same source applies to Croatia and Kosovo below.

96. Ding, "Yugoslavia."

97. This refers to per capita regional income in 1981 (Jovan Ilic, "Characteristics and Importance of Some Ethno-National and Political-Geographic Factors Relevant for the Possible Political-Legal Disintegration of Yugoslavia," in Stanoje Ivanovic, ed., *The Creation and Changes of the Internal Borders of Yugoslavia,* Beograd: Srbostampa, 1991.

98. Some sections of Krajina have fertile agricultural land and high agricultural yields; however, there is great regional disparity.

99. This number refers to the percent of Croatia's income, rather than Yugoslavia's income (Ilic, p. 89).

100. The explanation for such a high proportion of income from the secondary sector is that the total income provided by the official statistics does not include income from private agriculture (which in these regions is not insignificant). Savezni Zavod za Statistiku, *Statisticki Godisnjak Jugoslajive,* Beograd, 1990, Table 3.3.

101. Ibid.

102. Ding, "Yugoslavia."

103. This incredibly high proportion of income from industries may be explained by the following: Kosovo has much mining, and the industrial classification provided by the Yugoslav official statistics includes mining (in dinars [constant, in thousands], the total income is 859, while that derived from industries is 388). See Savezni Zavod Za Statistiku, *Statisticki Godisnjak Jugoslavije,* Beograd, 1990, Table 205-1.

104. The economic statistics for Slovakia are taken from *PlanEcon Report,* vol. 6, no. 52, December 20, 1990.

105. Slovakia's contribution to the national income is less than proportional to its population of 31 percent (Robert Dean, *Nationalism and Political Change in Eastern Europe: The Slovak Question and the Czechoslovak Reform Movement,* Monograph Series in World Affairs, no. 1, University of Denver, 1973, p. 22).

106. According to Schopflin, Transylvania "has traditionally been an underdeveloped area—this was so even when the region was part of Hungary" (George Schopflin, "Transylvania: Hungarians Under Romanian Rule," in Stephen Borsody, ed., *The Hungarians: A Divided Nation*, New Haven: Yale Center for International and Area Studies, 1988, p. 136.

107. International Bank for Reconstruction and Development, *The Economic Development of Nigeria*, Lagos: Federal Government Printer, 1954, p. 398. This indicates that the income per capita of the eastern region, which at the time included South Cameroons also, was at the national average. That persisted until the exclusion of the Cameroons and the increase in the importance of petroleum.

108. At the time of independence, the southerners, including the Ibos, tended to be among the most literate peoples in Africa (see Walter Schwartz, *Nigeria*, London: Pall Mall Press, 1968). Their high levels of education may be attributed to the extensive missionary activity in the region. The literacy rate for Nigeria refers to 1985, and thus is not strictly applicable to the period of the Biafran secession.

109. According to Epstein, the mineral production of Katanga represented almost one-half of the nation's earnings (Howard Epstein, *Revolt in the Congo 1960-64*, New York: Facts on File, 1965, p. 177). This was also found by Fernand Hernan, *Courrier Africain*, March 4, 1960.

110. According to Gerard-Libois, 36.2 percent of the Katanga labor force was employed outside the "traditional milieu" (agriculture and small-scale household industries). See Jules Gerard-Libois, *Katanga Secession*, Madison: University of Wisconsin Press, 1966, p. 4.

111. It has been claimed that by the end of the 1950s, Belgian Congo was enjoying the highest literacy rate in tropical Africa (see Howard Epstein, *Revolt in the Congo*). The literacy rate for the state refers to Zaire in 1985.

112. M. R. Sharif, *Modern Economic Development of Pakistan*, Dacca: Mullick Brothers, 1966, p. 306.

113. Ibid.

114. Relative to West Pakistan, East Pakistan had a lower income per capita. Indeed, per capita income as a multiple of per capita income of East Pakistan (1.00) is 1.63 for West Pakistan (and 1.27 for India). Azizur Rahman Khan and Mahabub Hossain, *The Strategy of Development in Bangladesh*, New York: St. Martin's Press, 1990, p. 7.

115. For lack of statistics on previous years, this figure is included, although it refers to 1981-82 (Khan and Hossain, p. 68, Table 4.1).

116. Ibid.

117. Ibid., p. 4, Table 1.1. In 1985, the literacy rate of Bangladesh was 67 percent.

118. Amina Tyabji, "The Economy," in Jon S. T. Quah, Chan Heng Chee, and Seah Chee Meow, eds., *Government and Politics of Singapore*, Singapore: Oxford University Press, 1985, p. 25.

119. At the time of its independence, Singapore's economy was based in services. The manufacturing sector was developed only in the subsequent decade.

120. Tyabji, p. 29, Table 2.1.

121. This number refers only to ethnic Chinese, but it is used as a proxy for the entire labor force since the Chinese make up 75 percent of the population. Chiew Seen-King, "The Socio-Cultural Framework of Politics," in Jon S. T. Quah, Chan Heng Chee, and Seah Chee Meow, eds., *Government and Politics of Singapore*, p. 62, Table 3.6.

122. The first number refers to ethnic Chinese, and the second to ethnic Malays (Chiew Seen-Kong, p. 59, Table 3.5).

123. See Harold Lydall, *Yugoslavia in Crisis*, Oxford: Clarendon Press, 1989, p. 188.

124. *The Wall Street Journal*, January 3, 1990.

125. Ibid.

126. Griffin, p. 118.

127. Reserve Bank of India, "Analysis of Estimates of State Domestic Product," *Reserve Bank of India Bulletin*, September 1981.

128. The Economist, May 26, 1990.

129. SVIMEZ, Associazione Per Lo Sviluppo Dell'Industria Nel Mezzogiorno, *Rapporto 1990 Sull'Economia Del Mezzogiorno*, Bologna: il Mulino, 1990.

130. *The New York Times*, April 19, 1990.

131. Gertrude Schroeder, "Nationalities and the Soviet Economy," in Lubomyr Hajda and Mark Beissinger, eds., *The Nationalities Factor in Soviet Politics and Society*, Boulder: Westview Press, 1990, p. 47.

132. Deutsche Bank, *The Soviet Union at the Crossroads: Facts and Figures on the Soviet Republics*, Frankfurt: Deutsche Bank, 1990, p. 19.

133. Z. Baletic and B. Marendic, "The Policy and System of Regional Development," in Rikard Lang, George Macesich, and Dragan Vojnic, eds., *Essays on the Political Economy of Yugoslavia*, Zagreb: Informator, 1982, p. 251.

134. Henryk Flakierski, *The Economic System and Income Distribution in Yugoslavia*, Armonk, N.Y.: M. E. Sharpe, 1989.

135. Copper accounted for 70 percent of the region's mining production (Rene Lemarchand, *Political Awakening in the Belgian Congo*, Berkeley: University of California Press, 1964, p. 234.

136. Gerard-Libois, p. 3.

137. Fernand Hernan, *Courrier Africain*, March 4, 1960, also cited in Gerard-Libois, p. 5.

138. The relationship between population characteristics and economic growth was drawn by Lucien Pye, *South East Asia's Political Systems*, Englewood Cliffs, N.J.: Prentice-Hall, 1967.

139. Simpson describes this phenomenon in detail. In 1978 the GDP per capita of Northern Ireland was 77 percent of that of the United Kingdom, while it was 12 percent higher than that of the Republic of Ireland. John Simpson, "Economic Development: Cause and Effect in the Northern Ireland Conflict," in John Darby, ed., *Northern Ireland: The Background to the Conflict*, Belfast: Appletree Press, 1983, pp. 94-100.

140. Slovakia was the recipient of a large infusion of capital in an effort to industrialize the region. This is discussed in detail in chapters 4 and 5.

141. World Bank, p. x.

142. United Nations Development Programme, *Human Development Report 1991*, New York: Oxford University Press, 1991.

143. David Morawetz, *Twenty-five Years of Economic Development*, Baltimore: Johns Hopkins University Press, 1977.

144. Simon Kuznets, *Modern Economic Growth: Rate, Structure and Spread*, New Haven: Yale University Press, 1966.

145. World Bank, Table 1, as well as *PlanEcon Report* 6, no. 52, December 28, 1990, p. 6.

146. Servizio Stampa Della Giunta Regionale Della Lombardia, *La Lombardia Si Presenta: 2*, La Geografia Milan: Arti Grafiche Reina, 1980, p. 6.

147. *The New York Times*, June 24, 1990.

148. International Bank for Reconstruction and Development, *The Economic Development of Nigeria*, Lagos: Federal Government Printer, 1954, p. 398.

149. Like Quebec, Bougainville, Punjab, and Katanga, the economic and geographical position of Biafra relative to the national union was largely determined by colonial rulers insofar as they directed investment according to their policies, which in this case focused on the exploitation of natural resources.

150. Harold Nelson, *Nigeria: A Country Study*, Washington: U.S. Government Printing Office, 1982, p. 162.

151. For a breakdown of the value of imports and exports that pass through the various ports of Nigeria, see Reuben Udo, *Geographical Regions of Nigeria*, Berkeley: University of California Press, 1970, p. 61.

152. Indeed, when the Eritrean army captured the port city, the tide of the war began to change since its blockade had a devastating impact on the Ethiopian economy.

153. No statistics are available for Assam, where the census was prevented from occurring during the past two census years (Government of India, *Statistical Abstract of India*, New Delhi: Department of Statistics, 1984, Table 225).

154. The Indian average is 20.8 percent in 1976-78. These data are from *Reserve Bank of India*, p. 818.

155. Milica Zarkovic Bookman, p. 82, Table 4.3.

Notes to Chapter 4

1. Forty-five percent of total foreign exports derive from the copper mine (*The Wall Street Journal*, January 3, 1990).

2. The economy of Papua New Guinea is highly regulated with respect to prices. Goodman, Lepani, and Morawetz describe the price policy in wages, commodities, and manufactured goods, indicating a price structure that supports efforts at import substitution (Raymond Goodman, Charles Lepani, and David

Morawetz, *The Economy of Papua New Guinea,* Canberra: The Australian National University, Development Studies Center, 1985, pp. 59, 89, 128).

3. Despite the central government's large involvement in the economy of the region, the central policy of export promotion, coupled with the largely foreign ownership of the mines, resulted in the exclusion of copper from trade barriers. See Philip Daniel and Rod Sims, *Foreign Investment in Papua New Guinea: Politics and Practices,* Canberra: The Australian National University, Pacific Research Monograph no. 12, 1986.

4. There is evidence of capital infusions from the center in the development of the mines. However, most of the capital to finance construction and operation came from foreign sources.There has been no indigenous input of technology on the island.

5. The copper mines in Bougainville employed labor from other parts of Papua New Guinea, due to the lack of sufficient locals that were either willing or able to satisfy the demands of the foreign managers. This inflow of migrants had far reaching effects on the established economy, land rights, social network, et cetera. (Azeem Amarshi, Denneth Good, and Rex Mortimer, *Development and Dependency: The Political Economy of Papua New Guinea,* Melbourne: Oxford University Press, 1979, p. 209).

6. This outflow consists of copper and other mined goods.

7. The central government established the Mineral Resource Stabilization Fund to accumulate receipts from the mining sector and to redistribute them, through the national budget, to the rest of the economy in other locations. See Herb Thompson, "Economic Theory and Economic Development in Papua New Guinea," *Journal of Contemporary Asia* 21, no. 1, 1991, p. 62.

8. Tibet's principal outputs are wool and wool products, and its proportion of total Chinese production in these items is low (.16 percent), and therefore it is inferred that the proportion of Tibet's output in foreign exports is also low (State Statistical Bureau, People's Republic of China, *Statistical Yearbook of China 1985,* Oxford: Oxford University Press, 1985, pp. 350, 503).

9. As before World War II, Tibet's principal trading partners were the Chinese, followed by the Indians. Its exports consisted of mostly wool, as well as hides, furs, yak tails, and musk. The construction of roads following the Chinese invasion enabled faster and greater trade.

10. The central Chinese government has freely used pricing policy on goods traded with Tibet in order to achieve its goals. For example, when the United States began its boycott of Tibetan wool, Beijing responded by purchasing Tibet's entire wool production and paying three times the market price for it, with the goal of endearing the population (A. Tom Grunfeld, *The Making of Modern Tibet,* Armonk, N.Y.: M. E. Sharpe, 1987, p. 110).

11. The central government invested heavily in the system of transportation within Tibet. This road system of over 21,000 kilometers linked villages and capitals of adjoining countries and Chinese provinces, enabling the intensification of trade. Industrial development, funded from the center, proceeded much more slowly during the cultural revolution, but increased dramatically thereafter, both in the urban and rural areas. Technological innovation came in the form

of the telephone and telegraph in 1952, a coal mine in 1958, and a blast furnace in 1959. In the decade from 1964-1975, the number of industrial enterprises increased from 67 to 250 (Grunfeld, p. 175). In addition, the Tibetan diaspora has transferred money into the region.

12. Much to the chagrin of the Tibetans, the Chinese policy of assimilation entailed the in-migration of the Han population to teach, build, and partake, as cadres, in the reconstruction and administration of Tibet. No accurate numbers exist on their size. Lucien Pye has claimed that in 1976, the Han had come to outnumber the Tibetans two to one (Lucien Pye, "China: Ethnic Minorities and National Security," *Current Scene* (Hong Kong) 14, no. 12, 1976, pp. 6-7).

13. Tibet does not pay taxes to the central government, but instead gets a yearly inflow of $275 million in subsidies (*The New York Times*, October 7, 1990). One-third goes to salaries, and the rest goes for infrastructure, health, and education.

14. It is inferred that the region's exports are low since the principal exports of the entire state are tea and rubber (38 and 16 percent respectively), neither of which are produced in the Tamil regions (The Economist, *The World in Figures 1981*, London: The Economist Newspaper, p. 197).

15. For lack of other statistics on internal trade, the following information is offered: In the early 1970s, the Northern Province produced over 15 percent of the island's chilies and 83 percent of the domestic requirements for onions, implying that their principal produce was exported to the southern regions of the state (Chelvadurai Manogaran, *Ethnic Conflict and Reconciliation in Sri Lanka*, Honolulu: University of Hawaii Press, 1987, p. 138).

16. The government of Premadasa in 1988 introduced a series of changes in an effort to create a free market economy based on the export promotion policies of the four dragons of East Asia. In that effort, rules on foreign investment were liberalized and exchange controls eliminated. The price controls and subsidies on fertilizer, fuel, rice, cooking oil, and other products have been lifted (*The Wall Street Journal*, April 4, 1991).

17. First, prior to 1977, the importation of agricultural goods that were produced domestically was subject to a ban. This was lifted in 1977, causing great hardship to the cultivators of crops such as onions. Second, there has been a liberalization during the last years of the civil war: in 1988, tariffs have been simplified and capped at 50 percent, while import licenses were vastly reduced (*The Wall Street Journal*, April 4, 1991).

18. Manogaran describes the lack of central government investment in the Tamil regions. He claims that "since the 1950s, no . . . major industries have been established in the region." (Manogaran, p. 139).

19. The central government sponsored migration of people (largely Sinhalese) into the sparsely populated areas of the Northern and Eastern Provinces (Robert Kearney, "Ethnic Conflict and the Tamil Separatist Movement in Sri Lanka," *Asian Survey* 25, no. 9, September 1985, p. 904).

20. This is the only available figure. It refers to international exports in 1982, in tons per 100 population (Christine Drake, *National Integration in Indonesia:*

Patterns and Policies, Honolulu: University of Hawaii Press, 1989, p. 297, Appendix 2).

21. This refers to exports into Indonesian provinces in tons per 100 population in 1982 (Drake).

22. The local government is in charge of regulating the prices of numerous goods produced in East Timor, including coffee (M. Hadi Soesastro, *East Timor: Questions of Economic Viability, in Unity and Diversity: Regional Economic Development in Indonesia Since 1970,* Singapore: Oxford University Press, 1989, p. 225).

23. There is evidence that since 1975, the Indonesian government made investments into the infrastructure such as roads and bridges, as well as education and health. Indeed, transfers from the government for various economic and social programs were the highest in the state throughout the 1980s. In 1985–86, this inflow was seven times that of the Java provinces (Soesastro, p. 219).

24. There is evidence of in-migration into East Timor of two different groups of individuals. First, as part of a transmigration project, the central government has engaged in the moving of retired or near-retired army personnel, largely for the purposes of national security (Timothy Babcock, "Transmigration: The Regional Impact of a Miracle Cure," in Colin MacAndrews, ed., *Central Government and Local Development in Indonesia,* Singapore: Oxford University Press, 1986 p. 179). Second, in order to satisfy manpower demands, as well as to relieve population pressures in overpopulated regions, the government sponsored migration. This included the movement of active government personnel into the public sector of the region (20 percent of the population of East Timor employed in the public sector).

25. The region remains a deficit producer in numerous agricultural goods and must rely on imported goods such as rice and maize. Although these goods are not used in production, they are food crops necessary for the survival of the population.

26. Two studies have found that the inflow of funds into East Timor from the central budget is positive, and indeed, that on a per capita basis, it is the highest in the state. See Soesastro, pp. 219-220 (he claims that in the peak year of central government transfers, 1985-86, the equivalent of 85 percent of regional GDP was transferred). Similar results were found by Drake (p. 165). For a discussion of transfers from the center to the regions, see Anne Booth "Efforts to Decentralize Fiscal Policy: Problems of Taxable Capacity, Tax Effort and Revenue Sharing" in Colin MacAndrews, ed., *Central Government and Local Development in Indonesia.*

27. Foreign exports of wheat, the primary agricultural product of Punjab, have been insignificant during the 1970s: between 2 and 13 percent of the product, depending on the year, was destined for international or local use. A breakdown of those two categories is not available (see Milica Zarkovic Bookman, *The Political Economy of Discontinuous Development,* New York: Praeger, 1990, p. 151).

28. In 1970-71, the percent of wheat destined to national markets was 85 percent, in 1975-76; 77 percent and in 1977-78, 98 percent (see Bookman, p. 151).

29. There are two aspects to the price policy of India. First, some prices are biased against agricultural goods in an effort to promote industrialization. Second, food price policy has been characterized by a complex system of price supports. One of these, procurement prices, was created so as to provide the producer with incentive to produce while guaranteeing low-income consumers the possibility to purchase grain at a "fair" price (see T. Prabha, "Government Intervention and Marketed Surplus Disposal: A Case Study of Tamil Nadu," *Economic and Political Weekly* 19, nos. 51-52, 1984).

30. The Indian government, in its effort to satisfy domestic demand for grains, placed a ban on the export of wheat applicable in all years except those of surplus production.

31. Punjab is a unique case among developing regions insofar as it was extremely successful in adapting foreign technology to the local environment. The green revolution package of technologies, introduced in the mid-1960s, was adapted to local conditions because of an infrastructure capable of this transformation (see M. Zarkovic, *Issues in Indian Agricultural Development*, Boulder: Westview Press, 1987).

32. With the exception of peak agricultural periods, during which migrant day laborers from adjoining states in-migrated, Punjab has satisfied its labor demand with its own population (see P. Bardhan, *Land, Labor and Rural Poverty*, New York: Columbia University Press, 1984).

33. The author has made a study (discussed below in the text) of the interregional flows by observing the share of central taxes, the central budget transfers, and central assistance for annual plans in India, and found that the evidence is inconclusive. The high-income states, including Punjab, do not consistently contribute more to the center than the low-income states, nor do they receive less than others.

34. Given that the region's principal output is tea, and that tea is India's principal export, we might infer that the portion of the region's output for the international markets is high.

35. Given that Assam produces half of the total national petroleum and natural gas needs of India, it may be inferred that most of Assam's supply is exported to other Indian states.

36. Regulations restrict the sale of petroleum and natural gas in the open market unless there has been satisfaction of national demand.

37. Three of the four tea plantation owners are foreign, and they are responsible for the import of capital and technology in this crucial segment of the Assamese economy.

38. According to per capita taxes paid to the center, Kashmir ranks among the highest of the Indian states, while according to contribution to state plans, the percentage of Indian contribution is high (relative to the region's population). See I. S. Gulati, ed., *Center-State Budgetary Transfers*, Bombay: Oxford University Press, 1987.

39. For decades, the Karens have dominated trade across the important Thai-Burmese border. This black market thrives to compensate for the inability of local or state production to satisfy consumptive and industrial needs (Wolf estimated

that 80 percent of the consumer goods entering the country did so through the Karen areas (Jim Wolf, "Asia's Civilized Insurgents," *Bangkok Post,* November 9, 1983, p. 5). With respect to exports, lumber is exported from the Karen regions, mostly to Thailand. It is estimated that in the Karen region, 65 saw mills are engaged in preparing teak for export (Ronald Renard, "The Karen Rebellion in Burma," in Ralph R. Premdas, S.W.R. de A. Samarasinghe, and Alan B. Anderson, *Secessionist Movements in Comparative Perspective,* New York: St. Martin's Press, 1990, p. 107).

40. See previous note.

41. The central government of Myanmar ignored the black market trade involving the Karen regions for decades until 1983, at which point they imposed restrictions in order to divert some of this lucrative trade to themselves.

42. Since the mid-1980s, hundreds of thousands of refugees from the Karen regions have out-migrated, mostly to Thailand, thus depleting the labor force.

43. The region's trade with Thailand and other Asian countries mostly consisted of the export of raw materials such as teak, precious stones, and cattle.

44. No statistics are available pertaining to the flow of revenue across the Karen borders. However, it is known that in order to compensate for the lack of sufficient central government inflow, the Karen have imposed their own tax on trade. A 5 percent tax is assessed on all goods crossing their area (Ronald Renard, p. 107).

45. The southern regions are net exporters of water and oil to the northern regions (see Charles G. Gurdon, "The Economy of Sudan and Recent Strains," in Peter Woodward, ed., *Sudan After Nimeiri,* London: Routledge, 1991).

46. It was calculated that the three southern regions, which contain 30 percent of the population, received only 7 percent of government investment (Tim Niblock, *Class and Power in Sudan,* Albany: State University of New York Press, 1987, p. 145, Table 4.10). Johnson points out that the southern region of Equatoria was the recipient of foreign development funds, especially in the agricultural sector (Douglas H. Johnson, "North-South Issues," in Peter Woodward, ed., *Sudan After Nimeiri,* p. 124.

47. The population exodus, in terms of refugees that have been forced out of the region by the famine and the civil war, has depleted the local labor force.

48. See note 45.

49. Johnson notes that the regional government of Southern Sudan "was always short of money" and depended on monthly inflows of cash from the Central Ministry of Finance (Johnson, p. 124). Also, see Al-Agab Ahmed Al-Teraifi, "Regionalisation in the Sudan: Characteristics, Problems and Prospects," in Woodward, ed., *Sudan After Nimeiri,* pp. 100-106.

50. As a result of the ongoing conflict with Morocco, large numbers of people have migrated out of Western Sahara and become refugees, depleting the labor force.

51. The principal raw material, phosphates, flows out of the region. However, guerrilla activity has decreased this export dramatically during the late 1970s and 1980s.

52. The price interventions that most affect the Eritrean economy are those pertaining to port duties and agriculture. In the case of the former, these were kept artificially low in order to reduce costs to the center, which had no access to the waterways other than the Eritrean ports. When the Eritreans came to power in May 1991, they eliminated this price bias and proceeded to extract income from the ports. With respect to agricultural prices, these were set by the Agricultural Marketing Corporation so as to provide food at cheap prices for the urban population, mostly of Addis Ababa. This policy hurt the Eritrean farmers. See Okbazghi Yohannes, *Eritrea: A Pawn in World Politics*, Gainesville: University of Florida Press, 1991, p. 266.

53. There has been an inflow of capital from the Arab countries to support the war and capital from Eritrean exiles, mostly residing in Sudan (Tekle Mariam Woldemikael, "Political Mobilization and National Movements: The Case of Eritrean Peoples Liberation Front," *Africa Today* 38, no. 2, 1991, p. 36).

54. Before the end of the civil war in 1991, large numbers of people left the labor force and fought in the war. It is estimated that some 95,000 people were in the Eritrean Front. However, after the war, these people are flooding the labor markets. One way in which the government is coping with this labor surplus problem is by requiring all non-Eritreans to vacate the region (*The New York Times,* magazine section, September 22, 1991).

55. The predominant part of the oil produced in Cabinda is exported into the international market. Indeed, the 330,000 barrels a day that are produced account for some 60 percent of Angola's export earnings (*The New York Times,* March 24, 1992).

56. Ibid.

57. The American Gulf Oil Company invested capital and technology into the region.

58. The inflow of technical staff occurred in order to support the functions of the oil company in Cabinda. The migrations of the indigenous populations have not been recorded, since the Bakongo tend to flow between Zaire and northern Luanda and Cabinda.

59. This refers to the outflow of crude oil.

60. No exact data are available; however, given that the production in Casamance is not of cash crops, but rather corn, rice, and cotton (for regional industry), it is likely that those crops, unlike export crops such as groundnuts, are not exported in the international markets.

61. Trade between the north of Senegal and Casamance has been hampered due to the lack of a transportation network and the reality of geography. In other words, the shortest way from Casamance to Dakar is through Gambia, an unwilling transit partner. The building of a bridge and dam in Gambia in the 1980s has significantly increased the possibilities for interregional trade within Senegal. For a discussion of these trade constraints, see Sheldon Gellar, *Senegal: An African Nation Between Islam and the West,* Boulder: Westview Press, 1982, p. 74.

62. In the agricultural sector there exists a government marketing system that distorts prices, often to the disadvantage of the Casamance cultivators (see Rita

Cruise O'Brien, "Introduction," in *The Political Economy Of Underdevelopment: Dependence in Senegal,* Beverly Hills: Sage, 1979, p. 22).

63. The development of tropical cash crops in Casamance was identified by the World Bank as a potential for capital absorption that would have lucrative returns (Donald B. Cruise O'Brien, "Ruling Class and Peasantry in Senegal, 1960-1976: The Politics of a Monocrop Economy," in O'Brien, ed., *The Political Economy Of Underdevelopment,* p. 212).

64. The principal flow of migrants tends to be from the rural areas of Casamance to the urban center of Dakar, despite the perceptions of discrimination against their entrance into the labor market in a language that they do not speak. There is some evidence of migration into Casamance (when groundnut expansion occurred in some pockets of the region), as well from Casamance by temporary laborers into regions that have different agricultural cycles (see Martin Klein, "Colonial Rule and Structural Change: The Case of Sine-Saloum," in O'Brien, *The Political Economy of Underdevelopment,* pp. 80 and 86).

65. Cotton production is expanding rapidly to feed into the single most important industry, textile production. In this way, the dependency of Casamance on the imports of cotton is eliminated (ibid., p. 84).

66. Ninety-eight percent of Iraq's exports consist of crude oil (1978). Since the area surrounding Kirkuk is among the highest oil-producing regions, it may be inferred that a large portion of those exports have originated in the Kurdish region (The Economist, p. 174).

67. Especially during the time of the Ba'th authority in Baghdad, the flow of financial resources into the Kurdish areas was, according to Helms, substantial. Funds were provided for hospitals, farms, housing projects, and so on. (Christina Moss Helms, *Iraq: Eastern Flank of the Arab World,* Washington: Brookings Institution, 1984, p. 33).

68. The outflow of raw materials, in the form of oil, is the largest outflow from the region.

69. *The Wall Street Journal,* April 13, 1990.

70. Although the trade with Canada, especially Ontario, is large in absolute numbers, as a proportion of total exports it is low, especially in comparison with the proportion directed to international markets (77 percent).

71. Various macroeconomic policies of the central government are unacceptable to the Quebec government, among them central intervention in interest rates that keeps them high and thus slows down investment and production, and the policy of an artificially high Canadian dollar that negatively affects Quebec's competitiveness in the world markets.

72. There is evidence of little economic benefit from the center. According to the Frazier Institute in British Columbia, the outflow from the province to the federal government is roughly equal to what it gets back in various social payments and government contracts. Indeed, the net flow from the center has been calculated at a mere $300 per year per head (Quebec manages its own social security and pension fund), certainly not sufficient to create dependency on the center (*The New York Times,* June 24, 1990). Some even argue that during 1986-90, Quebec was a donor province, giving more to the federal

government than it got in return (*The Wall Street Journal,* April 13, 1990). Leslie and Simeon claim that the data are inconclusive in this respect (Peter Leslie and Richard Simeon, "The Battle of the Balance Sheets," in Richard Simeon, ed., *Must Canada Fail?,* Montreal: McGill-Queens University Press, 1977).

73. The principal outputs of Puerto Rico are chemicals, crude oil, and machinery, and these are not aimed for domestic markets.

74. Presently, Puerto Rico does not have the right to create its own barriers to trade and enter into trade agreements without the approval of the federal government.

75. In 1989 there was $22 billion in private investment on the island. Most of this was capital from U.S. companies attracted to the region because of its special tax benefits.

76. The majority of the Puerto Ricans residing outside of the island are forced to do so for lack of adequate employment opportunities on the island. Indeed, unemployment on the island was 14.6 percent in 1989, twice that of the mainland (*The Philadelphia Inquirer,* January 6, 1991).

77. There has been an inflow of raw materials in order to supply inputs for the industrial concerns that have proliferated in the island, such as the chemical and pharmaceutical industries.

78. The island receives $6 billion per year in federal funds, while its commonwealth status implies that the population does not pay federal taxes (*The Philadelphia Inquirer,* January 6, 1991).

79. "The small size of the domestic market dictated an export-oriented production which in turn tended to result in light industries with relatively low transport costs": Sabine Wichert, *Northern Ireland since 1945,* London: Longman, 1991, p. 58.

80. Ibid.

81. Northern Ireland's agriculture benefited from price guarantees and subsidies and its secure access to the British market. The importance of these price interventions are recounted by Wichert, p. 59.

82. There has been a sporadic inflow of capital from the rest of United Kingdom. However, the inflow that has made a great impact on the economy is the recent capital from foreign sources, mostly due to the success Ireland has achieved in attracting overseas moves and therefore entering the sphere of service export production. See R. R. MacKay, "Regional Policy," in Donald MacKay, ed., *Scotland 1980: The Economics of Self-Government,* Edinburgh: Q Press, 1977, p. 191.

83. During 1961-71, 6.9 per 1000 of Roman Catholics and 2.8 of non-Catholics emigrated from Northern Ireland (John Simpson, "Economic Development: Cause of Effect in the Northern Ireland Conflict," in John Darby, ed., *Northern Ireland, The Background to the Conflict,* Belfast: Appletree Press, 1983, p. 102, Table 4.13).

84. Northern Ireland has few natural resources to fuel development and expansion of industry, and hence depends on an inflow of resources. However, due to the transportation costs and separateness (due to its geography), these are not forthcoming. See Wichert, p. 58.

85. John Darby (p. 92): "It is indisputable that Northern Ireland, as a relatively unprosperous region, has received a net inflow of government funds over and above its own tax payments."

86. McGilvray claims that there are no precise data on trade with the rest of the United Kingdom, but he claims that Scotland has a high degree of trade dependence and is extremely interlinked with the U.K. economy (J. W. McGilvray, "Economic Policy and Management," in MacKay, ed., *Scotland 1980*, p. 52.

87. As in Ireland, there has been some inflow of capital from the rest of the United Kingdom and significant inflow from foreign sources. See R. R. MacKay, p. 191.

88. Scotland has been unable to absorb labor for years, resulting in a consistent out-migration of its labor force. See J. W. McGilvray, p. 49.

89. The outflow of raw materials pertains to oil.

90. According to Birch, the citizens of Scotland contribute less than average to government revenues but enjoy public services that are more expensive than average. Indeed, central government expenditures per head in 1968-69 were 42 percent higher in Scotland than in England (Anthony H. Birch, *Nationalism and National Integration*, London: Unwin Hyman, 1989, p. 84).

91. According to Clark, one of the Basque Provinces, Navarra is taxed at special rates and is given more local autonomy than other regions to gather taxes (Robert P. Clark, *The Basques: The Franco Years and Beyond*, Reno: University of Nevada Press, 1979, p. 221).

92. There has been both an influx of capital and technology into the Basque regions as well as an outflow into the rest of Spain. According to Clark, technological innovation for the Basque industries has been largely introduced from abroad, while simultaneously the Basque Provinces constitute "a significant source of private investment capital for the rest of Spain" (Clark, pp. 220, 223).

93. According to Buchanon, the revenue derived from the Basque area by the government of Spain is approximately three times greater than what it infuses into that region. (Allen Buchanon, *Secession*, Boulder: Westview Press, p. 105). According to Clark, the Basque Provinces contribute 13 percent of Spain's taxes, so that their per capita tax burden is twice the national Spanish average (Clark, p. 220).

94. Generalitat de Catalunya, p. 116. Moreover, Catalonia exports 23 percent of total Spanish exports (*The Economist,* March 21, 1992, p. 54).

95. Generalitat de Catalunya, p. 116.

96. Catalonia is one of the largest recipients of direct foreign investment in Spain (see Generalitat de Catalunya, p. 160).

97. Catalonia contributes more to the center than it gets back. It is estimated that of every three pesetas sent to Madrid, only two come back (*World Press Review* [reprinted from *Veja*], April 1992, p. 24).

98. Estimated on the basis of data in Istituto Nazionale di Statistica, *Le Regioni in Cifre,* Roma: Istat, 1992, Table 12.6.

99. Lombardy absorbed migrant labor, especially from the labor-surplus regions of the south, and especially during the 1960s and 1970s.

100. Lombardy pays 25 percent of the national taxes, while it receives only 18 percent of that back in the form of various services. (*The New York Times*, June 24, 1990).

101. The trade statistics for the former Soviet republics are taken from the sources listed at the bottom of Table 4.2.

102. The ex-Soviet regional economies were reaping the benefits of subsidies that enabled production and consumption at lower rates than would be the case if it were purchasing them on the free market. For example, the Bridai Collective Farm in Lithuania had been paying 34 rubles for a ton of oil, and upon withdrawal from the USSR, that was estimated to increase to the equivalent of 74 rubles in hard currency (*The Wall Street Journal*, February 14, 1990). Independence and the removal of price distortions would cut regional GNPs dramatically: Hanson estimated that the Baltic states would reduce their GNP by ten percent in the first year of adoption of world prices (Philip Hanson, quoted in *The Economist*, October 20, 1990, Survey: The Soviet Union, p. 9). With independence, the former republics continued to subsidize their own economies by imposing various export and import restrictions (IMF Economic Review, Common Issues and Interrepublic Relations in the Former USSR, Washington: IMF, 1992).

103. The existence of foreign sources of capital in the region is shown by the fact that 39 joint ventures were registered in April 1990 (Deutsche Bank, *The Soviet Union at the Crossroads*, Frankfurt: Deutsche Bank, 1990, p. 47, Appendix 3).

104. See Bahry for an explanation of inflows into all the Soviet regions in this table (Donna Bahry, "The Evolution of Soviet Fiscal Federalism," in Rachel Denber, ed., *The Soviet Nationality Reader*, Boulder: Westview Press, 1992, p. 314). She describes how the determination of how much of revenues is kept within the region depends upon the regional level of development. For example, the higher deductions (from payments to the center) went to the less developed republics, so that regions such as Tadzikhistan and the Tatar Autonomous Region kept almost 100 percent of some taxes, while regions such as Latvia had to give close to 50 percent of their receipts to the all-union budget.

105. Although only one joint venture was registered in April 1990 (Deutsche Bank, *The Soviet Union*), the region was a recipient of industrial funds from the Soviet center. See Bahry, p. 312.

106. Forty-one out of 1,542 joint ventures were registered in Georgia in April 1990 (ibid.).

107. Ukraine has been the recipient of 99 out of the total 1,542 joint ventures registered in April 1990.

108. Tatar Autonomous region exports more oil to the rest of the Soviet Union than it imports. *The Economist*, September 7, 1991, p. 46.

109. As a less developed region, it too received an inflow of industrial capital from the center, although the exact proportion of this inflow relative to internally generated income varied over time. For a discussion of this variation, without data, see Bahry, "The Evolution of Soviet Fiscal Federalism."

110. There has been an inflow of non-Tatar peoples, mostly Russians, into Tatar Autonomous Region. This group has been mostly concentrated in the capital,

Kazan, which is over 50 percent Russian. Indeed, in 1991, 43 percent of the population of the entire region is Russian.

111. Tatar Autonomous Region produces 600,000 barrels of oil per day, roughly the same as Algeria.

112. Estimates of the spatial destination of Slovenia's products indicate that they are almost evenly split between the international markets, the Yugoslav markets, and the regional markets (Milica Z. Bookman, "The Economic Basis of Regional Autarchy in Yugoslavia," *Soviet Studies* 42, no. 1, 1990).

113. Pricing policy has often been in favor of industrial goods, at the expense of agricultural goods.

114. Yugoslavia engaged in policies of export promotion, due to the high demand for foreign currency.

115. Evidence indicates that Slovenia is the principal recipient of foreign technology, which embodies the transfer of both know-how and equipment and is measured by foreign investment and collaborative contracts among domestic and foreign firms. At the same time, it is the most self-sufficient region within Yugoslavia with respect to technology. It has the most qualified labor force and the highest concentration of investment in science and research in the nation (and training tends to be associated with technological innovation). See Bookman, chapter 9.

116. Although from World War II until 1981, Slovenia was a net population absorber, the percentage of the population that were migrants remained relatively low (1960s: 0.8 percent of population; 1970s: 2.2 percent of the population) (Savezni Zavod za Statistiku, *Saopstenje*, no. 365, Beograd, 1984). According to Prout, migrants form an insignificant proportion of the Slovenian labor force, mostly the unskilled or semiskilled laborers (Christopher Prout, *Market Socialism in Yugoslavia*, Oxford: Oxford University Press, 1985, p. 135). However, Schrenk estimates that 20 percent of total employment in Slovenia is performed by workers of other ethnic groups not permanently settled in the region (Martin Schrenk, Cyrus Ardalan, and Nawal A. Tatawy, *Yugoslavia: Self-Management Socialism and the Challenges of Development*, Baltimore: Johns Hopkins University Press, 1979, chapter 10).

117. There is evidence that some 50 percent of Slovenian foreign imports are in the category of raw materials (Statisticki Zavod za Statistiku, *Statisticki Godisnjak Jugoslavije*, Beograd, 1985 (Table 218-3), 1986 (Table 218-3), and 1987 (Table 219-3). At the same time, trade in raw materials never exceeded 3.3 percent of wholesale trade (Bookman, *Political Economy*, p. 180). This leads to the conclusion that there was much local input into industry.

118. Slovenia received close to 40 percent of the total Yugoslav grants for investments from federal sources, while paying only 18.5 percent of the Federal Fund (ibid., chapter 11). There may be other payments that have been incurred, but data for these is not available to the author.

119. This number refers to the percent of total trade that is accounted for by foreign trade, not the percent of regional production that is destined for foreign markets (Savezni Zavod za Statistiku, *Statisticki Godisnjak*, Belgrade 1990, Table 220-5).

Thus, the entries for Croatia and Kosovo are not comparable with the entry for Slovenia.

120. This refers to wholesale and retail trade. See preceding note.

121. Croatia's participation in the Federal Fund is approximately 25 percent (during the 1980s), while its benefit from investment funds from federal sources is approximately the same (25.6 percent of the Yugoslav credits in 1987). Bookman, *Political Economy,* chapter 11.

122. Given that Krajina is largely agricultural, the same policies apply to its food products as to those from Vojvodina, which that were described by the author (Bookman, "The Economic Basis of Regional Autarky"). Namely, the export of all foodstuffs, with the exception of wheat and corn in deficit years, is encouraged with export subsidies.

123. The population of Krajina has been on the decrease, due to the out-migration of the Serbian population. This is true both in absolute numbers and a proportion of the population of Croatia, and the proportion of the Serbian population in Croatia. (In 1971, the population of Krajina made up 6.5 percent of the Croatian population, and this percentage dropped to 5.8 in 1981 (Jovan Ilic, "Characteristics and Importance of Some Ethno-National and Political-Geographic Factors Relevant for the Possible Political-Legal Disintegration of Yugoslavia," in Stanoje Ivanovic, ed., *The Creation and Changes of The Internal Borders of Yugoslavia,* 1991, p. 89).

124. See note 119 for Croatia.

125. See note 120 for Croatia.

126. There has been an inflow of capital and resources into Kosovo in an effort to develop the region as part of the Yugoslav regional development plans, especially during the 1960s and 1970s. See text of chapter 4.

127. There has been a simultaneous inflow and outflow of population to and from Kosovo. The inflow has been mostly of illegal Albanians: this has been reported in the popular press, but official estimates are not available to the author (according to Dragnich and Todorovich, between 200,000 and 240,000 Albanians entered the region in the aftermath of World War II). At the same time, Serbian residents have been leaving the region (Dragnich and Todorovich estimate this to be 100,000 during World War II, and between 150,000 and 200,000 during 1961-81). This migratory pattern (together with the high fertility rates among the Kosovars) has altered the demographic picture of Kosovo. See Alex N. Dragnich and Slavko Todorovich, *The Saga of Kosovo,* Boulder: East European Monographs, 1984, p. 158.

128. Kosovo has been linked to the more developed regions of Yugoslavia mostly by the provision of raw materials for manufacturing. Indeed, Slovenian imports of raw materials largely originate in Kosovo.

129. The regional proportion of investments into Kosovo exceeds the regional proportion of payment to the Federal Fund (from which it mostly benefits). Bookman, *Political Economy,* chapter 11.

130. Given the largely agricultural and subsistence base of the Slovak economy during the Austro-Hungarian Empire and the interwar period, the region did not generate its own capital. Its principal source of capital was the center, which

during the course of 1949-65 contributed over one-third of its allocations to Slovakia (See Milica Zarkovic Bookman, "Economic Issues Underlying Secession: The Case of Slovenia and Slovakia," *Communist Economies and Economic Transformation* 4, no. 1, March 1992).

131. Slovakia is a net out-migrating region, as employment opportunities in the growing sectors of the Czech economy attracted manpower. Steiner estimated that tens of thousands of Slovaks were forced to emigrate to the Czech lands for employment, while Koctuch claims that the oversupply of labor in Slovakia is on the order of 200,000 people (Eugen Steiner, *The Slovak Dilemma,* Cambridge: Cambridge University Press, 1973, p. 134; Hvezdon Koctuch, *The Economic and Social Development of Slovakia,* Bratislava, 1968, quoted in Steiner, p. 136).

132. Dean claims that raw materials were brought from Slovakia to the Czech lands for manufacturing, and then returned as finished products for sale (Robert Dean, *Nationalism and Political Change in Eastern Europe: The Slovak Question and the Czechoslovak Reform Movement,* Denver: Monograph Series in World Affairs, no. 1, University of Denver, 1973).

133. The Slovak population of 33 percent received 38.5 percent of the federal budget in 1990 (*The New York Times,* May 18, 1990). However, Kosorin argues that Slovakia contributes 19 billion crowns to state offices but receives only 17 in return. He argues that the Slovak economy received from Prague 115 billion crowns in funds from taxes, and that if it were independent, it would collect 200 billion crowns. This is taken from Stanislav J. Kirschbaum, "Slovakia in the Post-Communist Constitutional Process," paper delivered to the American Association for the Advancement of Slavic Studies, Miami, November 23, 1991, p. 12.

134. Verdery claims that, as a result of the economic priorities set by all the governments from the Hapsburgs to the Communists, industry has been preferred to agriculture. (Catherine Verdery, *Transylvanian Villagers, Three Centuries of Political, Economic and Ethnic Change,* Berkeley: University of California Press, 1983, p. 356). The economy of the Transylvanian region has suffered in pricing biases that were aimed in providing foodstuffs and raw materials to the urban population and industrial needs at lower prices.

135. Schopflin describes the investments of the Romanian government into the area of Transylvania and claims that the sum invested there was "considerable." Just 22 factories were built in Covasna and Harghita between 1966 and 1975 alone (George Schopflin, "Transylvania: Hungarians under Romanian Rule," in Stephen Borsody, ed., *The Hungarians: A Divided Nation,* New Haven: Yale Center for International and Area Studies, 1988, p. 136).

136. The data on this out-migration is unclear. Secondary evidence points out that population movements in Romania are part of the minority or industrialization policy of the central government. This implies that no citizen is allowed to relocate without specific permission. However, in the effort to break up the Hungarian minority, the government has consistently assigned Hungarian graduates to jobs outside their native communities, while Romanians are brought into the area to fill positions that could be filled by Hungarians (Bulcsu

Veress, "The Status of Minority Rights in Transylvania: International Legal Expectations and Romanian Realities," in John F. Cadzow, Andrew Ludanyi, and Louis J. Elteto, eds., *Transylvania, The Roots of Ethnic Conflict,* Kent: Kent State University Press, 1983, p. 285).

137. Approximately one-half of the petroleum reserves of Nigeria are concentrated in what was the Eastern Region, and earnings from oil in 1970 were four-fifths of all export earnings (Harold Nelson, *Nigeria: A Country Study,* Washington: U.S. Government Printing Office, 1982, p. 162).

138. The Ibo population was culturally predisposed for high levels of achievement, which are related to the technological capacity of the region. Indeed, they were more educated and had adopted aspects of European political systems, technology, and values. In short, they became more modern than their counterparts in the north. Hence, they were more adaptable to absorbing and creating technology.

139. The Ibos had to migrate to urban centers outside of their region to make use of greater employment opportunities, most often in the civil service.

140. This outflow refers principally to oil.

141. Prior to the increased importance of oil in the national economy, regional revenues derived from federal payments were allocated on the basis of contribution from the region. The Eastern Region was at a disadvantage. Then, when oil was discovered, this system of allocation was reversed, greatly angering the government of the Eastern Region. See Kenneth Post and Michael Vickers, *Structure and Conflict in Nigeria 1960-1966,* London: Heinemann, 1974, p. 55.

142. Mining in Katanga represented 80 percent of Congolese mining production, and the region was the sole producer within Congo of copper, cobalt, silver, and platinum. (Howard Epstein, *Revolt in the Congo, 1960-64,* New York: Facts on File, 1965, p. 178). This 80 percent contributed strongly to ranking the Congolese production of copper at 8 percent of global production. The region also contains most of the world deposits of cobalt and industrial diamonds.

143. At the time of independence, the Katanga's mines were in the hands of a single foreign company, the Union Minière du Haut-Katanga, which invested immense amounts of capital and technology into an obviously lucrative region. It covered an area of some 20,000 square kilometers, and was one of the world's largest producers of cobalt and uranium and the world's third largest producer of copper. See Rene Lemarchand, *Political Awakening in the Belgian Congo,* Berkeley: University of California Press, 1964, p. 234.

144. Newcomers from adjoining regions (mostly from Kasai) migrated into Katanga in search of employment and were often recruited by the mining companies.

145. This outflow refers to mineral resources.

146. The only estimate of interregional flows that was available to the author claims that while Katanga contributes 50 percent of the center's earnings, its share of central budgetary expenditure is some 20 percent (Jules Gerard-Libois, *Katanga Secession,* Madison: University of Wisconsin Press, 1966, p. 5).

147. Raw jute, which is grown almost exclusively in East Pakistan, is the country's most important foreign exchange earner, accounting for 60 percent of total export earnings in 1957-58 (M. R. Sharif, *Modern Economic Development of Pakistan*, Dacca: Mullick Brothers, 1966, p. 320). From 1948-49 to 1966-67, East Pakistan had a surplus in its foreign trade balance, largely due to this jute export. However, it is claimed that this jute was exported into international markets by the West Pakistanis, who acted as exporters and traders, thus buying the jute in local currency while earning foreign currency for its resale (Harun-or-Rashid, "Bangladesh: The First Successful Secessionist Movement in the Third World," in Ralph R. Premdas, S.W.R. de A. Samarasinghe, and Alan B. Anderson, *Secessionist Movements in Comparative Perspective*, New York: St. Martin's Press, 1990, p. 88).

148. Some of East Pakistan's manufactured goods were traded in West Pakistan (such as matches and paper), but mostly the region exported its goods, such as jute and jute manufactures, into the international markets (see preceding note). The principal international market that it sold to, India, was a closer trading partner than West Pakistan (Azizur Rahman Khan and Mahabub Hossain, *The Strategy of Development in Bangladesh*, New York: St. Martin's Press, 1990, p. 103).

149. The central government discriminated in its protection of various goods. In the case of jute, it issued licenses in order to keep the supply up when it varied due to weather conditions, for example. In so doing, it managed the inflow of foreign currency. This obviously had an impact on the production of other crops and the diversification of the East Pakistani agricultural sector.

150. Import duties existed on goods to be imported by the East Pakistani government for manufacturing. See Sharif, pp. 161-162.

151. Sharif indicates that there has been a consistent inflow of capital into East Pakistan from both the center as well as foreign sources but that this inflow was always lower than that of West Pakistan, despite the larger population in the East. For example, with respect to internal funding for investment into industry, West Pakistan got 57.9 crores rupees (1964-65) while East Pakistan received 32.6; with respect to foreign involvement in industries, the numbers are 27.5 and 11.8 respectively. Sharif, pp. 274 and 145.

152. There were two sources of out-migration from Bangladesh, both due to the high population pressure on scarce employment, as well as the density of population (922 per square mile), pressure on social services, and infrastructure. One destination of migrant flow was the sparsely populated region of West Pakistan (population density: 138 per square mile), in response to incentives supplied by a resettlement scheme. The second outflow of population was into India, the Philippines, Indonesia, Singapore, and South and East Africa in search of employment. With the proliferation of oil-related industries in the Middle East, that region became an attractive destination.

153. The principal cash crop grown in East Pakistan is jute, while the major manufacturing industry is jute manufacture. Therefore, the principal input into that industry is grown domestically. See Sharif, p. 153.

154. According to government statistics, in 1960-61, tax receipts in East Pakistan amounted to 19.1 crores Rs. while those of the West were 26.3 crores Rs. At the same time, the distribution of central revenues was as follows: East Pakistan received 14.5 crores Rs. while West Pakistan received 23.0 crores Rs. (Sharif, pp. 284, 281).

155. Initially, Singapore had the benefit of tax-free importation of raw materials. However, since the rest of the federation was also industrializing, it protected itself from goods manufactured in Singapore by introducing a tariff (C. M. Turnbull, *A History of Singapore 1819-1988,* Singapore: Oxford University Press, 1989, p. 279).

156. During the period of federation, there was no free trade between Malaysia and Singapore, and restrictions increased following Singapore's independence as a result of Malaysia's desire to protect its industries and its ports (R. S. Milne and Diane K. Mauzy, *Singapore, The Legacy of Lee Kuan Yew,* Boulder: Westview Press, 1990, p. 131).

157. After independence, Singapore wooed foreign investment to stimulate industrialization. It supported these efforts by legislation that would make foreign investment attractive to foreigners (Turnbull, p. 295). However, in the process, Singapore became very dependent on capital and technology from the industrialized countries.

158. Given the fact that the Singapore's economy was more active than that of its neighboring regions, it attracted migrants in search of labor. Despite strict immigration policies, this resulted in migrant workers accounting for 12 percent of the labor force in 1972 (Turnbull, p. 297).

159. At the time of federation, financial guarantees were given to Singapore whose leaders feared the region would bleed in center-state relations. Indeed, the agreement called for special center-state financial relations, which Singapore insisted had to be renegotiated on a yearly basis, in case its contribution became too large (B. H. Shafruddin, *The Federal Factor in the Government and Politics of Peninsular Malaysia,* Singapore: Oxford University Press, 1987, p. 23).

160. The following statistics were printed in *The Wall Street Journal,* April 17, 1990, as well as *Newsweek,* March 26, 1990. Also see Frederic T. Harned, "Lithuania and the Lithuanians," in Zev Katz, Rosemarie Rogers, and Frederic Harned, eds., *Handbook of Major Soviet Nationalities,* New York: Free Press, 1975.

161. Among these, Vladimir Capelik, "Anti-Monopoly Policy in the USSR," paper presented to the IIASA Conference on Soviet Economic Reform, Sopron, Hungary, July 1990, and quoted in Havrylyshyn and Williamson, p. 21.

162. V. Cao Pinna, *Analisi delle Interdipendenze Settoriali di un Sistema Economico,* Torino: Boringhieri, 1958; M. Di Palma, *L'Analasi Delle Interdipendenze Strutturali Strumento Per Una Politica di Industrializzazione,* Roma: Comitato dei Ministri per il Mezzogiorna, Quaderni di Studi e Ricerche, no. 2, 1968.

163. Bruno Ferrara, *Nord-Sud, Interdipendenza di Due Economie,* Milano: Franco Angeli Editore, 1976.

164. *PlanEcon Report* 6, nos. 31, 32, 33, August 17, 1990, p. 6.

165. Alice Teichova, *The Czechoslovak Economy 1918-1980,* London: Routledge, 1988, p. 25.

166. Ibid., p. 15.

167. Eugen Steiner, *The Slovak Dilemma,* Cambridge: Cambridge University Press, 1973, p. 134.

168. Hvezdon Koctuch, *The Economic and Social Development of Slovakia,* Bratislava, 1968 (quoted in Steiner, p. 136).

169. Milica Z. Bookman, "The Economic Basis of Regional Autarchy in Yugoslavia," *Soviet Studies* 42, no. 1, January 1990.

170. I. Bicanic, "Fractured Economy," in Dennis Rusinow, ed., *Yugoslavia: A Fractured Federalism,* Washington: The Wilson Center Press, 1988; C. Ocic, "Integracioni i Dezintegracioni Procesi u Privredi Jugoslavije," *Marksisticka Misao* 4, 1983. The study by Ding uses data compiled from the Yugoslav press to show that trade with other republics accounts for roughly one-third of Slovenia's trade (Wei Ding, "Yugoslavia: Costs and Benefits of Union and Interdependence of Regional Economies," *Comparative Economic Studies* 33, no. 4, 1991, p. 22).

171. Clearly, there is a great difference between products, ranging from 5 percent of production exported to foreign markets (textiles), 37 percent of foodstuffs, 41 percent chemical, and 50 percent machinery. These data refer to 1985 (Bookman, "The Economic Basis of Regional Autarchy," Table 4).

172. Ibid., p. 102.

173. During the 1960s, 0.8 percent of the population were migrants, whereas during the 1970s, this number increased to 2.2 percent. (*Saopstenje*).

174. Prout, p. 135.

175. Schrenk, et al., *Yugoslavia: Self-Management Socialism and the Challenges of Development,* Baltimore: Johns Hopkins University Press, 1979, p. 29.

176. Savezni Zavod za Statistiku, *Statisticki Godisnjak Jugoslavije,* Beograd 1987, Table 207-2.

177. In 1986, 24 percent; in 1985, 22 percent. In addition, Slovenia is also the largest exporter of "highly manufactured goods," amounting to 22 percent of the national volume in 1986 (ibid., Table 218-3).

178. E.A.A.M. Lamers, *Joint Ventures Between Yugoslav and Foreign Enterprises,* Tilburg: Tilburg University Press, 1976, p. 129.

179. *The Wall Street Journal,* April 13, 1990.

180. *The Wall Street Journal,* January 3, 1990.

181. *The Economist,* January 20, 1990, p. 36.

182. James Griffin, "Movements for Separation and Secession," in Anthony Clunies Ross and John Langmore, eds., *Alternative Strategies for Papua New Guinea,* p. 118.

183. However, most of the capital to finance construction and operation of the mines came from foreign sources.

184. Most of this research was published in the following: M. Zarkovic, *Issues in Indian Agricultural Development,* Boulder: Westview Press, 1987.

185. Punjabi institutions were highly successful in adapting HYV seeds in the 1950s and producing strains of seeds locally.

186. This number varies with the years. These numbers are taken from the Government of Punjab, *Punjab Statistical Abstract,* Chandigarh: Department of Statistics, 1984, Tables 23.1, 7.8, and 6.3.

187. A comparison of local, procurement, and international prices of wheat is contained in Milica Zarkovic, "Linkages With the Global Economy: The Case of Indian and Yugoslav Agricultural Regions," *Peasant Studies* 16, no. 3, 1989, Table 5, p. 151.

188. Government of India, *India, a Reference Annual,* New Delhi: Ministry of Information and Broadcasting, 1983, pp. 476-77.

189. As Bahry points out correctly, center-region relations are not static over time, nor is the relative economic position of regions within the state (Bahry, p. 305).

190. Due to data shortcomings, different flows are observed in the various states: for example, tax flows in India, and federal budget and fund flows in Yugoslavia. The federal budget in Yugoslavia is also funded by taxation, hence the flows in both countries are in effect a form of taxation. It is also noted that the constitutions of both countries give the right to the center to tax and redistribute income in accordance with certain policies.

191. Peter Aranson, quoted in Allen Buchanon, *Secession,* Boulder: Westview Press, 1991, p. 104.

192. *The New York Times,* June 24, 1990.

193. This low number must be viewed in light of the fact that Quebec is alone among the provinces to manage its own social security and pension fund.

194. *The Wall Street Journal,* April 13, 1990.

195. Peter Leslie and Richard Simeon, "The Battle of the Balance Sheets," in Richard Simeon, ed., *Must Canada Fail?* Montreal: McGill-Queens Press, 1977, pp. 243-58.

196. Herman, in Jules Gerard-Libois, *Katanga Secession,* p. 5.

197. Lemarchand, p. 235.

198. Post and Vickers, *Structure and Conflict in Nigeria 1960-1966,* p. 55.

199. In India, the term *state* refers to regions within the federation, as in the United States. In this section, state will be used to refer to subnational regions and should not be confused with the state as it is used throughout the book.

200. Through which financial institutions are the transfers for these programs to take place? Given that 85 percent of the Indian banking system is in the public sector, central outlays per region are transmitted through banks, operating at a state or federal level. There are several of these, classified by the type of development finance they provide (e.g., Industrial Finance Corporation of India, Industrial Development Bank of India, Credit Guarantee Corporation, Agricultural Finance Corporation, among others). These are the intermediaries through which flows from the center to the regions take place.

201. Under the Third and Fourth Finance Commissions, the weights were respectively 80 and 20 percent.

202. I. S. Gulati, "Possible Routes of Change" in *Center-State Budgetary Transfers,* Bombay: Oxford University Press, 1987, p. 145.

203. Reserve Bank of India, *Reserve Bank of India Bulletin,* Bombay, October 1987, Current Statistics, Appendix I, pp. 866-889.

204. I. S. Gulati and K.K. George, "Inter-State Redistribution through the Budget," in I. S. Gulati, ed., *Centre-State Budgetary Transfers,* Bombay: Oxford University Press, 1987, p. 271.

205. K. N. Prasad, *Problems of Indian Economic Development,* New Delhi: Sterling Publishers, 1983, p. 323.

206. Ibid., p. 326.

207. K. K. George, "The Fiscal Transfer Mechanism in India: An Appraisal," in L. S. Bhat, et al., *Regional Inequalities in India,* New Delhi: Aruna Press, 1982.

208. This fund is part of the federal spending, which also included military spending, administrative spending, and miscellaneous expenditures. Payment into the fund comes from individual republics, which is one of the three sources of funds for the federal government (the other two are federal sales taxes and import duties).

209. Savezni Zavod Za Statistiku, *Statisticki Godisnjak Yugoslavije,* Belgrade, 1988, Table 207-7.

210. Ibid., Table 207-6. This paragraph draws heavily from the findings in Bookman, *Political Economy,* chapter 11.

211. In per capita terms, this translated into the following: Slovenia, $360; Croatia, $188; Vojvodina, $178; and Serbia, $132 (Wei Ding, p. 8).

212. Fred Singleton and Bernard Carter, *The Economy of Yugoslavia,* London: Croom Helm, 1982, p. 220.

213. This changed after the reforms of 1965, when there was a clear shift in policy, and the emergence of a trend in investment toward "political factories" became clear. According to this trend, investments were located in less developed regions despite their obvious economic drawbacks.

214. Branko Petranovic and Momcilo Zacevic, *Jugoslovenski Federalizam: Ideje i Stvarnost,* Beograd: Prosveta 1987, p. 326.

215. The research of Bogden Denitch of the Bureau of Applied Social Research at Columbia University, is cited and discussed in Louis Snyder, *Global Mini-Nationalisms: Autonomy or Independence, Westport: Greenwood Press, 1982, p. 278.*

216. *Interviju,* April 27, 1990, p. 24.

217. Mijatovic claims that 90 percent of capital used for investment during this reconstruction period was from foreign sources (*Interviju,* April 27, 1990, pp. 25-27).

218. This point underlies discontent in Serbia, since this state contributed funds for the development of the tourist industry in the form of loans for hotels and infrastructure, but the issue of profit sharing was not clearly agreed upon. Repayment with interest did not seem to cover the opportunity costs associated with the inflows into Croatia.

219. *The New York Times,* September 22, 1991.

220. Robert P. Clark, "Spanish Democracy and Regional Autonomy: The Autonomous Community System and Self-Government for the Ethnic Homelands," in Joseph R. Rudolph, Jr., and Robert J. Thompson, eds., *Ethnoterritorial Politics, Policy and the Western World*, Boulder: Lynne Rienner, 1989, p. 18.

221. Since its creation in 1830, the French speakers dominated the Belgian state, even though they were outnumbered by the Flemish. However, by the 1950s, Flanders became the wealthier province, causing resentment among the population.

222. *The Economist*, October 12, 1991, p. 50.

223. Belgium has had ingenious ways and compromises of solving the problem of heterogeneity of population, such as the fourons, French-speaking communities living in Flanders.

224. The Trudeau government did allow bilingualism and encouraged francophones in Canada, but vehemently rejected Quebec nationalism.

225. *The Economist*, June 29, 1991, p. 5 (Canada survey).

226. For detail on these, see Peter Leslie, "Ethnonationalism in a Federal State: The Case of Canada," in Rudolph and Thompson, eds., *Ethnoterritorial Politics*, pp. 74-81.

227. *The New Republic*, April 23, 1990.

228. These amendments required that all federal legislation be approved by the Chamber of Nationalities and that the number of representatives in it was to double. See Steven Burg, *Conflict and Cohesion in Socialist Yugoslavia*, Princeton: Princeton University Press, 1983, chapter 1.

229. Cochrane, "Republic and Provincial Barriers in Yugoslav Agricultural Marketing," paper presented at the meeting of the Association for the Advancement of Slavic Studies, Washington, 1990.

230. Harold Lydall, *Yugoslavia in Crisis*, Oxford: Clarendon Press, 1989, p. 81.

231. According to *Borba*, April 26, 1982, "One republic exports, and acquires foreign exchange, while another imports the same goods."

232. Published in *Borba*, October 8, 1990, p. 4. This proposal has been rejected by the central authorities.

233. This compromise has been suggested by the Bosnian president Alia Izetbegovic in 1990. *The Economist*, March 2, 1991, p. 50.

234. These reforms, introduced in January 1990, would not have been possible without the cooperation of all republics. Consisting of measures to decrease inflation and increase production, they are the most successful joint endeavor of the republics in the recent time (Savezno Izvrsno Vece, Sekretarijat za Informisanje, *Ekonomska Reforma i Njeni Zakoni*, Beograd, 1990).

235. *Pravda* (Bratislava), cited in Steiner, p. 197.

236. Planning chief Hula announced this at the 1970 CC Plenum (Dean, p. 47).

237. Dean, p. 47.

238. During these elections, the Slovak government became composed of a fragile coalition between Public Against Violence, the Christian Democratic Movement, and the Democratic Party. The first of these strongly favors federation. The National Party, which only holds 22 seats in the 150-member parliament,

is in favor of independence for Slovakia. *The New York Times,* October 25, 1991.

239. *The New York Times,* December 13, 1990.

240. Center-state relations underwent a transformation since independence. See T. V. Sathyamurthy, "Impact of Centre-State Relations on Indian Politics," *Economic and Political Weekly* 24, no. 38, September 1989, p. 2133.

241. See Anirudh Prasad, *Centre and State Powers Under Indian Federalism,* New Delhi: Deep and Deep Publications, 1981, and Tarun Chandra Bose, ed., *Indian Federalism: Problems and Issues,* New Delhi: K. P. Bagghi and Company, 1987.

242. The local level consists of the village, the block, and the zila.

243. See S. P. Singh, *Centre State Relations in Agricultural Development,* New Delhi: Vikas Publishing House, 1973, chapter 1.

244. For a discussion of the financial responsibilities of the center and the states, see Amarjit Narang, "Decentralization to Remove Regional Disparities," in L. S. Bhat et al., *Regional Inequalities in India,* New Delhi: Aruna Press, 1982, p. 61.

245. Because of the very limited nature of Kashmir's special status, it was not included in the section below on "special status decentralization." Despite this special status, Indian Kashmir has less autonomy than Azad Kashmir, the Pakistani part of Kashmir, where the population elects its own government, collects its own taxes, runs its own police force, administrative services, and educational system, and can directly enter into foreign development projects and business ventures (*The New York Times,* January 27, 1990).

246. William Saffran, "The French State and Ethnic Minority Cultures: Policy Dimensions and Problems," in Rudolph and Thompson, *Ethnoterritorial Politics,* p. 147.

247. After this referendum, the popularity of the SNP (Scottish Nationalist Party) dropped dramatically, so that in 1987 it captured only 14 percent of the votes and merely three seats in Parliament (Birch, p. 95).

248. According to *The Economist* (April 18, 1992, p. 60), the campaign for a referendum pertaining to the question of a Scottish parliament has increased in momentum at the time of the elections of April 1992.

249. See D. M. Fenbury, *Practice Without Policy: Genesis of Local Government in Papua New Guinea,* Canberra, The Australian National University, Development Studies Center Monogram no. 13, 1980, and Harry Gailey, *Bougainville 1943-1945: The Forgotten Campaign,* Lexington: University Press of Kentucky, 1991.

250. Papua New Guinea was an Australian colony during 1951-63.

251. These regions are the Gazelle Peninsula and Papua; however, the movements in these regions did not sustain themselves after independence.

252. Ralph R. Premdas, "Decentralization and Development in Papua New Guinea," in Premdas, Samarasinghe, and Anderson, *Secessionist Movements in Comparative Perspective.*

253. Alex Dragnich and Slavko Todorovich, *The Saga of Kosovo,* East European Monographs no. 170, Boulder, 1984, p. 161.

254. Prior to this declaration, the President of Kosovo, Ibrahim Rugova, visited Albania to request that government's support and subsequently Washington's. (*The New York Times,* November 3, 1991).

255. Raphael Zariski, *Italy: The Politics of Uneven Development,* Hinsdale, Ill.: Dryden Press, 1972, p. 136.

256. Joseph La Palombara, *Italy: The Politics of Planning,* Syracuse: Syracuse University Press, 1966, pp. 117-119.

257. For a discussion of Chinese policy towards minorities in its various regions and the power that they have, see Thomas Heberer, *China and Its National Minorities: Autonomy or Assimilation?* Armonk, N.Y.: M. E. Sharpe, 1990.

258. Conrad Brandt, Benjamin Schwartz, and John K. Fairbank, eds., *A Documentary History of Chinese Communism,* New York: Athenaeum, 1960, pp. 223-24.

259. A. Tom Grunfeld, *The Making of Modern Tibet,* Armonk, N.Y.: M. E. Sharpe, 1987, pp. 147-60.

260. The Dalai Lama fled to India in 1959, although he officially remained part of the Preparatory Committee until 1964, when he was branded a traitor following the discovery of evidence that the Tibetans were resisting efforts at socialization.

261. *The New York Times,* November 12, 1990.

262. *The Economist,* April 14, 1990, p. 39.

263. *The New York Times,* March 9, 1992.

Notes to Chapter 5

1. The Mezzogiorno refers to the southern Italian states that are grouped together on the basis of their low levels of income. At this time, they do not have a secessionist movement.

2. Furthermore, despite the fact that the Slovenes (as well as the Croats) entered the union with Serbia voluntarily and remained a part of the Yugoslav union for 70 years, in some ways they remain Central European in orientation and harbor a distrust and intolerance of the regions that are more Mediterranean or Balkan in outlook. This intolerance has been aimed mostly at Serbia, the largest republic in the nation.

3. The full name, rarely referred to as such in the literature, is the Federal Fund for Financing Faster Development of Economically Underdeveloped Republics and Autonomous Provinces. This move by the Slovenes led to a discussion in the federal chambers about the wisdom of blocking Slovenian funds in retaliation (*Politika,* March 15, 1990). In addition, this withdrawal from the Federal Fund has been viewed as the strongest attack on Yugoslav unity since the interregional crisis began (*Politika,* July 20, 1990).

4. The military heavy industry is located outside of Slovenia, and an insignificant percent of rank and file military personnel are from Slovenia.

5. Vojislav Kostunica, "The Constitution and the Federal States," in Dennison Rusinow, ed., *Yugoslavia: A Fractured Federalism*, Washington: Wilson Center Press, 1981, p. 81.

6. *The New York Times*, December 24, 1990.

7. The remainder had no opinion (*Interviju*, March 30, 1990).

8. Calculated from Savezni Zavod za Statistiku, *Statisticki Godisnjak Jugoslavije*, Beograd, 1988, p. 412, Table 201-10.

9. Indeed, as noted above, during the summer of 1990, Slovenia has withdrawn its support from the Federal Fund as a sign of protest and as a part of its general effort to divorce itself from the nation (*Politika*, July 20, 1990). As of February 1991, the Slovenian leadership proclaimed that it does not wish to abandon its involvement in the less developed regions of Yugoslavia, but it wants to assist them on the basis of bilateral agreements (Danas, February 19, 1991, p. 9).

10. See Prout on a discussion of this regulation and the steps leading to its repeal. Christopher Prout, *Market Socialism in Yugoslavia*, Oxford: Oxford University Press, 1985.

11. Komalek in *Rude Pravo*, March 27, 1968, quoted in Robert Dean, *Nationalism and Political Change in Eastern Europe: The Slovak Question and the Czechoslovak Reform Movement*, Monograph Series in World Affairs, no. 1, Denver: University of Denver, 1973, p. 56.

12. Hvezdon Koctuch, *The Economic and Social Development of Slovakia*, Bratislava, 1968, cited in Eugen Steiner, *The Slovak Dilemma*, Cambridge: Cambridge University Press, 1973, p. 135.

13. Robert Dean, p. 56, and Alice Teichova, *The Czechoslovak Economy 1918-1980*, London: Routledge, 1988.

14. Dean, p. 22.

15. Steiner, p. 137.

16. Ibid., pp. 11-13.

17. Ibid., p. 14.

18. Carol Skalnik Leff, *National Conflict in Czechoslovakia*, Princeton: Princeton University Press, 1988, p. 281. This was most strongly associated with the views of Victor Pavlenda, a Secretary of the Central Committee of the Slovak Communist Party responsible for economic affairs during the rule of Dubcek (also see Steiner, pp. 131-32).

19. See Joshua Sharap, Karel Dyba, and Martin Kupka, "The Reform Process in Czechoslovakia: An Assessment of Recent Developments and Prospects for the Future," *Communist Economies and Economic Transformation*, 4, no. 1, 1992, pp. 16 and 18.

20. Oleh Havrylyshyn and John Williamson, *From Soviet Disunion to Eastern Economic Community*, Washington: Institute for International Economics, Policy Analyses in International Economics no. 35, 1991, p. 9

21. *The Wall Street Journal*, 1991.

22. Estonia, for example, deregulated prices on cigarettes and liquor and was sharply criticized by Moscow in early 1990 (The New York Times, February 11, 1990).

23. Anthony H. Birch, *Nationalism and National Integration,* London: Unwin Hyman, 1989, p. 90. The following paragraph draws heavily from this study by Birch.

24. Ibid., p. 91.

25. Ibid., p. 91.

26. Ibid., p. 83.

27. Michael Keating, "Territorial Management and the British State: The Case of Scotland and Wales," in Joseph R. Rudolph, Jr., and Robert J. Thompson, *Ethnoterritorial Politics, Policy and the Western World,* Boulder: Lynne Rienner, 1989.

28. *The New York Times,* March 3, 1992.

29. Indeed, some Sikhs actually proclaimed the existence of such a homeland. In 1980 in London, Jagjit Singh Chauhan proclaimed the formation of Khalistan, of which he was the president of the government in exile. This government went so far as to issue passports, postage stamps, and currency notes. See Bhabani Sen Gupta, "Punjab: Fading of Sikh Diaspora," *Economic and Political Weekly* 25, nos. 7, 8, February 17-24, 1990, p. 365.

30. The popular sentiment also incorporates cultural and political aspects. All regions want to assert their independence: although their national constitutions allow them the use of their language and support their heritage, as minorities their languages and cultures do not take supremacy within the nation.

31. *India Today,* March 1-15, 1979, p. 36.

32. Holly Hapke, "Agrarian Sources of Sikh Nationalism," in Surjit Dulai and Arthur Helwig, eds., *Punjab in Perspective,* South Asia Series Occasional Paper no. 39, Michigan State University, 1991, p. 61.

33. Part of this discrimination, if it indeed exists, comes from the geographical proximity of Punjab to the Pakistani border. Given two wars with Pakistan, as well as the animosity among the countries that exists in times of peace, it is unlikely that too much investment will be made within easy reach of the Pakistani tanks.

34. Reserve Bank of India, "Analysis of Estimates of State Domestic Product," in *Reserve Bank of India Bulletin,* September 1981, p. 825.

35. In the international markets, Punjab could be receiving a greater revenue for wheat than it is by selling to the national markets. See various tables in United Nations, *World Wheat Statistics,* New York, 1985.

36. Anand Mohan, "The Historical Roots of the Punjab Conflict," *Conflict* 11, no. 2, April-June 1991, p. 152.

37. Azeem Amarshi, Kenneth Good, and Rex Mortimer, *Development and Dependency: The Political Economy of Papua New Guinea,* Melbourne: Oxford University Press, 1979, p. 209.

38. As such, this case of secession differs from the others: although the region in question has an economic asset that the remainder of the region depends upon, its claims to secession are not based on the desire to exclude outsiders from the benefits of that asset, as is the case in Punjab, Lombardy, Katanga, and Biafra.

39. James Griffin, "Movements for Separation and Secession," in Anthony Clunies Ross and John Langmore, eds., *Alternative Strategies for Papua New Guinea*, p. 124.

40. Ibid., p. 118.

41. See, among others, M. Leifer, "Singapore in Malaysia: The Politics of Federation," *Journal of Southeast Asian History* 6, no. 2, 1965, and P. Boyce, "Policy without Authority: Singapore's External Affairs Power," *Journal of Southeast Asian History* 6, no. 2, 1965.

42. C. M. Turnbull, *A History of Singapore 1819-1988*, 2nd ed., Singapore: Oxford University Press, 1989, p. 288.

43. R. S. Milne and Diane K. Mauzy, *Singapore, The Legacy of Lee Kuan Yew*, Boulder: Westview Press, 1990, p. 60.

44. Turnbull, p. 279.

45. Like Quebec, Bougainville, Punjab, and Katanga, the economic and geographical position of Biafra relative to the national union was largely determined by colonial rulers insofar as they directed investment according to their policies, which in this case focused on the exploitation of natural resources.

46. An excellent statistical source for the regional distribution of manufacturing activity according to both the 4 and the 12 state division of Nigeria is found in: Ludwig Schatzl, *Industrialization in Nigeria, A Spatial Analysis*, Munchen: Weltforum Verlag, 1973.

47. See Table 3.1.

48. Harold Nelson, *Nigeria: A Country Study*, Washington: U.S. Government Area Handbook for Nigeria, 1982, p. 162.

49. For a breakdown of the value of imports and exports that pass through the various ports of Nigeria, see Reuben Udo, *Geographical Regions of Nigeria*, Berkeley: University of California Press, 1970, p. 61.

50. Indeed, in this respect they resembled the Chinese spread out throughout Southeast Asia.

51. It produced more than 90 percent of its beer, soap, and cigarettes, 80 percent of its sacks and cement, 60 percent of its paint and shoes, and 50 percent of its cotton fabric and blankets. See Howard Epstein, ed., *Revolt in the Congo 1960-64*, p. 177.

52. Ibid., p. 178.

53. Copper accounted for 70 percent of the regions mining production. Rene Lemarchand, *Political Awakening in the Belgian Congo*, Berkeley: University of California Press, 1964, p. 234.

54. Jules Gerard-Libois, *Katanga Secession*, Madison: University of Wisconsin Press, 1966 p. 3.

55. Fernand Herman, *Courrier Africain*, March 4, 1960, also cited in Gerard-Libois, p. 5.

56. *The New York Times*, April 7, 1992.

57. See an interview with the Senator Bossi in "Quei Lombardi in Guerra con Roma," *La Repubblica*, June 21, 1990, as well as *The Economist*, July 21, 1990.

58. The central government is viewed as too corrupt to rule in the best interest of the region.

59. *The New York Times,* June 24, 1990.

60. Regione Lombarda, *Guida Pratica Della Lombardia,* Milano: Amilcare Pizzi, 1990, p. 14.

61. The Lega does explain that it perceives the money Lombardy has contributed thus far to the south has not been properly used because of the corruption and nonproductive mentality of the southern regions.

62. Given the concentration of urban and industrial units in Lombardy, this region attracted a large proportion of the immigrant workers.

63. However, at least with respect to the foreign immigration, this position is no longer perceived negatively. All of Italy, as well as most of northern Europe, is undergoing a period of reexamination due to the dramatic consequences of open immigration policies toward, for example, North Africa.

64. See chapter 3.

65. Less significant sectors include the following: finance, real estate, and insurance, 14 percent; retail and wholesale trade, 13 percent; construction, 9 percent; and transportation and telecommunications, 9 percent (*The New York Times,* June 24, 1990).

66. Peter Leslie, "Ethnonationalism in a Federal State: The Case of Canada," in Rudolph and Thompson, eds., *Ethnoterritorial Politics,* p. 48.

67. A few decades ago, the leaders in the economy tended to be English-speaking. That has changed dramatically, so that presently, vital industries are in control of the French-speaking population.

68. D. Clift, *Quebec Nationalism in Crisis,* Kingston and Montreal: McGill-Queen's University Press, 1982.

69. Pierre Corbeil and Andre Montambault, "Secession and Independence for Quebec: How Legitimate?" in Ralph R. Premdas, S.W.R. de A. Samarasinghe, and Alan B. Anderson, *Secessionist Movements in Comparative Perspective,* New York: St. Martin's Press, 1990, pp. 186-90.

70. The federal government enacted policies of protection and subsidies to the textile and clothing industries (at a cost to taxpayers in other provinces) and in 1986 awarded the contract for a fighter aircraft to Montreal rather than Winnipeg although it was clear that the latter offered lower prices.

71. This interview was conducted by *The Wall Street Journal* and published on August 17, 1990.

72. *The New York Times,* February 24, 1992.

73. Secession would rectify the injustice perpetuated since 1947 when, under the terms of the British transfer of power in 1947, Kashmir was to choose between union with India or Pakistan. The Hindu Maharaja chose to join the Indian union despite the predominantly Muslim population (Kashmir was divided between Pakistan [Azad Kashmir], India [Jammu and Kashmir], and China [Aksai Chin]). U.N. resolutions of 1948 and 1957 guaranteed the population a vote for self-determination, but this was ignored by the Indian government. Today independence is the preferred path, as was shown by the events of February 1992, compared to unification with Pakistan (Pakistan has always

supported fundamentalist groups that favor accession to Pakistan. See *The Economist,* February 15, 1992).

74. India exports $400 million of tea yearly, and approximately 60 percent of that originates in Assam (*The New York Times,* November 25, 1990).

75. That perception is rooted in colonial times,when Bengali professionals and officials ran the region and Bengali was made the official language.

76. *The New Republic,* July 23, 1990, p. 19.

77. *The Economist,* March 31, 1990, p. 34.

78. *The New York Times,* January 28, 1990.

79. The passports are sold for $10 each. *The New York Times,* September 22, 1991.

80. *The New York Times,* September 22, 1991.

81. *The New York Times,* April 22, 1990.

82. *The New York Times,* June 2, 1990.

83. *The New York Times,* March 27, 1991.

84. Vera Beaudin Saeedpour, Director of the Center for Research at the Kurdish Library in Brooklyn, in her letter to the editor of *The New York Times,* February 16, 1992.

85. *The New York Times,* February 6, 1992.

86. Robert Kearney, "Ethnic Conflict and the Tamil Separatist Movement in Sri Lanka," *Asian Survey* 25, no. 9, September 1985, p. 906.

87. Chelvadurai Manogaran, *Ethnic Conflict and Reconciliation in Sri Lanka,* Honolulu: University of Hawaii Press, 1987, pp. 137-38.

88. Ibid., p. 139.

89. Kearney, p. 905.

90. Edgar O'Ballance, *The Cyanide War: Tamil Insurrection in Sri Lanka 1973-88,* London: Brassey's, 1989, pp. 121-28.

91. Birch, pp. 105-6.

Notes to Chapter 6

1. An interview with Leimann at the Ministry of Economics, Tallinn (*The New York Times,* January 24, 1992).

2. Indeed, the case of the Baltic republics of the Soviet Union has been so successful and quick that they were granted their independence without having to go through the five-year period that was insisted on by Gorbachev just one year before. Indeed, up to four months before the coup of August 1991, the central government opposed the idea of a breakup of the Soviet Union and proposed a simple modification of relations.

3. In this way, sovereignty has become a panacea behind which are often masked opportunists, who hail statements against the center while pursuing their individual ends.

4. This is a seminar entitled "Children Cope with Divorce: Seminar for Divorcing Parents" that must be taken by divorcing parents in various counties across the United States (*The New York Times*, January 23, 1992).

5. *The Wall Street Journal*, November 1991.

6. This was elaborated upon in chapter 4 in the discussion of interregional flows. Investment capital was the focus of the argument, but since some of that comes from the public debt, the arguments are similar.

7. *International Herald Tribune*, March 23, 1990.

8. This raises important questions, such as whether the Slovak government today can legally or morally hold the federal government responsible for using the available technology in the past—the same technology that was used in other parts of the country. It is analogous to suing a doctor for malpractice today, with the benefit of today's knowledge, for an operation some decades ago using the technology available then.

9. *The New York Times*, March 14, 1992. Some estimates of the debt are as low as $60 billion (Felix Rohatyn, "The New Domestic Order," *The New York Review of Books*, November 21, 1991, p. 6) and $70 billion (Norbert Walter "The Soviet Union in the Trough: A Call to Action" in *Gateways to Trade and Investment in the Changing Soviet Landscape*, Geonomics Institute: East-West Seminar Report, Spring 1991, p. 4).

10. Valery Semyonov, "Republics Agree to Divide Federal Cake," *Commersant*, July 29, 1991, p. 2.

11. *The New York Times*, December 1, 1991.

12. The agreement with Ukraine also calls for Vneshekonombank, the former Soviet State Bank for Foreign Economic Affairs, to be under joint CIS control, rather than strictly Russian jurisdiction, and for it to handle debt servicing.

13. *The New York Times*, January 17, 1992.

14. Allen Buchanon, *Secession*, Boulder: Westview Press, 1991, p. 107.

15. This unilateral decision caused the central bank in Lagos to retaliate by blocking the transfer of all foreign currency to the region. See Peter Schwab, ed., *Biafra*, New York: Facts on File, 1971.

16. It has been proposed by Havrylyshyn and Williamson that the creation of a currency board would be preferable to a central bank because this would avoid the pressure to monetize the public debt that the new states might have. (Oleh Havrylyshyn and John Williamson, *From Soviet Disunion to Eastern Economic Community*, Washington: Institute for International Economics Policy Analyses in International Economics no. 35, 1991, pp. 39-42).

17. This is the rate in Serbia in May 1992. Its dimension is largely due to the printing of money to finance the war and provide livelihood to the refugees from Croatia and Bosnia.

18. *Politika*, July 20, 1990. The issue of the currency is especially important, given the hardships caused by the monetary policies of the central government in 1989-90. Former President Markovic's economic program of reform had succeeded in drastically decreasing the inflation rate, but it had brought with it a liquidity crisis, high interest rates, and a decrease in productivity. Slovenes

believed that an independent monetary policy would reverse some of these problems, and that it must begin with the creation of an independent currency.

19. *The New York Times,* July 16, 1990.

20. *The New York Times,* January 17, 1992.

21. *The New York Times,* October 30, 1990. This tender is issued by a private company and is officially unapproved by the government, although it is accepted by about 80 percent of businesses throughout Slovenia.

22. One solution that has been suggested for Russia is to use its gold deposits to solve its monetary problems. It has been suggested by Rohatyn that one way to aid the Soviet economy would be to gradually increase the price of gold by international agreement to, for example, $500 per ounce. This would enable Russia, the world's largest gold producer, to back its currency with gold, and thereby make it acceptable internally and externally (Rohatyn, p. 6).

23. *The New York Times,* January 24, 1992.

24. Indeed, the Movement for a Democratic Slovakia, the largest party of Slovakia, has recently made the withdrawal of state subsidies from Slovak factories and its concomitant unemployment one of the principal rallying points against Prague (*The Economist,* May 30, 1992).

25. This kind of pressure was evident in Croatia, when the nationalist government of Tudjman endorsed pressure on Serbs in Croatia to vacate their positions in their traditional places of employment, namely the government bureaucracy and the police.

26. A Russian reported recently that he could not buy a suit because the shopkeeper said there was a shortage and what there is is being saved for ethnic Estonians.

27. *The New York Times Magazine,* September 22, 1991, p. 56.

28. An analysis of the training and educational expenses in Slovenia is contained in Milica Z. Bookman, "The Economic Basis of Regional Autarchy in Yugoslavia," *Soviet Studies* 42, no. 1.

29. *The Economist,* March 7, 1992.

30. This was covered in various issues of *Politika* during January and February 1992.

31. See chapter 5 for a detailed description of the territorial demands of the Sikhs in Punjab.

32. The question of compensation for the army has also arisen in international relations between countries, such as between Hungary and the Soviet Union. When the Soviet army withdrew from Hungary in 1990, they came to an agreement with the Hungarians that Hungary didn't have to pay for what the Soviet military built in the country, and the military didn't pay for the ecological and physical damage it did to the countryside.

33. *The New York Times,* October 30, 1991.

34. In March 1992, the Ukrainian government halted the transfer of tactical nuclear weapons to Russia because, according to President Kravchuk, there was no guarantee that Russia was destroying them, as previously agreed. Consequently, he wants to keep them on Ukrainian soil (The New York Times, March 13, 1992).

35. *The New York Times,* March 21, 1992.

36. *The Economist,* February 22, 1992.

37. *The New York Times,* May 6, 1992.

38. This is the case of Eritrea, which has issued stamps two years before it is due to have a referendum (*The New York Times,* March 12, 1992).

39. Indeed, Tito also created a Macedonian Orthodox Church in the mid-1960s, giving the Macedonian population a religious identity they previously shared with the Serbs through the Serbian Orthodox church.

40. It is unclear why Macedonia does not hurry to gain international recognition, in the hope that that act would serve as somewhat of an obstacle in the possible dismemberment of the region. More so than any of the other regions of former Yugoslavia, Macedonia is likely to become divided up and its territory distributed to its neighbors whose populations inhabit the region: Serbs in the north, Kosovars in the western part, and Bulgarians in the east.

41. *The New York Times,* April 1, 1992.

42. Turkey has applied and been rebuffed by the EEC. Cyprus and Malta have applied, and it is likely they will be asked to come back at a later date.

43. The Commonwealth of Independent States came into being in December 1991.

44. See the Model on Confederacy proposed by the Slovenian and Croatian leadership in 1990, and published in Borba, October 8, 1990.

45. *The New York Times,* May 6, 1992.

46. Anders Aslund, "Should the Soviet Union Get Western Assistance after the Coup?" Stockholm: Stockholm Institute of Soviet and East European Studies, 1991, quoted in Havrylyshyn and Williamson, From Soviet Disunion to *Eastern Economic Community, p. 17.*

47. Havrylyshyn and Williamson, chapter 3.

48. There was dispute between the regional level administration and Moscow as to who held the power to make decisions pertaining to oil exploration in this potentially lucrative region (*The Economist,* May 2, 1992, p. 87).

49. Indeed, this has led former President Nixon to admonish the Bush administration for missing a historic opportunity by not offering more financial help to Russia. The Nixon memo caused a furor in Washington, eliciting a defensive response from the White House (*The New York Times,* March 10-12, 1992).

50. *The New York Times,* January 24, 1992.

51. *The New York Times,* February 25, 1992.

52. Michel Piessel, *The Secret War in Tibet,* Boston: Little, Brown, 1972, p. 126.

53. Janos Kornai, *The Road to a Free Economy,* New York: W. W. Norton, 1990; Manuel Hinds, "Issues in the Introduction of Market forces in Eastern European Socialist Economies," *World Bank Report,* Washington: World Bank, April 1990; John Williamson, "The Economic Opening of Eastern Europe," *Policy Analysis in International Economics* 31, Washington: Institute for International Economics, 1991.

54. Graham Allison and Grigory Yavlinsky, *Window of Opportunity: The Grand Bargain for Democracy in the Soviet Union,* New York: Pantheon, 1991.

55. It is interesting to note that German policymakers and academics have encouraged a slower transition from planned to market economy. This may be due to the fact that their economy has a large public sector and that they do not have an ideological ax to grind.

56. Susan Collins and Dani Rodrik, "Eastern Europe and the Soviet Union in the World Economy," *Policy Analyses in International Economics* 32, Washington: Institute for International Economics, 1991, p. 11.

57. It is unclear to what degree such adverse conditions are the result of a legacy of communism, and how much is due to the speed of the application of these changes.

58. Perhaps the economic problems were accentuated there because of the lack of energy resources coupled with internal dissension among nationalities.

59. R. S. Milne and Diane K. Mauzy, *Singapore: The Legacy of Lee Kuan Yew*, Boulder: Westview Press, 1990, p. 137.

Notes to Chapter 7

1. *The New York Times*, December 6, 1991.

2. *The Economist*, February 15, 1992, p. 54.

3. Allen Buchanon, *Secession*, Boulder: Westview Press, 1991, p. 92.

4. The independence government was changed in March 1992.

5. The issue of fragmentation of the national economy was addressed in chapter 4.

6. This was briefly discussed in chapter 4 and is treated at length in M. Zarkovic, *Issues in Indian Agricultural Development*, Boulder: Westview Press, 1987.

7. Regulation of the national food markets prohibited Punjab from entering the more lucrative global markets (see chapter 4).

8. See the discussion pertaining to Canada in chapter 3.

9. See the discussion pertaining to Canada in chapter 3.

10. Regione Lombarda, *Guida Pratica Della Lombardia*, Milan: Amilcare Pizzi, 1990, p. 14.

11. *The New York Times*, June 24, 1990.

12. Deutsche Bank, *The Soviet Union at the Crossroads: Facts and Figures on the Soviet Republics*, Frankfurt: Deutsche Bank, 1991, p. 24.

13. That self-interest may also reflect inertia or the perception of a lack of options.

14. Louis Snyder, *Global Mini-Nationalisms: Autonomy or Independence*, Westport: Greenwood Press, 1982, p. 186.

15. *The New York Times*, June 24, 1990.

16. *The New York Times*, March 29, 1992.

17. James Griffin, "Movements for Separation and Secession," in Anthony Clunies Ross and John Langmore, eds., *Alternative Strategies for Papua New Guinea*, Melbourne: Oxford University Press, 1973, p. 126.

18. M. Zarkovic, *Issues in Indian Agricultural Development*, chapter 5.

19. Howard Epstein, ed., *Revolt in the Congo 1960-64*, New York: Facts on File, 1965, p. 177.

20. Rene Lemarchand, *Political Awakening in the Belgian Congo*, Berkeley: University of California Press, 1964, p. 234.

21. Fernand Hernan, *Courrier Africain*, March 4, 1960.

22. Deutsche Bank, pp. 38-39.

23. Buchanon, p. 92.

24. *The New York Times*, March 8, 1992.

25. Slovenia dumped its dinars after introducing its own currency, and thus aggravated inflation in the dinar zone.

26. Papua New Guinea has doubled its production of gold in 1992 from 1990 levels and is likely to become the sixth biggest gold producer in the world (*The Economist*, January 18, 1992, p. 34).

27. One large impediment that Quebec is likely to face at the time of its secession is the issue of territory. It is very likely that the region will not be allowed to take with it all its present territory. English-speaking Quebecois have questioned Quebec's right to the land between the St. Lawrence River and the U.S. border where they are concentrated. Furthermore, the Cree and Eskimo leaders have claimed as much as two-thirds of the area, saying it was ceded to Quebec only after the establishment of the Canadian confederation. If Quebec secedes, it will remain with Canada.

28. This might come as no surprise, given the recent Gallup poll, according to which more than a third of Canadians polled recently expect their country to become part of the United States in the next 50 years. This represents more than a 50 percent increase over the sentiment in 1988 (*The Toronto Star*, quoted in *World Press Review*, March 1992, p. 3).

29. In the June 1989 elections, the Lega conquered 40 percent of the vote in some parts of the state (*La Repubblica*, June 22, 1989).

30. *The New York Times*, February 5, 1990.

31. *The Wall Street Journal*, January 15, 1990.

32. *The Economist*, January 20-26, 1990.

33. Areas around Dubrovnik have for two decades experienced an increase in their standards of living due to the income from tourist-related industries, such as restaurants, bed and breakfast establishments, souvenir shops, et cetera. Already during the summer of 1991, before the war broke out, these regions suffered from lack of tourists. Nineteen-ninety-two will be the second consecutive year that these people, who have forgotten to fish and farm, are without income. The public relations damage associated with the war will last beyond the final ceasefire.

34. Peter Reddaway, "The End of the Empire," *The New York Review of Books*, November 7, 1991, p. 54.

Notes to Chapter 8

1. The cases of Singapore, Bangladesh, Katanga, and Biafra are included in this group, although their secessionist efforts took place during the 1960s and 1970s.
2. These are Tibet, East Timor, Western Sahara, Tadzhikistan, and possibly northern Sri Lanka and Corsica.
3. The violence in regions of Moldova, Georgia, and Azerbaijan are the result of internal and interregional conflicts, not conflict with the center.
4. The winning of independence in much of Africa and Asia was relatively peaceful; however, it often did not involve changes in the existing borders. Obvious exceptions that come to mind are the creation of the state of Israel, the arbitrary drawing of the borders between Pakistan and India, the disputed area of Kashmir, and so forth.
5. William L. Langer, *An Encyclopedia of World History*, 5th ed., Boston: Houghton Mifflin Company, 1972.
6. The role of the Catholic church in anti-Serbian war activities in Croatia during World War II is discussed in the following: *The Economist*, August 22, 1992, p. 36; and Stewart Lamont, *Church and State: Uneasy Alliances*, London: Bodley Head, 1989, p. 146. Furthermore, the Croatian minister of the interior of the independent fascist government during World War II, A. Artukovic, stated at his trial that whatever he and his Ustashas had done conformed to the principals of morality of the Catholic church (*Borba*, December 26, 1988).
7. This secret conspiracy was revealed in the popular press in February 1992.
8. This has provoked new disputes between the Orthodox and Catholic churches. See Domenico Del Rio, "La Chiesa Ortodossa Va Alla Riscossa," *La Repubblica*, November 21, 1991.
9. Conor Cruise O'Brien, *Godland: Reflections on Religion and Nationalism*, Cambridge: Harvard University Press, 1988, p. 40.
10. The lopsided international support in the Serbo-Croat conflict is all the more pronounced given that Russia and France, Serbia's traditional allies, are both battling internal problems and are in no position to take a strong stand against Germanic demands.
11. For example, there was as much local sensitivity in Czechoslovakia in February 1992 when German Chancellor Kohl delayed the signing of a good-neighbor treaty, because of the question of the Sudetens expelled after World War II, as there was in Poland in 1990, when Kohl delayed the recognition of the Oder-Neisse line as Poland's western frontier.
12. *The New York Times*, February 25, 1992.
13. A discussion of the efforts of Serbs and Croats in Bosnia-Hercegovina to carve out autonomous ethnic enclaves is not discussed here because it is not clear how much of the impetus for the creation of the Serbian Republic of Bosnian Krajina and the Croatian Community of Herceg-Bosna comes from within the former republic of Bosnia-Hercegovina, and how much comes from Serbia and

Croatia respectively. In other words, it is not clear if the war in Bosnia-Hercegovina is the result of land grab directed from Belgrade and Zagreb or an internal ethnic struggle for territory.

14. Paul Lendvai, *Eagles in Cobwebs: Nationalism and Communism in the Balkans,* New York: Anchor Books, 1969, p. 20.

15. This was an excerpt from an annual session of the Croatian Democratic Union general convention, marking its second anniversary. Quoted in *UPI Reports,* February 23, 1992.

16. While the world focuses on minority guarantees in the former Yugoslav regions, little attention is paid to a discussion of similar issues some 100 kilometers away in Alto Adige. This Italian state was attached to Italy, from Austria, at the end of World War II. Under the Paris accord of 1946, and ratified by the Italian parliament in 1969, the region was granted autonomy status, including the use of the German language and its guaranteed equality with Italian. However, that status was never really put into action. In January 1992, the Italian government announced that it reached some decisions pertaining to the question of the Alto Adige, called "il pacchetto Alto Adige." This package consists of the following: 1) a set of laws regulating state and local rights under the status of autonomy; 2) agreement pertaining to regional finances; 3) reversal of some rules that previously were in the domain of the center, such as hunting rights; and 4) rules pertaining to the mixed use of languages in education. However, the leading party of the region, the Sudtiroler Volkspartei, refuses to accept this set of proposals without international guarantees that the Italian government cannot reverse the measures included in this package. The Italian government refuses to accept this, since it claims that this is an internal matter of the Italian state and not something up for international deliberations. It is interesting that such a statement should come from a government that has been so supportive in Croatia's efforts to secede and has found no problem in recognizing Croatia's independence, thereby interfering in the internal affairs of a neighboring state, while in the same month refusing such intervention in its regions.

17. To this day, some claim that the Armenian genocide never occurred, just as some claim that the Holocaust and Stalin's gulag are figments of the imagination.

18. The western region is the bastion of Ukrainian nationalism, the eastern is more russified, and the south, including Crimea, has few Ukrainian roots.

19. *The New York Times,* March 3, 1992.

20. The tax was in the form of forced labor. See Barbara Tuchman, *The March of Folly,* New York: Ballantine Books, 1984, pp. 8-10.

21. Anthony Birch, *Nationalism and National Integration,* London: Unwin Hyman, 1989, p.72.

22. The recognition of Croatia and Bosnia-Hercegovina by western states ruined any possibility of a negotiated compromise to the territorial issue in former Yugoslavia. The EEC set standards that had to be met prior to recognition, and while only Slovenia and Macedonia met those standards, Croatia and Bosnia-Hercegovina were recognized. This odd behavior on the part of the western

leaders is inconsistent and unprincipled and points out either ignorance or ulterior motivations in the region.

23. The World Bank, *World Development Report 1989*, New York: Oxford University Press, 1989, p. 230.
24. Hans Kohr, "Disunion Now: A Plea for a Society Based Upon Small Autonomous Units," *Commonwealth*, September 26, 1941. Kohr in 1941 attributed the longevity of the Swiss confederation not to the strength provided by the center, but rather the strength of the cantons. His suggestion that Italy, Germany, and other countries should be composed of numerous small national states led him to the conclusion that peace could better be maintained if no single region could become too strong to threaten others. He did, however, allow for microwars such as those in Croatia and Azerbaijan, but these would not have the power to dissipate into world wars.
25. Dean Keith Simonton thus claims that Eastern Europe presently shows the greatest promise because there, as in the city-states of Italy that produced the Renaissance and the small German states that produced Goethe, Hegel, and Mozart, there is no cultural homogeneity (*The New York Times*, March 22, 1992).
26. Nigel Harris, *National Liberation*, London: I. B. Tauris, p. 225.
27. *The New York Times*, January 24, 1992.
28. *The Wall Street Journal*, December 4, 1991.
29. Francis Fukuyama, *The End of History and the Last Man*, New York: The Free Press, 1992.
30. Nathan Gardels, "Two Concepts of Nationalism: An Interview with Isiah Berlin," *The New York Review of Books*, November 21, 1991, p. 21.
31. *The New York Times*, December 28, 1990.
32. Abraham Lincoln, *Letters and Addresses of Abraham Lincoln*, New York: Unit Book Publishing, 1905.
33. Craig Baxter, "Pakistan and Bangladesh," in Frederick Shiels, ed., *Ethnic Separatism and World Politics*, Lanham: University Press of America, 1984, p. 240.
34. This was said in August 1965 by President Tunku Abdul Rahman (C. M. Turnbull, *A History of Singapore 1819-1988*, 2nd ed., Singapore: Oxford University Press, 1989, p. 288).
35. According to a recent Gallup poll, more than one-third of the Canadians polled expect their country to become part of the United States in the next 50 years (*The Toronto Star*, quoted in *World Press Review*, March 1992, p. 3).
36. *The New York Times*, October 30, 1991.
37. Dennison Rusinow, "Ethnic Politics in the Habsburg Monarchy and Successor States: Three Answers to the National Question," in Richard L. Rudolph and David F. Good, eds., *Nationalism and Empire: The Habsburg Empire and the Soviet Union*, New York: St. Martin's Press, 1992.
38. Indeed, numerous people in former Yugoslavia have come to associate the new freedom and democracy associated with the demise of communism and free multiparty elections with nasty forms of nationalism that could not but result

in war. The sentiment of the population of war-ravaged Yugoslavia may be summed up in the words of one citizen of Vukovar: "Here democracy has set people against each other, it has encouraged people to hate and kill" (*The New York Times,* March 4, 1992).

39. *The New York Review of Books,* November 21, 1991, p. 20.

40. Liberal democracy and economic development seem to go hand in hand. A worldwide study was recently conducted by Greenwood and Ogus that extends the concept of freedom and democracy to include economic freedom of various sorts and links it to economic growth (the study is discussed in *The Economist,* March 14, 1992, p. 42). The present trend towards the market economy as a quick way to achieve economic development is also compatible with democratic institutions. Individualism is important in both. For an application of the link between economic and political liberalism and economic development in the Third World, see Christopher Colclough and James Manor, eds., *States and Markets: Neo-Liberalism and the Development-Policy Debate,* Oxford: Oxford University Press, 1992.

41. "The dissolution of ethnicity. The transcendence of nationalism. The internationalism of culture. These have been the dreams and expectations of liberals and rationalists in practically every country." Anthony Smith, *The Ethnic Revival,* Cambridge: Cambridge University Press, p. 1.

42. Not all regions are experiencing secessionist drives are engulfed in hardship. Furthermore, as noted in chapter 1, not all regions in this study are experiencing secessionist drives. It is interesting to question why this is true, especially in light of the fact that secession has been so easily achieved in many parts of Eastern Europe and the Soviet Union. Indeed, elections in the spring of 1992 in Britain, Italy, and Spain, all states with regional autonomy seekers, showed that while there was a desire for regional affirmation, the secessionists did not perform as well as it might have been expected. The critical reason for this is likely to be that the move toward the unification of Europe is changing the structure of Europe and redefining what it means to be a state and within Europe.

43. Morocco requested an advisory opinion from the World Court on the issue of Western Sahara. The court determined in 1975 that the region had a right to self-determination. See James Mayall, *Nationalism and International Society,* Cambridge: Cambridge University Press, 1990, p. 63.

REFERENCES

Official Sources

The Economist, *The World in Figures*. London: The Economist Newspaper, various annual volumes.

Generalitat de Catalunya. *Catalunya Endavant*. Barcelona, 1982.

Government of India. Central Statistical Organization. *Statistical Abstract*. New Delhi, annual volumes.

Government of India. Ministry of Information and Broadcasting. *India*. New Delhi, annual volumes.

Government of Pakistan. *Twenty-Five Years of Pakistan in Statistics 1947-1972*. Karachi: Central Statistical Office, 1972.

Government of Punjab. Economic and Statistical Organization. *Statistical Abstract of Punjab*. Chandigarh, annual volumes.

Minister of Supply and Services. *Canada Yearbook 1988*. Ottawa: Statistics Canada, 1987.

Regione Lombarda. *Guida Pratica Della Lombardia*. Milano: Amilcare Pizzi, 1990.

Republique Francaise. Ministère de L'Economie, des Finances at de la Privatisation. *Annuaire Statistique de la France 1986*. Paris: Institut National de la Statistique et des Etudes Economiques, 1986.

Savezni Zavod za Statistiku. *Statisticki Godisnjak Jugoslavije*. Beograd, annual volumes.

Savezni Zavod Za Statistiku. *Jugoslavija 1918-1988*. Beograd 1989.

Savezni Zavod Za Statistiku. *Saopstenje* no. 365, Beograd 1984.

Savezni Zavod Za Statistiku. *Statisticki Bilten* no. 1320, Beograd 1981.

Savezno Izvrsno Vece. *Ekonomska Reforma i Njeni Zakoni*. Beograd, 1990.

Savezno Izvrsno Vece. *Constitutional System of Yugoslavia*. Beograd, 1980.

Servizio Stampa Della Giunta Regionale Della Lombardia, *La Lombardia Si Presenta: 2*. La Geografia Milan: Arti Grafiche Reina, 1980.

State Statistical Bureau. People's Republic of China. *Statistical Yearbook of China 1985*. Oxford: Oxford University Press, 1985.

U.S. Congress. Joint Economic Committee. *Gorbachev's Economic Plans*. Washington, D.C.: U.S. Government Printing Office, 1987.

The World Bank, *World Development Report 1989, 1990, 1991*. New York: Oxford University Press, 1989, 1990, 1991.

Books and Articles

Anderson, J. "Nationalism and Geography." In *The Rise of the Modern State*. Brighton: Harvester Press, 1986.

Banac, Ivo. *The National Question in Yugoslavia*. Ithaca: Cornell University Press, 1984.

Birch, Anthony, *Nationalism and National Integration*. London: Unwin Hyman, 1989.

Breuilly, John. *Nationalism and the State*. Chicago: University of Chicago Press, 1985.

Bookman, Milica Z. "The Economic Basis of Regional Autarchy in Yugoslavia." *Soviet Studies* 42, no. 1 (January 1990).

Bookman, Milica Zarkovic. *The Political Economy of Discontinuous Development*. New York: Praeger, 1991.

Buchanon, Allen. *Secession*. Boulder: Westview Press, 1991.

Buchheit, Lee. *Secession: The Legitimacy of Self-Determination*. New Haven: Yale University Press, 1978.

Chazan, Naomi, ed. *Irredentism and International Politics*. Boulder: Lynne Rienner, 1991.

Conquest, Robert, ed. *The Last Empire: Nationality and the Soviet Future,* Stanford: Hoover Institution Press, 1986.

Despres, Leo, ed. *Ethnicity and Resource Competition in Plural Societies*. The Hague: Mouton, 1975.

Deutsche Bank. *The Soviet Union at the Crossroads: Facts and Figures on the Soviet Republics*. Frankfurt: Deutsche Bank, 1991.

Ding, Wei. "Yugoslavia: Costs and Benefits of Union and Interdependence of Regional Economies." *Comparative Economic Studies* 33, no. 4 (1991).

Dragnich, Alex, and Slavko Todorovich. *The Saga of Kosovo*. East European Monographs 25, Boulder, 1984.

Gelfand, Donald, and Russell Lee, eds. *Ethnic Conflicts and Power: A Cross-National Perspective*. New York: John Wiley, 1973.

Glazer, Nathan, and Daniel Moynihan, eds. *Ethnicity*. Cambridge, Mass.: Harvard University Press, 1975.

Gleason, Gregory. *Federalism and Nationalism*. Boulder: Westview Press, 1989.

Griffin, James. "Movements for Separation and Secession." In Anthony Clunies Ross and John Langmore, eds., *Alternative Strategies for Papua New Guinea*. Melbourne: Oxford University Press, 1973.

Gulati, I. S., ed. *Centre-State Budgetary Transfers*. Bombay: Oxford University Press, 1983.

Hall, Raymond. *Ethnic Autonomy: Comparative Dynamics*. New York: Pergamon, 1979.

Harris, Nigel. *National Liberation*. London: I. B. Tauris, 1990.

Hartshiorne, R. "A Survey of the Boundary Problems of Europe." In C. C. Colby, ed., *Geographical Aspects of International Relations*. Port Washington, N.Y.: Kennikat Press, 1970.

Havrylyshyn, Oleh, and John Williamson. "From Soviet Disunion to Eastern Economic Community?" *Policy Analyses in International Economics* 35. Washington: Institute for International Economics, 1991.

Heberer, Thomas. *China and Its National Minorities: Autonomy or Assimilation?* Armonk, N.Y.: M. E. Sharpe, 1990.

Hobsbawm, E. J. *Nations and Nationalism Since 1780*. Cambridge: Cambridge University Press, 1990.

Hobsbawm, Eric. "Some Reflections on the Break-Up of Britain." *New Left Review* 105 (September-October 1977).

Hroch, Miroslav. *Social Preconditions of National Revival in Europe.* Cambridge: Cambridge University Press, 1985.

Johnston, R. J., David B. Knight, and Eleonore Kofman, eds. *Nationalism, Self-Determination and Political Geography.* London: Croom Helm, 1988.

Johnston, Ray F., ed. *The Politics of Division, Partition and Unification.* New York: Praeger, 1976.

Kaplan, Robert. "Croatianism: The Latest Balkan Ugliness." *The New Republic* (November 25, 1991).

Katz, Zev, Rosemarie Rogers, and Frederic Harned, eds. *Handbook of Major Soviet Nationalities.* New York: Free Press, 1975.

Kearney, Robert. "Ethnic Conflict and the Tamil Separatist Movement in Sri Lanka." *Asian Survey* 25, no. 9 (September 1985).

Koropeckyj, I. S., and Gertrude Schroeder, eds. *Economics of Soviet Regions.* New York: Praeger, 1981.

Kratochwil, Fredrich, Paul Rorlich, and Harpreet Mahajan. *Peace and Disputed Sovereignty: Reflections on Conflict over Territory.* Columbia University Institute of War and Peace Studies. Lanham: University Press of America, 1985.

Krejci, Jaroslav, and Vitezslav Velimsky. *Ethnic and Political Nations in Europe.* New York: St. Martin's Press, 1981.

Leslie, Peter. "Ethnonationalism in a Federal State: The Case of Canada." In Joseph Rudolph, Jr., and Robert Thompson, eds., *Ethnoterritorial Politics, Policy and the Western World.* Boulder: Lynne Rienner, 1989.

Leslie, Peter, and Richard Simeon. "The Battle of the Balance Sheets." In Richard Simeon, ed., *Must Canada Fail?* Montreal: McGill-Queens Press, 1977.

MacKay, Donald. *Scotland 1980: The Economics of Self-Government.* Edinburgh: Q Press, 1977.

Mathos, Michael. *Communist China and Tibet: The First Dozen Years.* The Hague: Martinus Nijhoff, 1964.

Manogaran, Chelvadurai. *Ethnic Conflict and Reconciliation in Sri Lanka.* Honolulu: University of Hawaii Press, 1987.

Mayall, James. *Nationalism and International Society.* Cambridge: Cambridge University Press, 1990.

Nahaylo, Bohdan, and Victor Swoboda. *Soviet Disunion: A History of the Nationalities Problem in the USSR.* New York: Free Press, 1990.

Nairn, T. *The Break-Up of Britain: Crisis and Neo-Nationalism.* London: New Left Books, 1977.

Nelson, Daniel. "Europe's Unstable East." *Foreign Policy* 82 (Spring 1991).

Ocic, C. "Integracioni i Dezintegracioni Procesi u Privredi Jugoslavije." *Marksisticka Misao* 4 (1983).

Paris, Edmond. *Genocide in Satellite Croatia 1941-1945.* Chicago, 1962.

Petranovic, Branko, and Momcilo Zacevic. *Jugoslovenski Federalizam: Ideje i Stvarnost.* Beograd: Prosveta, 1987.

Pockney, B. P. *Soviet Statistics Since 1950.* New York: St. Martin's Press, 1991.

Premdas, Ralph R., S.W.R. de A. Samarasinghe, and Alan B. Anderson. *Secessionist Movements in Comparative Perspective.* New York: St. Martin's Press, 1990.

Pryor, Frederick. *A Guidebook to the Comparative Study of Economic Systems.* Englewood Cliffs, N.J.: Prentice-Hall Inc, 1975.

Rokkan, Setin, and Derek Urwin, eds. *The Politics of Territorial Identity.* London: Sage Publications, 1982.

Ronen, Dov. *The Quest for Self-Determination.* New Haven: Yale University Press, 1979.

Rothenberg, Gunther E. *The Military Border in Croatia 1740-1881.* Chicago: University of Chicago Press, 1966.

Rudolph, Joseph J.,Jr., and Robert R. Thompson. *Ethnoterritorial Politics, Policy and the Western World.* Boulder: Lynne Rienner, 1989.

Rudolph, Richard L., and David F. Good, eds. *Nationalism and Empire: The Habsburg Monarchy and the Soviet Union.* New York: St. Martin's Press, 1992.

Rusinow, Dennison, ed. *Yugoslavia: A Fractured Federalism.* Washington: Wilson Center Press, 1988.

Russel, Peter, and Storrs McCall. "Can Secession Be Justified? The Case of the Southern Sudan." In Dunstan M. Wai, *The Southern Sudan, The Problem of National Integration*. London: Frank Cass, 1973.

Sarkar, R.C.S. *Union State Relations in India*. New Delhi: National Publishing House, 1986.

Schroeder, Gertrude. "Nationalities and the Soviet Economy." In Lubomyr Hajda and Mark Beissinger, eds., *The Nationalities Factor in Soviet Politics and Society*. Boulder: Westview Press, 1990. Shiels, Frederick, L., ed. *Ethnic Separatism and World Politics*. Lanham: University Press of America, 1984.

Shoup, Paul S. *The East European and Soviet Data Handbook*. New York: Columbia University Press, 1981.

Simpson, John. "Economic Development: Cause and Effect in the Northern Ireland Conflict." In John Darby, ed., *Northern Ireland, The Background to the Conflict*. Belfast: Appletree Press, 1983.

Smith, Anthony. *The Ethnic Revival*. London: Cambridge University Press, 1981.

Snyder, Louis. *Global Mini-Nationalisms: Autonomy or Independence*. Westport: Greenwood Press, 1982.

Suhrke, Astri, and Lela Garner Noble, eds. *Ethnic Conflict in International Relations*. New York: Praeger, 1977.

SVIMEZ. Associazione Per Lo Sviluppo Dell'Industria Nel Mezzogiorno. *Rapporto 1990 Sull'Economia Del Mezzogiorno*. Bologno: il Mulino, 1990.

Szporluk, Roman. *Communism and Nationalism*. New York: Oxford University Press, 1988.

Talmon, J. L. *The Myth of the Nation and the Vision of Revolution*. London: Secker and Warburg, 1981.

Teichova, Alice. *The Czechoslovak Economy 1918-1980*. London: Routledge, 1988.

Verdery, Catherine. *Transylvanian Villagers: Three Centuries of Political, Economic and Ethnic Change*. Berkeley: University of California Press, 1983.

Whalley, J., and I. Trela. *Regional Aspects of Confederation.* Toronto: University of Toronto Press, 1986.

Williams, Colin, ed. *National Separatism.* Cardiff: University of Wales Press, 1982.

Wood, John. "Secession: A Comparative Analytic Framework." *Canadian Journal of Political Science* 14, no. 1 (March 1981).

INDEX

Africa 1, 15, 160
Akali Dal Party 22, 191
Alsace 15, 37
Ambonese 23
anarchy 17, 35
Angola 11, 16
armed forces 40, 118, 133-35; Yugoslav, 43, 96, 134; Indian, 43
Armenia 7, 131
Asia 1, 15
Assam 27, 32, 53, 66, 75, 77, 110
Austro-Hungarian Empire 1, 9,
  13, 19, 22, 28, 35, 71, 97, 136,
  174, 179
autonomy 12, 16, 18, 22, 23, 29,
  31-34, 49, 82, 88, 91, 97, 111,
  112, 123, 126, 168
Azerbaijan 7, 14, 24, 131, 134,
  162

Balkan Wars 162, 166
Baltic republics of the USSR 22,
  23, 38, 45, 58, 98-100
Bangladesh 2, 14, 30, 34, 36, 55,
  68, 137
banking system 99, 118, 124-26
barriers to trade 85, 99
Basques Provinces 29, 34, 54, 62,
  68, 81, 111, 158, 190, 197
Basques 23
Belgium 18, 36, 81, 82, 133, 232
Belarus 70, 99, 130, 131, 134
Biafra 21, 24, 29, 34, 41, 55, 68,
  104-5, 121, 124
Bohemia 22, 98

borders 1, 6, 7, 11, 12, 15-16, 17,
  19, 20, 22, 23-24, 39, 40, 131-
  33, 134, 136, 162
Bosnia-Hercegovina 7, 20, 78,
  134, 138, 162, 245, 246
Bossi, U. 107
Bougainville 2, 19, 20-21, 26, 31,
  45, 52, 66, 73, 80, 89, 102, 153,
  183
Bourassa, R. 108-9
brain drain 129-30
Buchanan, A. 4, 37, 45, 145
budget (central) 76, 77, 94, 120,
  129, 148

Cabinda 7, 21, 27, 32, 53, 67, 185,
  193, 206
Canada 1, 2, 7, 23, 73, 82, 107,
  119, 152, 158
capital flows 66-69, 71, 140-41
capitalism 20, 26-30, 141, 163,
  169
Casamance 27, 32, 53, 60, 67,
  185, 218
Catalonia 10, 12, 21, 28, 34, 54,
  62, 68, 80, 111, 208
center-state relations 20, 36, 48,
  80, 86, 90, 148, 161
central bank 20, 77, 100
Central Bank of Nigeria 125
central revenue 57, 103
centralization 20, 80, 87, 92, 130
China 91, 110, 203
civil war 22, 23, 41, 76, 86, 95,
  105, 113, 132, 153, 218

cold war   2, 15, 16, 17

Commonwealth of Independent
State (CIS)   9, 134, 137, 151,
156

communism   13, 14, 16, 97, 130,
163, 169

confederation   65, 96, 137, 138,
145, 168, 174, 182

Conference on Security and Cooperation in Europe   136

confiscation   121

conflict   21-22, 47, 114, 137, 158,
226

Congo   22, 58, 106, 155

Conner, W.   8, 15, 45

constitution   19, 20, 23, 31, 81, 83,
84, 86, 91, 113, 196

Corsica   4, 29, 34, 54, 68, 80, 88,
189, 197

Corsicans   22, 23, 89

credits   121

Crimea   40

Croatia   4, 6, 10, 21, 22, 28, 33,
54, 68, 78, 123, 135, 175, 186,
195

currency   2, 86, 109, 124, 139;
earning capacity, 42, 49; establishment of, 40, 99

Czechoslovakia   11, 13, 22, 23,
71, 86, 141, 188

Dalmatia   37, 80

Danube   37

debt   118, 119-21

decentralization   20, 41, 42, 48,
80, 83, 84, 88, 101, 102, 106,
125, 129, 134, 147, 202

Deutsche Bank   40, 42, 43, 151,
156, 201, 211

development   42, 43, 127

disassociation   37, 41, 117

East Timor   11, 19, 20, 26, 31, 53,
66, 69, 204, 215

Eastern Europe   2, 16, 138, 157,
164

Eastern Region   77, 104, 198; see
also Biafra

economic development   36-37, 52,
56, 57, 113, 146, 176, 248

economic injustice   37, 44, 47, 56,
76, 94, 99, 101, 148

economic system   20, 26, 124

economies of scale   70, 71, 86

EEC   24, 109, 136, 137, 246

Eritrea   2, 11, 20, 24, 27, 32, 53,
57, 67, 206

Estonia   9, 41, 98, 119, 121, 125,
139, 172

Ethiopia   5, 11, 57, 128, 163

ethnic group   3, 13, 17, 35, 45, 60,
108, 128

ethnic homogeneity   20, 43, 108,
146, 151

ethnic purity   101, 172

ethnic tolerance   19

ethnicity   5, 8, 12, 13, 16, 21, 26,
132, 171

ethnoterritorial movements   3, 4,
180

export promotion   75

externalities   120, 130-31

federal budget   40, 78

Federal Fund   78, 95, 124, 224, 234

federation   13, 20, 26, 28, 30, 49,
82, 84, 86, 103, 182, 188

fiscal burden   79

fiscal policy   84, 142

foodgrains   75, 102, 155

foreign currency   40, 57, 63, 75,
99, 100, 105, 110, 120, 138, 143

fragmentation (markets)   72, 84

France 36, 111, 174
Fretilin 191
Front for the Liberation of the Enclave of Cabinda 193

Gagauz 41
Georgia 20, 28, 33, 54, 68
Germany 9, 18, 21, 59, 141, 165, 174
global economy 69, 109, 125, 139, 145, 151, 171
government intervention 75
government procurement 75
Greece 135, 136
green revolution 57
Griffin, J. 74, 154, 191
guerrilla warfare 21

Helsinki Final Act of 1975 24, 171
high-income regions 39, 44, 47, 56, 115, 149, 156
Hobsbaum, E. 14, 36, 40
Hong Kong 40, 171
Horowitz, D. 3, 4, 15
Hroch, M. 36
Hungarians in Romania 4, 111-12, 189, 225
Hungary 189, 241

IMF 74, 136, 141
incentives 75
independence 11, 12, 21, 23, 31, 41, 57, 106, 108, 109, 117, 135, 143
India 2, 6, 7, 19, 39, 74, 77, 87, 138, 205
Indonesia 9, 11, 36, 64, 91
industrial sector 72, 126, 153
industrialization 42, 64, 122
input-output analysis 70
integration 70, 122, 138, 146

interdependence 70, 86, 92, 155
international intervention 24, 31, 90, 94
interregional flows 65, 76, 110, 146, 152, 162, 213
investment 37, 39, 40, 47, 60, 73, 74, 94, 98, 110, 120, 123, 126-27, 140-41, 150
involuntary union 22, 31, 123
Iraq 19, 194, 219
Ireland 14
irredentist movement 3, 15, 16, 26, 111, 179
Istra 131
Italy 15, 18, 91, 106, 167

Karen 10, 12, 19, 26, 32, 53, 64, 67, 159, 184, 205
Kashmir 24, 27, 32, 53, 60, 66, 75, 88, 110
Katanga 20, 24, 29, 34, 41, 55, 59, 63, 68, 106, 154, 190
Kazakhstan 122, 126, 130, 134
Khalistan 10, 22, 158
Kosovar 13, 28, 90, 135, 188, 196
Kosovo 6, 21, 28, 33, 54, 58, 68, 155, 196
Krajina 4, 6, 10, 28, 33, 54, 68, 133
Kurdistan 4, 19, 27, 32, 53, 64, 67, 90
Kurdistan Democratic Party 112
Kurds 19, 112, 185; in Iran, 4; in Iraq, 4, 24, 112, 194; in Turkey, 4, 112

labor force 74, 118, 128, 129, 149
labor market 72
language 12
Latvia 13, 28, 33, 41, 54, 58, 68, 98

Law on Secession 118
Lega Lombarda 106-7, 150, 158
Lendvai, P. 166
Leslie, P. 82
Lincoln, A. 173, 175
literacy 45, 52-55, 106, 207
Lithuania 2, 7, 8, 70, 98, 127
Lombardy 2, 10, 18, 21, 29, 34, 39, 45, 54, 62, 68, 106-7, 150
low-income regions 44, 47, 56, 115, 155
Lydall, H. 85

Macedonia 24, 39, 135, 242
Macedonians 19
Malaysian Federation 18, 30, 41, 104, 198
market economy 49, 71, 122, 142
marketization 20, 141-43
markets 2, 139
Markovic, A. 86, 240
Meech Lake Accord 83, 158
Mezzogiorno 39, 57, 95, 107
migration 66-69, 72, 98, 110, 128-29, 137
minorities 14, 15, 90, 91, 146, 166, 170, 202
minority regions 22
modernization 35, 44, 45, 57, 104
Moldova 2, 4, 13, 20, 41, 121, 134
monetary policy 84, 87, 124, 142
money supply 125
Moravia 22, 98
Morocco 11, 248
multi-ethnic states 15
multi-party system 96
multiplier effect 74
Myanmar 10, 12, 18, 27, 67, 192, 217

Nagorno-Karabakh 131, 159, 164

national integration 35
National Salvation Front 111-12
nationalism 12, 13, 14, 16, 35, 45, 170, 177, 180, 200, 247
New Caledonia 11
Nigeria 4, 15, 24, 76, 104, 226
North Ossetian Autonomous Region 4
Northern Ireland 21, 29, 34, 54, 60, 67, 114, 164

oil-producing region 64, 87, 100, 104, 130, 151, 219
Ona, F. 102-3
Ottoman Empire 13, 19, 28, 35, 179

Pakistan 22, 24, 132, 227
Papua New Guinea 2, 45, 74, 89, 154, 203
Partition 6, 102
Patriotic Union of Kurdistan 112
perestroika 99
Polisario 11, 193
political culture 19
political structures 20, 26, 48, 80
President's Rule 88
prices 138, 146, 154, 212, 216, 218; adjustments, 66-69; bias, 94; determination of, 121, 122, 123, 127
privatization 98
Prout, C. 73, 235
public assets 121-23
Puerto Rico 18, 28, 33, 54, 67, 109, 186
Punjab 2, 9, 22, 26, 31, 53, 57, 59, 66, 74-75, 94, 101-2, 132, 154, 184
Punjabis 13, 101

Quebec 1, 2, 7, 12, 20, 28, 32, 45, 54, 67, 73, 76, 107, 123, 152-53, 157, 219

redefinition 40, 46, 48, 51, 117, 129
reequilibration 40, 44, 48, 51, 145
reevaluation 38-39, 45, 46, 51-94, 161
referendum 10, 12, 31-32, 96, 101, 103, 107, 109, 126, 135, 158, 163, 181
refugees 133, 163
regional disparities 58, 75, 78
regional potential 63
regulation 75
relative income 42, 44, 56
religion 2, 12, 26, 39, 95, 97, 110, 114, 141, 161-65
Reserve Bank of India 77
revenue 77, 105
Romania 111-12, 114, 179, 225
Rusinow, D. 175, 247
Russia 2, 20, 99, 120, 122, 126, 128, 134, 137, 138, 151, 241
Russian empire 13, 35
Russians 2, 41, 173

Sahrawi Arab Democratic Republic 193
Schrenk, M. 73
Scotland 29, 34, 54, 67, 88, 100, 101, 189
Scots 23, 170
Scottish National Party 100
secession aftermath 21; aspirations, 26, 39, 41, 45, 46, 49, 76, 93, 98, 108, 115; duration, 21; and ethnicity, 7-8; moral basis, 22, 25, 31, 35; peaceful, 14; and popular support, 10, 23; and

state unraveling, 8-9, 21, 118, 133, 143; and territory, 6-7
secessionist unit 5-6
self-determination 10, 11, 24, 49, 85, 91, 161, 167, 170, 195
self-sufficiency 69, 132, 146, 148, 155
separatist movement 3, 4
Serbia 7, 10, 119, 157
Serbs 1, 2, 4, 6, 7, 13, 133, 136, 187-88, 195
Shiels, F. 8, 93
Siberia 56
Sikhs 22, 27, 43, 102, 236
Singapore 18, 30, 34, 41, 55, 68, 94, 103, 143, 190
Sinhalese 113
Slavonia 6, 132, 133
Slovakia 2, 11, 21, 29, 33, 55, 68, 94, 97-98, 120, 128, 209
Slovaks 19, 120, 240
Slovenia 2, 9, 10, 20, 21, 28, 33, 45, 55, 68, 78, 85, 94, 95-97, 119, 121, 137, 153, 157, 175
Slovenians 9, 19
Smith, A. 37
social security 133
socialism 20, 26, 141
South Ossetians 4
Southern Sudan 4, 5, 12, 18, 21, 23, 26, 32, 53, 67, 184, 192
Soviet Bloc 2, 16, 20, 37, 141, 175
Soviet Union 2, 5, 9, 11, 13, 16, 17, 40, 43, 48, 70, 98, 120, 122, 126, 128, 134, 137, 139
Spain 21, 81, 208
Sri Lanka 4, 26, 31, 52, 64, 66, 113-14, 181, 184, 204
subsidies 41, 47, 138, 142
Sudan 2, 11, 19, 217

Sudanese People's Liberation
 Army 24, 192
Summers, L. 120
Switzerland 15, 16, 59

Tadzhikistan 28, 54, 58, 68, 155
Tamil Eelam 114
Tamil Tigres 114
Tamils 13, 114, 214
Tatar Autonomous Republic 5,
 17, 222
Tatars 1, 2
Tatarstan 28, 33, 55, 68
tax 40, 47, 66-69, 77, 83, 94, 97,
 118, 124, 140, 170, 220, 228
tax revolt 39, 47, 107, 176
technology 66-69, 71-72, 75, 85,
 130, 132, 146, 223
territorial integrity 7
Third World 1, 13, 107, 163
Tibet 20, 26, 31, 52, 66, 88, 91,
 141, 213
Tibet Autonomous Region 91, 183
Tibetans 13, 183, 214
Timorese 26
Tito 135, 159, 168, 174, 187
tourism 110
trade 37, 40, 46, 66-69, 74, 126,
 138-39, 146
trade dependency 39, 41, 46, 65,
 69-70, 71-72, 139, 148
Trans-Dniesterians 41
transition to capitalism 20, 141-43
Transylvania 20, 28, 33, 55, 68,
 88, 111, 197, 210
Turkmenia 21, 39

Ukraine 1, 2, 5, 20, 28, 33, 54, 68,
 99, 121, 126, 130, 134, 151-52
unitary political system 26, 27,
 29, 49, 88, 174, 185

United Liberation Front of Assam
 110, 192
United Nations 2, 10, 11, 48, 163,
 176, 185
United States 22, 24, 48, 107,
 118, 158
urbanization 74

vertical integration 72, 85
viability 2, 17, 25, 40, 41, 45, 49,
 63, 105, 144, 145-47, 151
Vojvodina 58, 78, 85
voluntary union 22, 123

Western Australia 23, 47
Western Europe 1, 36, 58, 91,
 137, 168, 175
Western Sahara 10, 11, 19, 22, 27,
 32, 53, 67
Wood, J. 37, 38
World Bank 44, 61, 90
World War I 1, 19, 22, 122, 165
World War II 19, 24, 71, 73, 79,
 107, 129, 135, 165

Yakutia 23
Yugoslavia 9, 10, 13, 19, 20-21,
 23, 78, 80, 84, 95, 121, 135, 165

Zaire 16, 32